the art of parenting

Aiming Your Child's Heart toward God

DENNIS AND BARBARA
RAINEY

with DAVE BOEHI

BETHANYHOUSE

a division of Baker Publishing Group
Minneapolis, Minnesota

© 2018 by Dennis Rainey and Barbara Rainey

Published by Bethany House Publishers
11400 Hampshire Avenue South
Minneapolis, Minnesota 55438
www.bethanyhouse.com

Bethany House Publishers is a division of
Baker Publishing Group, Grand Rapids, Michigan

Printed in the United States of America

ISBN 978-0-7642-1964-1 (cloth)
ISBN 978-0-7642-3175-9 (paper))

Library of Congress Cataloging-in-Publication Control Number: 2017961593

Unless otherwise indicated, Scripture quotations are from The Holy Bible, English Standard Version® (ESV®), copyright © 2001 by Crossway, a publishing ministry of Good News Publishers. Used by permission. All rights reserved. ESV Text Edition: 2011

Scripture quotations identified NASB are from the New American Standard Bible®, copyright © 1960, 1962, 1963, 1968, 1971, 1972, 1973, 1975, 1977, 1995 by The Lockman Foundation. Used by permission. (www.Lockman.org)

Scripture quotations identified NIV are from the Holy Bible, New International Version®. NIV®. Copyright © 1973, 1978, 1984, 2011 by Biblica, Inc.™ Used by permission of Zondervan. All rights reserved worldwide. www.zondervan.com

Scripture quotations identified NKJV are from the New King James Version®. Copyright © 1982 by Thomas Nelson, Inc. Used by permission. All rights reserved.

Cover design by Julie Sullivan, MerakiLifeDesigns.com

Authors represented by Wolgemuth and Associates

Baker Publishing Group publications use paper produced from sustainable forestry practices and post-consumer waste whenever possible.

23   24   25   26   27   28   29   7   6   5   4   3   2   1

Contents

Foreword

by David and Meg Robbins

One of the primary ways God is bringing the world back to Himself is through moms and dads making disciples of their own kids. We believe at our core that this is true, and we seek to be intentional in the formation of our four children. But many days it seems like we are doing more harm than good and barely hanging on by a prayer.

Are we being too strict? Or are we being too lenient?

Are we helping our kids pursue their own relationship with Jesus? Or are we just busying them with activity?

Are we displaying God's grace? Or are we being legalistic?

Are we focusing on the "majors"—on what's most important? Or the "minors"?

Dennis and Barbara have poured so much heart, wisdom, and experience into these pages, and we are so grateful for the profound encouragement and practical tools we've found in *The Art of Parenting*. We have loved reading other books from the Raineys over the years, but we've had the opportunity to get to know them and some of their children over the last year as they passed the leadership baton of FamilyLife to us. What a privilege to interact with their children and see how God has shaped them through the love and intentionality of Dennis and Barbara as parents. As we have talked with the Raineys and picked their brains about raising kids in the midst of all the challenges of the world, we have seen what a wealth of wisdom they gained from their own experiences.

This book is like a deep-dive into their years of parenting. It's a chance to be mentored, trained, and equipped by the Raineys as they share how God was at work in their family through both successes and missteps. We are in the thick of raising kids ourselves, ages two through twelve. So we appreciate the melding of biblical principles and practical advice and ideas to point our children to Jesus and to help them develop strong relationships, godly character, and steadfast identity—and discover their unique mission in life.

The timing of *The Art of Parenting* comes at an important cultural moment. God's plan A for the formation of the next generation is through parents. But what parents and kids must navigate today is certainly challenging—the pace of changing technology, an increasingly secular society, and a new set of questions encircling core identity (just to name a few). *The Art of Parenting* consistently draws upon the timeless, unchanging wisdom of Scripture to help us as parents navigate common challenges. Dennis and Barbara guide us in how to tenaciously build strong, grace-filled relational bridges in which character-forming truths and discipline can travel.

Recently, one of our kids began training for a cross-country team. Initially he began taking jogs on his own. But I (Meg) realized two things: First, I needed more exercise myself! Second, running *with him* would give me more opportunities to strengthen my relational bridge that is increasingly needed with my soon-to-be teen. So I pulled out my running shoes and started training with him. And although I've been very sore, I'm so grateful for this purposeful, consistent time with him. This is just one example of the many ways God has prompted us while reading this book to be more intentional with our kids.

We pray that you and your relationship with your kids will be shaped by *The Art of Parenting.* The Raineys beautifully steward the wisdom and experience gleaned from more than forty years of direct ministry to marriages and families. This is the culmination of countless interviews with experts on the *FamilyLife Today* radio show and the honest lessons from their own family.

One thing is sure: This book will draw you into closer relationship to the One who covers your imperfections as a parent and gives you supernatural power to pass on a living faith.

> One generation shall commend your works to another, and shall declare your mighty acts. . . . They shall pour forth the fame of your abundant goodness and shall sing aloud of your righteousness.
>
> Psalm 145:4, 7

David and Meg Robbins
President and CEO, FamilyLife

Eight Certainties for Every Parent

Having finished the journey of parenting, we understand the whole of the mission much like a coach who isn't on the playing field anymore but stands on the sidelines watching the team, noticing needed adjustments, and anticipating next plays. From his or her years on the field, the coach sees the value of both offense and defense. Decades of experience have led to strategic thinking that younger coaches, so engrossed in the demands of their specialties, haven't the time or experience to formulate.

So before you turn the page, here are eight truths we've learned in our decades of experience, certainties that will provide context to every word, every story in this book.

1. **All that follows in these pages is reflective of how God parents us, His children.** As parents ourselves, we sought to adopt His values and His definitions of character for our children's hearts. We are saying to you, "Here is what we learned, what we did reasonably well, and where we failed." Our goal is to encourage you, coach you, and cheer you on.

2. **Parents are complex.** Every parent brings into this journey a mixed bag of good and bad experiences from his or her family of origin. Those experiences need to be looked at with fresh eyes as you decide what to keep and repeat or what to set aside or overcome. Part of God's intent for you as parents is to continue growing you up, to continue transforming your heart. God *will* use children to change you as parents.

3. **Children are complex.** Every child is born with predispositions, gifts, handicaps, and talents that can't be seen clearly in the early years. Parenting is an adventure in discovering what God is up to in each uniquely created child He gives you. Pray and lean on Jesus for His specific, unique guidance with each one.

4. **Parenting is heart work.** It is fundamentally a relationship built on love and schooled in love. The ultimate parental goal each and every day is handing over to God's care the hearts of our children. He can be trusted to transform each of your children.

5. **There is no one-size-fits-all formula for parenting.** Yes, there are principles and clear teachings in the Bible, but the application of those to each individual child in each unique family setting must be done by listening to God's specific guidance. He knows everything about your child. Our stories and suggestions are what we did. Some will work for you and others won't. It's the beauty of God's creative genius. He doesn't want robots.

6. **No one raises perfect kids.** Even God. We sure didn't. Our children all have gaps in their lives from growing up in our home. They have told us we didn't meet them in some of their greatest needs. They've said they felt overlooked or excluded at times, and sometimes felt they didn't fit in the family. Those words hurt to hear, for we never intended harm for any of our six and loved them each passionately. We apologized and said how sorry we were for our mistakes. Every parent is full of limitations and flaws. No one parents perfectly.

7. **There are only two things guaranteed in life.** First, God's love will never end. We can confidently count on His unchangeable nature. Second, discord, disruption, and death will be with us for life, infecting all families and all relationships. Parenting, marriage, and life are lived in the tension of these two realities.

8. **Your work is not finished when your child turns eighteen.** Your child's character and convictions are not set in stone at eighteen. He or she may go on to college or marriage and still walk away from your teaching and guidance. Prodigal hearts can develop at any age or stage of life. Never stop praying for your child's heart to be wholly devoted to Christ.

A Parakeet Teaches God's Love

Whatever else may be said about the home, it is the single most influential force in our earthly existence. No price tag can adequately reflect its value, no gauge can measure its ultimate influence, for good or ill.

Charles Swindoll

When our daughter Deborah, aka Peanut, was sixteen, we had one of those father-daughter kitchen conversations. Amid the mealtime mess and clamor came this declaration: "Dad, I want to be able to do what I want to do . . . with whoever I want to do it with . . . whenever I want . . . for as long as I want."

I wasn't sure I had heard correctly. "What did you say?"

When she repeated her statement, I smiled and said, "Peanut, what if your parakeet came to you and said, 'Deborah, I'd like to go do what I want to do, with whoever I want to do it with, whenever I want to do it, for as long as I want to do it. And right now, I'd like to go on the porch and play with the cats!'"

Deborah loved her parakeet, affectionately named Sweet Pea. "Would you let Sweet Pea go play outside, Peanut?"

She quickly dismissed my fatherly attempt to reach her. "That's a silly illustration, Dad."

I said, "No, it's not. There's a cat on the porch right now. Sweet Pea is in the cage right now. The cage is actually a protection for Sweet Pea, don't you agree?"

Feeling uncomfortable, Deborah attempted to change the subject . . . and I let her. I knew she had heard.

Not long after that conversation, we went on a trip as a family and asked a friend to take care of Sweet Pea in our absence. After our dawn departure, she and her son drove to our house to take Deborah's parakeet home for the week. As twelve-year-old Tate was carrying Sweet Pea in her cage to their car, the bottom tray dropped open and Sweet Pea, being the free spirit she was, fluttered to freedom. Before flying the coop, unfortunately, Sweet Pea somehow failed to consider it was January in Arkansas.

Horrified, both mother and son tried for hours to coax the parakeet from the branches high above. Eventually they gave up.

A couple days later we got the message that Sweet Pea had escaped and was forever lost. The news of her feathered friend's defection ruined the rest of the trip for Deborah.

Like all parents do, we attempted to soothe, to understand, to provide possible solutions. "We'll go buy another parakeet when we get home," we said, hoping a replacement would eventually calm her heart. She remained unconvinced.

When we arrived at the airport, our friends messaged us to say they'd bought Deborah a new parakeet. But the new bird was no Sweet Pea. Deborah chased that wild and untrained bird around her room for hours. More disappointed than ever, she rejected the replacement and we returned the foul fowl for a refund.

Our home is in a very wooded neighborhood with only one neighbor in view amid hundreds of square miles of a greenbelt forest. Two days after we arrived home and bought and returned the new bird, our next-door neighbor, Bob, called to tell a beyond-belief story.

"About a week ago," he said, "I was watching TV in the living room and something kept hitting the window. *Thump, thump, thump.* . . . So I asked my wife to go see what it was."

Joann dutifully got up and went outside. When she didn't return after a few minutes, Bob made his way to the deck and found her watching a green parakeet flit from tree branch to window and back again. Bob stuck his finger out, and immediately the bird flew to his finger, which Sweet Pea was trained to do. Bob just happened to have an old empty bird cage in his basement, and that became Sweet Pea's new home.

Later that day Bob went to town for canary food, and then stopped to get a frozen yogurt. Standing in line, our ever-talkative neighbor started a conversation with the guy next to him. Small talk first. Then Bob said, "Strangest thing happened. We found a parakeet in the woods, so I came to town to buy feed."

The stranger asked, "Where do you live?" Bob named our neighborhood west of town, and the stranger said, "Is that near the Raineys?"

Bob said, "They live next door."

"I'm their kids' youth pastor. I think they have a parakeet."

The mystery appeared to be solved, so Bob was calling to ask if we were missing a parakeet!

Barbara and I marveled at how God cared about this bird and set in motion the circumstances to bring it back. It was so improbable that it seemed a divine declaration of love for our daughter. We wanted to make sure she heard loud and clear how much God loved her.

We kept the news to ourselves for the big reveal at dinner. We were seated at the table with our two girls who were still living at home (the other four kids were off to college or married). We asked about their days, and then I started talking about how much God loves us. I looked at Deborah and said, "I'm sorry about Sweet Pea, but I want you to know three things: First, it's not wrong to be sad over the loss of something you loved. Second, it's okay to question God—He can handle it. Third, God loves you, Peanut."

Deborah was unmoved by my words, so I repeated them: "Peanut, you don't understand . . . God really, really loves you."

Her younger sister, Laura, was bored to death and asked, "Do I have to listen to this?" We said yes. Disgustedly, she rolled her eyes, leaned her head back on her chair, and pulled her napkin over her face! She couldn't leave physically, so she escaped the conversation behind a mask.

For a third time I said, "Peanut, look at me. *God really loves you!*"

I paused, waited for eye contact, and then said, "Sweet Pea is alive. Mr. Nagle found her, and she's at his house!"

For just a moment Deborah's face was stoic—not a glimmer of a change. But not Laura! She jerked the napkin off her face, sat bolt upright, and yelled, "WHAT? MR. NAGLE HAS SWEET PEA?! YOU FOUND SWEET PEA?"

Slowly Deborah thawed, let it soak in; a sweet grin emerged. Minutes later all four of us walked up the hill to get Sweet Pea and brought him home.

That night before bed we reminded Deborah, and Laura, too, how God longs for us to know and experience His limitless love. Circling back to how this drama all began, I reminded them both that what kept Sweet Pea safe, his cage, was also what kept danger out. God knows what He is doing.

No one will ever convince us that the circumstances surrounding a sixteen-year-old girl's pet parakeet were orchestrated by anyone other than the God of the universe. He reached out to our daughter, who really needed to see His love for her at that moment in her life.

God wants to use the hard moments in your child's life to demonstrate His love, which is far greater for your child than yours. Paying attention to God, praying constantly or often, will open your eyes to His wonder-working involvement in the details of your family.

Good Years and Challenging Years

Of all the stories about raising six children we've told over the years, that is probably our favorite. It reveals so much about parenting—the difficulty, the heartbreak, the effort to point our children to Christ, and the joy of watching God work in His own mysterious ways to help the helpless parent.

Parenting is bursting with good, rewarding days, seasons, and years, but it also overflows with challenges most of us didn't anticipate, at least not like this!

We suspect you feel the same about your experience as a parent today. For everything you do right, you feel the anxiety of parents through the ages:

- "How can I get my child to obey me?"
- "How do I discipline my kids?"
- "Am I overprotective?"
- "Am I too lenient?"
- "Am I pushing them too hard in their education?"
- "Are they too busy?"

- "Why can't my kids get along with each other?"
- "Do I correct and criticize them too much?"
- "How do I control my anger?"
- "How can I help my children face all the changes they'll experience as they approach adolescence?"
- "Are my kids making good friends?"
- "How do I teach my children about right and wrong?"

But you also face some unique challenges in today's world:

- "How much screen time should I let my children have each day?"
- "When should we get them a mobile phone?"
- "Does too much technology hurt my child?"
- "How can I keep my child safe from bullying . . . or from sexual predators?"
- "How do I teach my child how to be a man or woman when the culture is changing the definition?"

In a 2017 survey by the Barna Research Group, nearly eight out of ten parents indicated they thought parenting was more difficult for them than it was for their parents. When asked what factors make it difficult, 65 percent said technology and social media, 52 percent said the world is more dangerous, and 40 percent pointed to a lack of common morality.[1]

Parents today have more information available to them than any previous generation. Type "how to be a better parent" into Google, and you can find millions of blogs, websites, and articles offering help. But how do you decide what advice to follow and what to ignore? Many parents today can relate to the lament of actor Ewan McGregor, who said, "The thing about parenting rules is there aren't any. That's what makes it so difficult."[2]

A Biblical Foundation

But there is a book that offers timeless advice to parents. The Bible is as relevant to today's parents as it has been for thousands of years.

Psalm 127:1 tells us, "Unless the Lord builds the house, those who build it labor in vain."

Our hope is that this book will help restore confidence in God's Word as the foundation for your lives and for your family relationships. In the Bible we find timeless words that apply to this generation just as it has to previous parents for over two thousand years.

Jesus says more about what it means for God to build your home on the solid foundation of His Word in Matthew 7:24–27:

> "Everyone then who hears these words of mine and does them will be like a wise man who built his house on the rock. And the rain fell, and the floods came, and the winds blew and beat on that house, but it did not fall, because it had been founded on the rock. And everyone who hears these words of mine and does not do them will be like a foolish man who built his house on the sand. And the rain fell, and the floods came, and the winds blew and beat against that house, and it fell, and great was the fall of it."

Jesus tutors parents in Homebuilding 101: You *will* build your house in the midst of storms. Count on it. And because these storms keep assaulting our homes, we need the very best foundation available—we need to teach His Word to our children and follow His Word in our homes.

Though we are no longer raising our children, and though we did not face all the challenges you confront today, there are two truths that unite all parents across all generations.

The first truth is that *God is the same yesterday, today, and forever.* His Word is enduring, and He will help you parent the children He gives you, working through you and with you for their good and for His glory.

Second, *while each new generation is different, most of the issues you face today are no different from those faced by past generations because the root is always about our hearts.* The Bible speaks to issues of the heart, and as we will share throughout this book, it will equip and transform the hearts of both parent and child.

Parenting Is an Art

Have you ever watched a sculptor at work? She works the clay with her hands, molding it, shaping it with thumbs that scoop, dig, and push the wet pliable earth into an image no one sees but the artist. Finally one day the work is finished. Though beautiful on its own, a clay sculpture is often only a model of what will eventually be chiseled out of marble.

God made Adam similarly, we imagine. Wet, clay-like earth, not loamy or sandy, filled God's hands as He worked to shape the design He envisioned. Full of texture and movement, with planes that rounded into curves or bent at angles, His handiwork was created to house His Spirit and reflect His image.

Can you picture those heavenly hands covered in mud?

Parenting is a messy art. To become an artist means getting clay under your fingernails, paint on your clothes, marble dust in your nostrils.

It means your hand cramps from hours of holding the paintbrush just so, and your knees will hurt and your heart will break for the passionate, protective love only a father and mother can feel for their little works of art. And it means only an artist who has been willing to try and fail and try again a thousand times can know the eventual satisfaction of a child who has grown up to become pliable clay in the Master's hand.

The handiwork is worth it all in the end.

Seeing God Work

So what do we, who are finished with parenting, offer you who are shaping the clay of your child's heart today?

As parents of six married kids who are all walking with Jesus today, we can show you how we followed God and His Word in every stage of raising our children. We can vividly illustrate what worked and what didn't. We are not afraid to share our failures. Several are epic!

So far, five of our children have birthed or adopted twenty-three little ones—who today range in age from eighteen months to nineteen years. And the additions are not yet complete; number twenty-four is on the way. We've interviewed all six of our children for this book. Some share what they learned from us that they are passing on, and others share about raising their own children today. Watch for their words of wisdom and stories throughout these pages.

We've also studied parenting for several decades. And while there are experiences we thankfully don't know firsthand, over twenty-five years of interviews on *FamilyLife Today* radio—with over a thousand subject-matter experts in marriage and parenting—have given us a library of information that can offer help and hope in just about any situation.

Many of those radio guests and other parenting veterans participated in the creation of FamilyLife's *The Art of Parenting Video Series*. These seasoned veterans provided more valuable insight than we could fit in the videos, so we're sharing it here, as well. Throughout this book you'll find nuggets of wisdom from Alistair Begg, Kevin DeYoung, Karen Fitzpatrick, Jim Keller, Alex Kendrick, Stephen Kendrick, Tim and Darcy Kimmel, Bryan Loritts, Meg Meeker, Judy Mok, Eric and Erikah Rivera, Phil Vischer, Dave and Ann Wilson, and Susan Yates. We've also included guidance from our FamilyLife colleague Ron Deal, an expert and author on the topic of blended families.

Finally, our history of seeing God work in challenging circumstances gives us great confidence in saying to you, *God will provide, guide, and deliver for you as you raise your children. When it feels impossible is when God loves to show up and transform.*

Whether you are cradling a newborn child in your arms, or you are trying to get your arms around an adolescent who is trying desperately to escape and break free of your love and limits, we hope this book gives help and hope to these and a host of other questions and perplexities.

The pages that follow unpack the essence of what we've learned from raising six children. We continually asked this question: *Since God created marriage and family, what is His counsel and instruction for raising children to become what He has in mind for them?*

We hope you will discover answers to questions about God, marriage, and children . . . and we'll weave in some lessons on faith.

Six Benefits for Parents as You Work through This Book

1. **We want to encourage you in the process of child-rearing.** Feelings of failure and discouragement are frequent visitors in every home. Your children aren't perfect. Ours weren't (and still aren't). Raising children in any generation demands courage, and we want to bolster your courage.

2. **We want to exalt the high calling and privilege of parenting.** Children are a gift from God, and He has a plan for each child, no matter how challenging. We want to give you a vision for what God can do in your kids' hearts.

3. **We want to help you develop a biblical game plan for parenting.** Whether you are married or a single parent, you can craft an individualized biblical plan for your kids and learn how to be intentional in your parenting.

4. **We want to challenge you to determine what your convictions are about God and life.** We want to state the obvious on the front end of this book: You won't agree with everything we did or didn't do in raising our children. You will think some of our standards were too high or too low. We're good with that. But if you don't know what you believe, you'll have a difficult time passing biblical standards on to your children.

5. **If you are married, we want to help you strengthen your teamwork as a couple.** Two-parent families, nuclear or blended, need a unified plan that will create stability in your children.

6. **We want to equip you to experience God and His guidance as you raise your children.** As parents, we don't always know what to do or say. But God can work in you and through you to accomplish His plan. And by the way, He loves the prayers of the helpless parent!

1 Like Arrows

Whenever I held my newborn baby in my arms, I used to think that what I said and did to him could have an influence not only on him but on all whom he met, not only for a day or a month or a year, but for all eternity—a very challenging and exciting thought for a mother.

Rose Kennedy, mother of President John F. Kennedy

When our son Benjamin was entering his teenage years, both Barbara and I knew that it would be a challenge for us to stay connected with him relationally. From our years of working with teenagers before we had kids of our own, we knew teens look for ways to assert their independence and push their parents away. We didn't want to be like many parents we had observed, who seemed intimidated by their teenagers and stepped back from their involvement at the very time they should have stayed connected.

So Barbara and I talked about finding something Benjamin and I could do together to grow a man-to-man relationship. He and I had enjoyed hunting together since he was about ten, but neither of us knew anything about bowhunting. We thought learning together would be fun and give us a common experience to share. And it did.

But learning to shoot arrows from a compound bow—both in practice at paper targets and in the woods as we stalked wild game—gave me some unexpected new insights into one of my favorite verses in the Bible. Psalm 127:4–5 tells us, "Like arrows in the hand of a warrior are the children of one's youth. Blessed is the man who fills his quiver with them!"

What an amazing statement. Think about those words. The psalmist refers to your child, both boys and girls, as an arrow—a *weapon*! And that is no mistake.

Did you know that God has great plans for your child, targets He has designed for them to reach and to redeem? Arrows are not meant to be kept safe in the quiver. God wants you, a warrior, to eventually release your arrows, your children, to make an impact on our world with the love of Christ.

Educator and cultural critic Neil Postman wrote that "children are the living messages we send to a time we will not see."[1] This long-term view of children should revolutionize the way you look at your responsibility as a parent. We raise children so that we can release them. They may make a greater impact on their world than we ever will in ours.

Interestingly, today our son Ben is doing archery with his fourteen-year-old daughter, Savannah, as a way for them to have father-daughter time together. Savannah has discovered she enjoys the skill of archery just as her dad did when he was her age, and we've enjoyed watching their adventures on Instagram.

Arrow Making 101

Parenting, as the title of this book states, is an art. Crafting your child to be an arrow in the hand of God is a design skill like painting or songwriting or hundreds of other hands-on creative endeavors that require individual attention to detail and nuances. Your child's life is in your hands to shape and direct for approximately eighteen years.

What sets arrow crafting apart from any other creative skill are the distinctives desired in the final result. To be useful, any arrow must have a *shaft*, a *nock* (the groove at the end of the arrow into which the bow string fits), a *point*, and *fletching* (feathers). In addition, arrow makers add *cresting* to differentiate one from another and to identify the arrow's creator.

If all of these elements are constructed well, always taking into account the uniqueness of the varying raw materials, the result is an effective arrow, handcrafted for flight and impact.

A Dad to All Girls

While I like to play sports and hunt and fish, most of my girls have not followed my passions in those areas. This is going to sound like the biggest no-brainer, but it's been difficult for me to learn to meet my daughters on their level and do what they like to do. I don't want to play with their dolls or watch Barbie movies. I hate that stuff! But I've come to love it over time because my kids love it.

Throughout a typical week, I find myself doing things I never ever envisioned—cooking, baking, designing websites, building computers, attending dance recitals, watching gymnastics practices. Each is important to my daughters and requires that I like who they are, not who I want them to be.

Each of our four girls is so very different. My wife, Marsha Kay, and I often joke that we somehow got four opposites. The point is, each daughter is unique and wonderful and deserving of being loved for who she is, not who I want her to be. So I put down my desire to sit and watch football and instead join them in *their* stuff, because not too long from now there will come a day when there are no little girls asking me to play or dance or bake or talk. And that day is going to be really sad.

Ben and Marsha Kay Rainey

These elements of an arrow also provide a glimpse into several crucial raw materials necessary for forming and shaping our children. Nearly every issue your children will encounter can be linked to the strength you build in these four areas.

1. The arrow's shaft: your child's character

The making of a fine arrow always begins with the shaft. If it is warped—not straight and strong—that child's flight in life will be wobbly. But know this: Perfection is not the goal in parenting or in arrow crafting, because there is no such thing as a perfectly straight arrow. Even with highly mechanized engineering techniques today, carbon fiber and composite metal arrows still fall short of perfection. Make your goal strong and straight, not perfect.

Barbara and I compare the shaft of an arrow to a child's character. From Genesis to Revelation, character development is a major theme of God's work, the purpose of His parenting of His people, you and me. From the first page to the last, God is calling our hearts to His. He invites us to let Him make our fallible broken character like His.

Character development is therefore one of the major assignments God gives earthly parents. When you think of building character into a child—in areas such as honesty, kindness, patience, and faithfulness—ultimately it's tied to teaching them God's ways as opposed to their own selfish ways.

Parenting becomes a training center to teach children to wait, to share, to trust Mom and Dad, and eventually to choose God and His Word as the best way to live life—with the goal eighteen years in the future of choosing God as their ultimate authority when they fly from you into the adventure God has ahead.

Partnering with God in the art of arrow crafting is the only hope for raising strong, wise children who will fly straight and safely into this world of enormous uncertainties.

2. The arrow's nock and freathers: your child's relationships

All of the pent-up power in a bow is of no value if it cannot be effectively transferred. That's why every arrow, at the rear of the shaft, has a small groove that holds the bowstring. This is called the nock. The nock keeps the arrow in place on the string until the power is released.

The feathers, or fletching, on an arrow create drag when the arrow is in flight, keeping the back end of the arrow smoothly following the front instead of flipping back over front from the propulsion of the release—a pretty important function! Fletching also keeps the arrow stabilized as it maintains its trajectory. An arrow without good fletching flies wildly and erratically, but with the right kind of feathers, properly installed, it will fly straight.

The nock and feathers can be compared to the second core ingredient necessary in a child's life: relationships. When your child's life intersects with God and with people, a power transfer occurs. None of us was intended to make a journey through life alone. We need the strength, comfort, encouragement, resources, and power provided by God and others.

The essence of every family is relationships—between parents in marriage, between parent and child, and between children as siblings. These lifelong relationships can be great gifts if nurtured and grown with care, or they can be sources of deep lasting pain.

Children need parents who will build into them the ability to love others. And this training can occur quite naturally in the context of relationship. The best school to learn about relationships and resolving conflict is in the

One of my favorite passages is Psalm 127. It talks about how children are a heritage of the Lord, a reward. And "blessed is the man whose quiver is full of them." I want to make sure that that arrow is aimed in the right direction. And so when it is released from my home, its purpose is fulfilled as God intended.

ALEX KENDRICK

University of Family, where the parental "professors" teach and train their students for more than eighteen years.

3. The arrow's cresting: a child's identity

If you look at arrows in a sporting goods store, you will see that they all seem to look alike. Modern arrows are made by machines and feature graphite shafts, slim metal points, and plastic feathers.

But in the days of King David, when Psalm 127 was written, arrows were works of art. The shaft was made of wood, the feathers came from birds, and the points were chipped from metal or stone. No two arrows were alike; each was unique.

Yet many of those arrows still *looked* alike from a distance. That's why cresting was necessary. Arrow makers added different colored stripes and other marks that told the world, "The markings of this arrow identify who its creator is and whom it belongs to."

This is very similar to a child's identity. As you raise your children, you will help them answer the question "Who am I?" You will help them understand what makes them different from other people—their personality, their interests, and their abilities. You will help them learn what it means to be male or female and how to hold on to God's design in a world that is trying to redefine the essence of gender identity.

You will also help your children understand their spiritual identity. What does it mean to be made in the image of God, to be valuable in His sight? How can we have a relationship with Him?

4. The arrow's point: mission

No finely crafted arrow would be complete without the tip, or arrowhead. Whether it's a chipped-stone arrowhead or a modern razor-sharp tip, the point of the arrow reminds us of the last essential quality we must give every child: a vision for the value and impact of his or her life. Every person needs

I Am Not God

I don't think anyone is ever ready to be a parent. We were the same way. Within the first week or two, it was clear that this was more than we had bargained for. We learned that parenting has way more to do with giving up control and living with a messy, tense process.

Kids don't do what we want them to do. Kids have helped me know that there is a God, and I am not Him! There's only so much I can do for them; I have to give them over to God. I get to be a shepherd and guardian. That's freeing for me, because I don't have to be in control. I don't have to fight to do things my way.

Samuel and Stephanie Rainey

a purpose, a driving passion or calling that provides meaning and impact. This is a person's mission.

Ultimately that means helping your child identify and embrace his or her unique, God-designed assignment. Every child, every human being wants and desires to experience an exhilarating adventure for a lifetime. We believe that mission can best be known by joining God for His unique purposes for your child, one of which is to reach and influence future generations and help them understand the grace and truth offered in Jesus Christ.

Think for a moment of this great privilege: God has given you the noble task of crafting each of your children into an arrow that will be released to help change the world. In this book and in our companion video series, *FamilyLife's The Art of Parenting*, we will help give you the tools you need to guide the development of each of your children into an arrow. We will break down these four essential elements—character, relationships, identity, and mission—and help you understand how to develop a biblical parenting plan for each of your children.

You will find that the art of parenting your unique, individual children—your arrows—requires patience, creativity, and persistence. In fact, that's why we titled this book *The Art of Parenting*, not *The Science of Parenting*. Science is built on studies, precisely controlled environments, and formulas. The Scriptures do not provide an exact equation we can follow and control for guaranteed results. How often we wished for the surety of simple rules, even one tried-and-true recipe that was foolproof. And you've wished for those prescriptions, too, we know. All parents do.

Instead, the Scriptures provide the wisdom that will guide you and give you skill as you form and shape your children's character, relationships, identity, and mission. While God's Word is eternal and true, each of your children is different. Each one will experience life in a different way and will require a different tailored plan.

As parents, we do not control the ultimate destiny of our children—the targets our arrows hit. But we do influence their direction and how true they will fly.

When God Changes the Script

Do you have faith in God? Do you trust Him and want His best for your family? Most of you would confidently answer yes.

But do you know God well enough to know how He will act and work? Tentatively you might reply, "Well, maybe," or, "I hope so." Wisely, you wouldn't say, "Of course," because the God who loves us is a mystery.

Over the decades of our parenting journey, God has been faithful beyond our deserving. He has also interrupted our plans and our expectations for reasons we couldn't understand or explain—all part of His greater designs, His greater good, His greater intentions for us and our children. And we have learned to trust Him in it all.

Our son Samuel was about eighteen months old when we began to see he was a natural athlete. His first word was "ball," and as soon as he could walk, he loved throwing anything round. He was adorable in every way. But when he got older, his precise aim and spin on the ball put everything in our house at risk.

At thirteen he changed from throwing balls to hitting them over a net with a racquet. His natural athleticism made it easy for him to quickly gain skill levels and start competing in tennis tournaments across our state.

Eventually he was ranked seventh in the state in his age bracket. But oddly, his game began to slide. His coach didn't understand why Samuel wasn't getting to balls he had reached earlier with ease, or why he was falling on the court. Soon we began a series of doctor visits to figure out what was going on. Eventually a neurologist diagnosed neuro-muscular degeneration. The bottom line was, Samuel's days of running were over, and his tennis, too.

Although Samuel's disease was not life-threatening, the result was as final as death. Our son's dream to achieve athletic success and our dream of delighting in watching him reach his God-given potential died that day. But the facts didn't stop his game immediately. He pushed against the verdict on the court for several months before the painful truth became real. As parents, we mourned, cried, asked God why, and prayed for mercy, for God to somehow use this for great good.

Late one afternoon I (Dennis) picked up Samuel from his job at Chick-fil-A. I was struggling to keep my emotions composed as he got in the car. Watching him walk with his new but now familiar gait still hurt to see, a constant visual reminder of the loss. As we drove away from the mall, I asked him how he was feeling about his disability. It was quiet for a few minutes. Then he said, "Well, Dad, I guess you don't need legs to serve God."

I couldn't talk. All I could do, as I brushed away a stream of tears, was reach across the seat and squeeze his shoulder.

In that moment, the God we as a family believed in, the God we taught our children to trust, became the only stability we knew. Everything had changed, it seemed, but God had not. And in Him our son found his strength to face a very uncertain future. He chose the unseen eternal truth over fleeting temporal physical strength.

When God interrupts your plans, when He changes the script, we as parents must be ready to both guide our children and respond on our own with hearts of faith. Thousands of variables will affect both the crafting of your arrows and the repeated releasing of them. Only God is unchanging and worthy of our ultimate trust.

2 What Every Child Needs

Before I got married I had six theories about how to raise children. Now I have six children and no theories.

Unknown (frequently attributed to John Wilmot)

I (Dennis) had just pitched my travel bag in the back of our Honda station wagon. I turned on the ignition and was about to back out of the garage to head off to the airport for a business trip when I saw Ashley had walked up to the driver's side window. I rolled the window down, smiled, and asked, "What's up, Princess?"

Ashley's eyes looked down. Quietly and slowly her words escaped: "Dad, I'm afraid your plane is going to crash." Then she gently placed her hand on my forearm.

A few weeks earlier, a Delta jet had crashed in Dallas. Our family heard the news live on the car radio as we were returning from vacation. Ashley had heard the reporters talk about first responders, billowing smoke, and casualties.

My eleven-year-old Princess was afraid.

So I did what every dad tries to do—I tried to fix it by addressing her fears with logic. "Airplane engines are among the best maintained pieces of machinery in all the world," I told her. I could tell she wasn't feeling comfort, so I continued. "Airplanes are much safer than cars—and you've never seen our car just quit driving down the road, have you?"

The pained look on her face wasn't going away. Finally, I got it. She didn't need an engineering lesson. She needed her daddy to speak to her soul about faith. I needed to seize this teachable moment.

I regrouped and silently prayed the prayer of the helpless parent: *Lord, help me know what to say here.* Then I put my hand on her hand, looked in her eyes, and said, "Princess, it's okay to feel afraid. I'm glad you told me. I have things that frighten me, too." She nodded.

"In a few moments I need to leave and go to the airport. I wish I could stay here with you, but I can't. But there is someone who is always with you. You can cast all your fears on Jesus Christ. He'll be with you after I leave . . . and for the rest of your life."

To help her visualize what I was saying, I explained, "Picture a bunch of cords coming from you to your mom and me. Our assignment as parents is to help you unplug those cords from us and help you plug them into God." I took her hand and "unplugged" one of those imaginary cords from me, and then stretched her arm above her head toward heaven and plugged her cord into God.

A tiny smile lit Ashley's sweet face. She reached above her head, unplugged her invisible cord from God, plugged it back into me, and said, "But what if I don't wanna plug into God?"

For a moment, silence and that invisible cord hung in the air. Then I looked her in the eyes, took her hand and unplugged her cord from me, plugged it back into God, and said, "But you gotta!"

We both smiled. Then I took her hands in mine and said, "I need to get to the airport. May I pray for you?" She nodded and I prayed, "Lord, help Ashley talk to You and trust You with her fears. And, God, please keep me safe on this trip!"

As I pulled out of the driveway, I waved at Ashley and she grinned back. My little girl was becoming a young lady. I thought about how the culture in which she was growing up didn't have many moorings, and how she would need to grow in her experience of depending on Christ.

A Vital Relationship with Christ

This treasured moment with our daughter is a snapshot of the most important job of a parent: to pass on a living faith, parent to child.

From our observations and experience over the years, it seems that most parents today have three basic goals for their children:

We want our children to be *safe*.
We want them to be *happy*.
We want them to be *successful*.

But how do we achieve those goals? You have only so much control as a parent.

No matter how much you protect your children, they will still be touched by danger, by injury, by sickness.

Our good friend Ann Wilson said it this way:

> Some people would say, "I just want my kids just to be happy." And I feel like that's not good enough. Because first of all, there's going to be so much hardship and heartache that our kids are going to experience. Happiness is just an emotion that comes and goes. But I want my kids in the long run to feel like I'm here for a purpose and on purpose. I am here to be on mission, because God has something for me, that he's put in me, that he wants me to do. I want them to live for Jesus.

She's so right. You can give your children happy moments and memories, but you can't prevent them from experiencing sadness or hurt or fear or disappointment.

You can help them build useful skills and a strong work ethic, and give them the best education you can afford. But at some point they will leave home and make their own choices, and you won't be able to control the outcomes.

That's why having a living faith and passing that faith on are so important.

When you encourage your children to establish and develop a relationship with the one true God, that connection will keep them *safe* in His hands no matter what they experience, it will give them a reason to be *happy* in the midst of fear and sorrow, and it will make them *successful* as they seek to follow God's will for their lives.

In fact, when you are closely connected to God, safety and happiness and success will look different, because God defines them differently than our culture does. Nothing is more important than connecting your children with their Creator, with the sovereign, unchanging, eternal God who ultimately controls their destiny. That's your real target as a parent.

And we guarantee that there is nothing more satisfying than watching your children grow into adults and work through everything life throws at them when you know at their core they walk with God. As verse 4 of 3 John says, "I have no greater joy than to hear that my children are walking in the truth."

The Top Ten Twitter List of What Every Child Needs

Newborns come with basic universal maintenance needs: to be fed, clothed, cleaned, held, and loved so that the nascent life in them can be cultivated into their full potential. But baby humans also have nonphysical needs that can't be purchased from Amazon and stored on your pantry shelf. Like the invisible framing of your home or apartment that supports the walls that protect and shelter your family, these needs of every child provide a framework of stability and security within which you provide the daily doses of love, care, and feeding your child needs to flourish.

So for simplicity and succinctness, we've created a top ten list of every child's needs, from least important to most important. And since we know you're busy, we've worked hard to follow the Twitter model and keep each item under 280 characters. Like providing the roof over your child's head, passing on a living faith is your number one goal, your child's number one need. All other needs of your child reside under this one.

#10: A home that is *not* child-centric. Your marriage is like the sun and your children like the planets revolving around the sun. Parents provide the gravity that pulls the family together, not the children. You are supposed to be in charge, not the kids.

#9: A home led by intentional and purposeful parents. Being intentional means investing lots of time planning, making wise decisions, and assuming responsibility for raising the next generation. Being purposeful means working to be consistent on discipline, boundaries, and standards.

> The single greatest desire for any Christian parent for their children is that they walk with the Lord, that they're born again, converted, repentant, and profess faith in Jesus Christ and walk with Him. That's what we want more than anything else.
>
> KEVIN DEYOUNG

> It's really important for kids to see that Mom and Dad love each other and have a life together that doesn't just center around the kids. It's so easy for marriage to become survival just managing this crazy household business. God is first and then your marriage second. Kids need to see Mom and Dad having fun together, laughing together, making it a priority to spend time together. Over time they find safety and security in that.
>
> KEVIN DEYOUNG

#8: A secure home. Security is far more than an alarm system, seat belts, and child safety locks. Children need emotional stability and peace. One of the biggest keys to your kids' feeling safe at home is building a strong marriage. Keep your covenant. Work on your marriage.

#7: Parents who pray together daily. We've done this almost every day since marrying in 1972. It has strengthened our marriage and kept us dependent on God as we raised our children. Single parents can find another single parent who would be encouraged by having a prayer partner.

#6: Parents who don't freak out when . . . their children fail or are caught lying, stealing, kissing, sneaking out, hiding things, making stupid choices, doing drugs, and more. And don't freak out when your children have doubts or push back against your faith!

#5: Parents who embrace God-given differences as male and female. Men and women are made in the image of God, male and female, and we are very different. Your children need to see you relating to one another, working together as a team, and modeling maleness and femaleness.

#4: A mom who is nurturer, lover, and vigilant protector of her kids. Children's souls need to be nourished by a mom who understands her indispensability. Mamas love, believe in, defend, rescue, encourage, and fight for their children like no one else on earth. Be there for them.

#3: A dad who is a servant leader, protector, and provider. Your children need to see what a real man does—pursuing relationship with God, his wife, and his children. Model humble leadership and provide spiritually, financially, educationally, and emotionally. Be there, dads.

#2: Parents who have surrendered to Christ because of His sacrificial love. Your children are like radar units locked in on what you say and how you live. We've not done it perfectly, but we have tried to model a life lived that glorifies God for our children and grandchildren.

#1: A personal relationship with Christ. As we've said, passing on a living faith to your child is your number one responsibility as a parent.

Another Teachable Moment

Not many days after my garage conversation with Ashley, I had the privilege of seizing another teachable moment with ten-year-old Benjamin.

It was evening and Barbara was away at a meeting. I read a few stories to the kids, tucked them into bed, and prayed with them. I told Benjamin that he could read until nine o'clock, but then he had to hit the hay. But five minutes after nine, as I was at work writing in my study, I felt a child's presence next to my chair. It was Benjamin.

Single-Parent and Blended-Family Wisdom

Children gain a sense of security when their parental caregivers (grandparents, parents and stepparents, mentors) are consistent and have a strong alliance. A healthy co-parenting relationship with his or her other biological parent also builds security in a child's heart. Respectful cooperation between these "bonus parents" and biological parents is a blessing to children.

Sometimes, one parent in a home is more serious about godliness than the other, and many children live between two homes that have slightly to vastly different spiritual values. This is confusing for kids. If that's you, be very intentional about modeling and teaching spiritual truths while children are in your home.

And finally, establishing your marriage as the basis for parenting in a blended family takes intentional effort. After the death of a parent or divorce, a single-parent home typically reorganizes around the parent-child relationships. When a stepparent enters the picture, the family has to reorganize again, this time around the couple. When kids precede your marriage, you have to work even harder to make your marriage a priority so that you can lead together as parents. This may not sit well with most children because initially it feels like another loss to them. Being united and supporting one another as you make the shift over time is vital to establishing a safe home environment.

Ron Deal

Pushing my chair back from the computer, I asked, "What's up, buddy? You're supposed to be in bed."

Sheepishly, Benjamin replied, "Dad, I was reading *Huckleberry Finn*, and there were these robbers. . . ." He paused, looking at the floor, then went on, "Dad, I'm afraid some robbers are going to come get me while I'm sleeping."

I pulled him close, gave him a firm hug, and said, "Hey, it's all right. Let me tell you what happened with Ashley the other morning." I went on to share about her fears and the promise of unplugging her dependence on me and plugging into God.

I took Benjamin's hand to pull out one of those invisible cords and plug it above his head into God. Then I felt another child's presence in the room. It was Ashley. "What's going on?" she inquired.

"Benjamin is a little afraid," I said.

"Benjamin, you mean *you* are afraid?" Ashley said with surprise sprinkled with a tiny bit of glee.

"Yeah," Benjamin sheepishly responded, trying not to, but finally admitting he had a need.

Ashley then told him about her garage theology class. After praying with them, I scooted them off to bed. I turned and looked over my shoulder, watching them walk up the stairs together. They were side-by-side, and Ashley had her arm around her brother. "It's okay, Benjamin," she said, "I'm going through the same thing."

Teachable moments are opportunities for us to imprint God's values on the next generation. They represent God's ordained means to pass on His agenda to our children.

3 What Every Parent Needs

The heartbeat of being a good parent is the same as the heartbeat of being a mature Christian. The thing that our kids need most from us is that we love and follow Jesus.

Kevin DeYoung

When Dennis and I married, I had no idea what I was getting myself into. I'm guessing you can identify. Most of us wake up bewildered one day, wondering how we ended up *here*, because it isn't all that we imagined when we said I do.

Spontaneous adventure seemed to be my new husband's middle name. To be sure, we had a lot of fun in those early years, and I'm grateful for the enthusiasm he brought to my world, but his impromptu ideas often left my head spinning. Like the time he had this grand idea that we should drive to Yellowstone National Park for the weekend. Why not?

We drove nearly ten hours from Boulder, Colorado, to Yellowstone, found our way to Old Faithful, and watched the geyser erupt as the sun set. Romantic, right? Then we meandered around the park loop until we found an open camping place, pulled in our car, fixed a meager camp dinner of who knows what, and spent the night in sleeping bags in the back of our car. The next morning we woke up, broke camp, and drove more than five hundred miles back home to Boulder. Over twenty hours in the car to watch one geyser, albeit a famous one, blow its top!

Life with my husband was quite the adventure.

And then we had children!

Sleepless nights, a two-year-old's asthma attacks, first steps, cereal ground into the car floor, learning to share, endless instructions like, "Don't throw your food," "Pick up your toys," "No, you can't hit your brother" . . . *It wore me out.* And then we had a few more kids to make an even half dozen.

An adventure with a thousand unknowns awaits parents when they bring a new child home. No instruction manual comes in the package. A few printouts, perhaps, on feeding, swaddling, and cord care, but like us, you probably had more than one late night of feeling that you had no idea what you were doing.

This chapter gives parents a packing list for this wild ride—eight best practices, essentials for you to keep in your purse or backpack at all times. Like the North Star or the Southern Cross, which have guided adventurers for millennia, these points of your compass will keep you on course along the way from start to finish.

Parents are in charge. It's you who must carry the load, and it's often a very heavy load. You start by providing the structure and atmosphere to meet your children's growing needs and help them to flourish—that's the Twitter list in chapter two. This list is for you. It's what you need personally to fuel, guide, and support your decisions, keeping you on course, steering you as you direct your children.

This list starts and ends with the most important items. Like two sides of a coin, you can't have one without the other.

1. A Bible That Isn't Dusty

If you want your children to choose to follow Jesus—to grow a real faith that is all their own—your number one go-to resource for life is the Bible. They need to see you with your Bible, one that is familiar to you, worn by your hands and with its pages marked.

Jesus commands His followers to abide in Him and His Word (John 15:1–11). One meaning of the word *abide* is to "draw your life's source from." It means you allow Christ and the Scriptures to be your primary source for doing life in good times, hard times, and all times.

The Scriptures give you the truth to guide decisions, big and small, in all of life, including parenting. Wisdom, which is essential in every aspect of raising kids, is godly skill in everyday living. Wisdom isn't a to-do list or the one and only way to raise kids. Wisdom develops from your being in the Word and the Word's being in you. There are no shortcuts, but God is faithful and delights to take all your small, often-interrupted-by-children's-needs attempts to read His words and multiply them in your heart.

I (Barbara) know you will want to quit reading the Bible. I wanted to quit and did at times. Life just squeezed it out. But don't let your Bible sit too long without your eyes falling on its inspired words for *you*. Always ask Him to meet you there. He will even if you don't feel like it.

Keep your Bible close-by all the time. It's your North Star.

2. An Understanding of the Times and the Wisdom to Act

In the Old Testament there's a story about the soldiers who were part of King David's army, the "mighty men who helped in war" (1 Chronicles 12:1). The descriptions are worthy of an epic Hollywood film with a cast of thousands. There were soldiers who could shoot arrows or sling stones with either hand, men "whose faces were like the faces of lions and who were swift as gazelles" (verse 8), and officers with supernatural reputations—"the least was a match for a hundred men and the greatest for a thousand" (verse 14).

Yet in the midst of this accounting of David's warriors was this notation about the men of Issacar: "men who had understanding of the times, to know what Israel ought to do" (verse 32).

These leaders were singled out for bringing wisdom to the mix. God knew it wasn't all about brawn and bravery. Leading an army is not unlike leading

> Our parents communicated very clearly who the parents were and who the children were, and that we were not the bosses. That was good for us. It's preparation for life. We are not the center of the universe; the Lord is. Part of the gospel is dying to ourselves and surrendering to Christ. Children do not need to grow up thinking they are the center of the home, the center of the marriage, and that what they say goes.
>
> STEPHEN KENDRICK

a family. Both require wisdom to not just know what to do next but when and how to do it. The men of Issachar brought tactical, practical, seasoned wisdom.

In every generation parents need an understanding of their times. What is going on in and around the lives of your children? What are the forces seeking to undermine you as you raise your children? What distractions are seeking to pull your children away from you and the truth? What challenges will your kids face in the years to come? As in battle, there will be unexpected surprises that will test you and take you off your game plan, but the more you antici-pate them, the better you will be prepared to adjust how your arrow will fly.

At times you will feel like you are in an all-out war, like the warriors who fought for King David. Your success is dependent on whom you trust for wisdom. Will you rely on your own opinions, the latest advice you find on the web, a friend's suggestion, or God Himself? Wisdom comes from under-standing what the Bible teaches. Ask Him to show you what to believe about these issues.

As you find answers, underline them or write down the supporting verses. You'll need to explain your case to your children sooner than you might believe.

- What is your worldview? How does God fit into your thinking?
- Are there moral absolutes, clear right and wrong, and what are you basing you convictions on?
- What does it mean to be a boy and not a girl? What did God build into man and into woman that makes them unique and why?
- What does the Bible say about sexual immorality, cohabitation/living together, divorce, pornography, abortion, bullying, and a hundred other questions your generation is asking today? Will you have convictions that can be explained to your children when they question you?

The men of Issacar could be described as thoughtful, prepared. They were paying attention and weren't caught off guard. Effective, intentional leadership is another descriptor for parenting, for both moms and dads.

Our friend Caleb Kaltenbach says, "Christians need to realize we are no longer the home team. We are the visitors." Our culture is growing increas-ingly hostile toward biblical Christianity. The truth is Christians have always been pilgrims here on earth, but our present prosperity in America has made us forget this earth is not our home.

Parents in every generation have faced an adversarial world: wars, epidemics, genocides, poverty, wicked rulers, and more. Parents need Jesus above all else. He will guide you and give you the wisdom you need.

Begin a journal with a page for each of the questions above, and record what you learn from your own Bible reading, from church, from a Bible study, or from this book.

3. A Big Vision of Children

God's plan has always been multigenerational. He has entrusted us, His frail children, with the big responsibility of sharing His good news with our children, and then launching them like arrows to carry the same message to their children.

In Genesis 1:28, God said to Adam and Eve, "Be fruitful and multiply and fill the earth." Those words are meant for us. Bearing and raising children is part of God's plan. Here's a quick reminder of God's big vision of children:

- They are a reward and a blessing (Psalm 127:3–5).
- They are made in His image (Genesis 1:26).
- They are messengers who will carry the Word and image of God from one generation to the next (Psalm 78:4; Genesis 18:19).
- They are a promise. In Matthew 19:14 Jesus says, "Let the little children come to me and do not hinder them, for to such belongs the kingdom of heaven." There is no future without them. They are a nation's greatest resource, your family's clearest message, and the disciple makers of tomorrow.
- They are a redemptive gift. In Matthew 18:3 Jesus says, "Truly, I say to you, unless you turn and become like children, you will never enter the kingdom of heaven." Little children are helpless, totally trusting in their parents. They offer nothing in the way of skills or accomplishments. In the same way, we enter the kingdom of God totally trusting in what God has done for us in Christ. In addition, children call us, as parents, away from selfishness. God gives us children to show us what we are really like and to help us become responsible.

Why Consistency Matters

When our twins were our only kids and very young, it was easy to assume Jake and I had the same values and same approach to training because we grew up in similar homes with similar Christian values.

But we soon realized we were assuming incorrectly, and in some situations we told our kids different things. They were confused because they didn't know how we were going to react.

Eight years later, we're in a much more stable, settled place. Most important, we've decided we will enact discipline *together* as often as possible, so our children know both of us are behind their consequences.

It's often easier to just let one parent do most or all of the discipline, but we want our kids to see that we are working as a team. Of course, it's not possible every time. When Jake is at work during the day, it necessarily falls to me, but he backs me when he comes home. This reinforces the fact that we are in this together.

Still, there are times we look at each other with eyes that ask, "What do we do this time?" If we aren't sure, we step away from the kids so they don't hear us discussing them and therefore have the opportunity to divide us. When we haven't talked in private, our smart kiddos know who the weak link is and will try to influence the one they perceive to be waffling.

Rebecca (Rainey) and Jake Mutz

Title another page in your journal "My Big Vision for My Children," and write these five bullets where you can remind yourself your children are of inestimable value even on days when you want to quit and scream and turn them over to someone else! Or print the list and hang it in your kitchen or on your bathroom mirror to see them every day. I wish I'd had this list.

4. A Clear Road Map

On your parenting journey there will be twists and turns and detours aplenty, but a map will help you see the big picture and stay on track more easily. Parenting as a journey is not unlike Christian's journey in John Bunyan's classic *Pilgrim's Progress*:

The starting point for your adventure is **receiving your child as God's gift.** For most of us, the moment of birth or adoption is a joyous occasion marked by announcements, celebrations, and great hopes. It is a clear point in time with no turning back.

The ending point is **releasing your child to God's purposes and care**—a significant launch point to college, marriage, military service, or a full-time job. These milestone moments are also usually marked by high hopes, announcements, and great celebrations to honor your child's successful arrival at the long-anticipated destination. Sandwiched in between the beginning and ending are thousands of practice runs for both receiving and releasing your child, essential steps toward arriving at the target satisfied that you've done your job well.

Re-receiving your child may seem like an odd concept, but as you walk this path of parenting, you will realize the need to accept each child as he or she is in key moments of life. You will discover surprising talents and traits you didn't expect that might or might not be easy to welcome into your world and experience. Unpleasant tendencies and sin patterns will require you to receive and trust God's good plan and design. You won't always like what you see in your child, but it's important that you accept the entire package—not just the parts of the package that you like. Each child is a gift to you for reasons you will learn and for purposes you'll never know. Trusting that God knows what He is doing is essential for continuing to receive your child.

There are also many **practice releases** during childhood and adolescence—times when your child takes steps toward more independence. The first day of kindergarten, sleeping away overnight, earning a driver's license . . . All these involve crucial instruction where you teach and coach about how to behave, what to do or say or not say, how to trust God while not with Mom and Dad. And then you let them go. After each mini-release, we encourage you to reflect on what you learned from the experience—about yourself and about your child.

When our six were in their senior years of high school, we intentionally talked often about their leaving home and what it meant to represent Christ without us there to guide them. It was a season of transition. Like letting out more and more string on a kite, we gave more and more freedom that last year for each one to exercise more self-government and make more decisions autonomously while still respecting our family values and boundaries. Some of our "kites" soared, and some crashed, with further lessons to be learned.

From start to finish, the long road of parenting involves staying on the road, repeatedly doing the often thankless work of teaching and training, receiving and releasing, always with an eye on the destination—grown children who know God and, we hope, will follow Him on their own because they want to, not because they have to.

Add a simple road map to your journal, with the beginning marked in the lower left corner of the page with the word *receive*, maybe with your child's name and date of birth and a little confetti drawn in the margins for fun. Draw a winding path in the direction of the upper right corner of the page and add the words *re-receive* and *practice release* several times along the way. Then mark the ending point. You can leave it vague, unless your child is already in high school, and then you might want to do some work on preparing for the big launch, making notes on this page for the big day.

5. A Team Approach

This may surprise you as it did me (Dennis). I remember my seminary professor Dr. Howard Hendricks telling our class that he would rather see a child raised in a non-Christian home where the two adults agree on their approach to parenting than in a Christian home where the mom and dad are divided and in constant disagreement. I will never forget sitting in class and struggling with that statement. The lesson stuck with me as a new dad—it was imperative for Barbara and me to work through our differences in parenting and be a united team as we raise our children.

Children are like radar units, "locked on" and constantly "reading" mom and dad. They are looking for signals, clues, and hints telling them how to feel about themselves, about their family, and about life in general. You are their true north, their stability, their peace. It's essential that both Mom and Dad work to be in agreement about how they raise their children. You won't always agree on everything, but consistency and a unified approach must be the goal.

Some of you know how this feels from your own experience. Do you remember going to the parent who was the easy touch when you wanted to do something? Children know how to wrangle and manipulate to get their way. Yours will seek to divide you, too, if you let them, sending a confusing signal to your children.

When they pressed us for a decision, on more than one occasion we called a time-out, explaining that we would let them know later. We would explain that we loved them and that if there was any way possible to give them what they wanted, we would. But if in our judgment it wasn't best for them, they

Team Harmony

Building harmony in your parenting team requires intentional effort. Your parenting context will impact how you achieve harmony. In biological two-parent homes, marital harmony supports your parental harmony, so work hard to strengthen your marriage. For a single parent dealing with an ex-spouse, finding cooperation with the other parent means overcoming the negativity of your relational past. It's critical to forgive and learn to set aside personal differences that led to your relationship breakup so you can focus on parental goals.

This dynamic is also a factor in blended families. Plus, you must incorporate the new stepparent into the parenting team and support his or her developing authority with the children.

In all of these situations, united *you* stand, but divided *they* fall. Children pay the biggest price for our lack of parental harmony. One significant reason for parental disharmony is different parenting styles. What if one parent (or home) is strict and the other permissive? Can one of you hold the children to a standard the other parent (or home) does not? Some differences are marginal in their impact, others are quite significant. Working toward cooperation and harmony is important because it reduces gaps in expectations and discipline.

Discussions about the principles can help you get on the same page. You do not have to be identical in your parenting, but within your home and between homes you do want to more alike than different.

Ron Deal

would need to trust us with our decision. We'd take a walk or go to another room to discuss alternatives, and then give them our decision.

Add to your map several islands of clarity and name them *teamwork*, *be united*, and *this is us—stand firm*.

6. A Core Values List

After we'd had three or four children, we began struggling to maintain a team approach as parents. It became clear that we had some different ideas about what was most important. Dennis loved having fun with the kids (he valued relationships), and Barbara wanted to teach them to work (she valued responsibility). We both appreciated the other's different approach, but we disagreed on how much time we spent playing versus working.

One weekend we went away to talk about our lives, our values, and what was most important to us as we raised our kids. We began with each of us making a list of what we valued most as outcomes for our children. After we wrote down as many qualities we could think of, we each narrowed our lists to ten qualities and ranked them from most important to least important.

Then we shared our lists with one another, explaining why we'd chosen each value and why we ranked them as we did. That alone was a meaningful and helpful experience as we learned more about each other and our backgrounds.

Finally we merged our lists and agreed on our top five shared values. *Knowing Jesus* and *being a lifelong disciple* topped our combined list. Eventually we had a list of over twenty-five things we wanted to teach our children. We added to it over the years, and it's now twice as long. (Check out the sidebar in this chapter for an edited list of forty.)

Agreeing on our top five core values early in our parenting journey gave us unity as we approached a wide range of decisions over the years ahead, from school choice to friends to sports. We were emboldened to break with the herd and do what was best for our family *because we both embraced the same values.*

Choose another page or two in your journal and start your own list of values you hope to impart to your children. It's worth the time.

7. A Commitment to Community

We have become increasingly convinced and alarmed that one of the most damaging changes in recent years is the loss of community in raising our children. We used to look out for the children of others far more than we do now.

When I (Dennis) was growing up in Ozark, Missouri, population 1,300, in the 1960s, I knew that if I peeled out from a stop sign at 8:00 p.m., by the time I parked in the driveway at 9:30 p.m., my parents would know about it. One night I got into a fight at the Dairy Queen. Fifteen minutes later when I walked through the door, my folks already knew what had happened.

We've called parents about behavior we have observed in their children and heard in response that they didn't want to hear it. They didn't want to know. One parent angrily chewed me out for calling about something his son had done that was clearly wrong.

Forty Things We Sought to Teach Our Children

1. Above all, know God and fear Him.
2. Be a lifelong disciple and focus on your relationship with Jesus.
3. Respect authority—trust and obey your parents.
4. Have a strong work ethic.
5. Keep your promises. Do what you say you will do.
6. Believe God for too much rather than for too little.
7. Real strength is found in serving, not in being served.
8. Understand the power of moral purity and a clean conscience.
9. Learn how to handle finances: God's view of giving, saving, and spending.
10. Learn how to handle failure—your own and those of others.
11. Have compassion for the poor and orphans.
12. The tongue is powerful—use it for good, not evil.
13. Give too much rather than too little.
14. Practice manners and common courtesies; they show respect for others.
15. View life through God's agenda—the Greatest Commandment (Matthew 22:37–38) and the Great Commission (Matthew 28:16–20).
16. Give thanks to God in all things.
17. Pray always. It's talking to God and listening, too.
18. Learn the art of asking good questions, of carrying on good conversation.
19. Live your life surrendered to the authority of Christ.
20. Learn how to handle temptation.
21. By faith, trust Christ as your Savior and Lord, and share with others how to become a Christian.
22. Seek wisdom—skill in everyday living. Know how to make good decisions.
23. Gain a sense of God's direction and destiny for your life.
24. Stay teachable and do not become cynical.
25. Obtain godly counsel.
26. Flexibility and adaptability are important for coping in life.
27. Truth is best passed on through relationships.
28. Leave a legacy of holiness.
29. Keep life manageable. Don't take on too much. Say no often.
30. Tame selfishness—you can't always get your way.
31. Choices are yours to make, and results are yours to experience.
32. Respect the dignity of other people—*all* people.
33. Be faithful in the little things.
34. Character is the basis of all leadership.
35. Life isn't fair—don't compare yourself with or be jealous of others.
36. Live by commitments, not by feelings.
37. Express grace and forgiveness.
38. Value friendships that help you grow and become more wise.
39. Learn grace. Express it often through forgiveness.
40. Learn how to motivate people without manipulating them.

We need to drop our defensiveness and fear and encourage others to offer observations to us about how our children are doing when we're not there to see for ourselves. Take the initiative by telling the parents of your child's friends, "If you see my teenager doing anything questionable, you have the freedom to tell me. I want to know."

There is a natural community to tap into for our children's accountability—our churches. Certainly, these groups of folks ought to have the right perspective on the value and worth our children possess. We are in this thing together, and that should pertain especially to raising the generation that is the future of the church. Why not call a meeting of all the parents of your children, say fifth through twelfth grade? Give one another the challenge and freedom to look out for one another's children.

8. Prayer

This final best practice for your parenting journey circles you back to the author of your guidebook, the Bible, the one whose wisdom, values, road map, and plan will provide clarity along the way. Without question, parenting did more to inspire us to pray than any other experience in life.

From the beginning, we were aware of our inadequacies, our fears, and our mistakes.

Like the time I (Barbara) hurriedly put a shoe on eighteen-month-old Samuel's little foot. An hour later I couldn't understand why he was so fussy, until I discovered his little pinky toe was bent back! I was mortified. Thankfully, his tiny toe was fine, and he was happy as soon as I fixed the problem.

Our mistakes were legion. Our needs for wisdom and clarity equally great.

In addition to regularly asking God for wisdom to be like the men of Issachar who knew what to do, we returned to a number of other oft-repeated prayers regularly:

"God, give us wisdom indeed to know what to do next in raising our children." We faced many forks in the road that demanded divine guidance.

"God, protect our children from evil and harm." This is just as important now as it was when we prayed for our children. Your children are arrows, but on the spiritual battlefield they are also targets. The apostle Paul admonishes us to put on the whole armor of God. And he specifically tells us to be "praying at all times in the Spirit" (Ephesians 6:18). Be on the alert; your children are in the sights of our enemy, and he is on the prowl (1 Peter 5:8).

"God, raise up quality friends for our children who love You, and remove those who will not be a good influence." Friends and peers are powerful as allies and as villains.

"God, help us catch our kids when they do wrong." One of the most important purposes of discipline is to help our arrows understand they are sinners who need a Savior. The word *sin* is an archery term that literally means to "miss the mark." The sin is the distance between where the arrow hits and the bull's-eye. The bull's-eye for us and our children is God's perfection. Your child needs to know that we have broken God's laws and need a Savior to remove the penalty for our sins.

When your child sins, it's a fresh opportunity to remind him of what Christ did for him.

We also wanted to catch our children doing wrong so that they could begin to understand that God sees and hears all. We did not want them thinking they could outsmart God.

And the flip side of this prayer was *"God, help us catch them doing what is right"*—making good choices so we could reward the positive, motivating them to continue choosing good.

Take a look at the list of things we wanted to teach our kids and begin to write in your journal those qualities that would comprise your list.

Relationships Matter

Relationship is central not only to the order of the universe God has created, but also to parenting. You, a parent, can't construct character in your children without having a deep relationship with each one of them.

Henry Cloud and John Townsend, *Raising Great Kids*

God's first choice for receiving and experiencing love is the family. Warmly snuggled in this incubator, love nurtures life, feeds souls, and calls forth the blossoming flower of God's unique individual design in every person He has created. Then Love calls for love to be given in return.

Home is where a child takes the first tentative steps from receiving love to giving love. At home parents *and* children learn that selfishness and love can't coexist. And at home we learn what to do when we hurt others and fail to love well.

The home is God's supreme training ground for the life skill of love. And as a parent, you are God's best choice for communicating His unfathomable love to your children. You are also His original choice for teaching and training your child to love others.

The most well-known verse in the Bible, "For God so loved the world, that he gave his only Son, that whoever believes in him should not perish but have eternal life" (John 3:16) sums up God's ultimate motivation toward us: His great unfathomable love.

Love sent Jesus Christ to dwell among flawed, broken humans . . . to be our Immanuel.

Love motivated Jesus to live a perfect life so that He might woo us back to the Father.

Love kept Jesus nailed to the cross when He could have called on a legion of angels to rescue Him from His agony.

Love did all this so that we might know the Father and live with Him forever.

All because He wants a relationship with us. First John 4:19 tells us, "We love because he first loved us." God reached out to us first. He made the first move.

He created us with our physical senses so that we could see, hear, smell, and touch one another. But most important, He fashioned our cognitive and emotional capacity to taste His love and to give it in return. As 1 John 3:11 says, "This is the message you have heard from the beginning, that we should love one another."

And because He wants His family to be full of healthy relationships with others. When asked, "Teacher, which is the greatest commandment?" Jesus answered, "You shall *love* the Lord your God with all your heart and with all your soul and with all your mind. This is the great and first commandment. And a second is like it: You shall *love* your neighbor as yourself" (Matthew 22:36–39, emphasis added).

Who are your closest neighbors? Your spouse and your children.

If you miss engaging in relationships at home, you've missed Life Himself.

As you craft your child—your arrow—you have the privilege of growing a child who knows the love of God personally and then how to love people well with healthy relational life skills. And because teaching the limitless love of God to our children is an impossible task, God graciously gives us wisdom to do what we cannot do on our own.

"Apple Tree Girl"

Our second son was full of boundless energy. My repeated reminders, "Don't throw balls in the house. Take it outside," usually jogged his memory, and off he'd run. But I (Barbara) couldn't always keep ahead of him.

One day, from the kitchen I heard a distinct crashing sound and subsequent tinkling of falling pieces. Samuel had ignored our house rule and had just broken something in the living room. Walking to investigate, I found lying in multiple pieces the little Hummel figurine my grandmother had purchased in the 1950s on a trip to Germany. Apple Tree Girl had been a happy sight to me when I caught glimpses of her perched on the top shelf out of children's reach. Why keep her wrapped in tissue in a drawer when I could enjoy the sweet memory of my grandmother's gift amid the daily drudgeries of my life?

I was greatly disappointed, both to lose this gift and to know my instruction had not taken deeper root in Samuel's five-year-old heart. How many times did I have to repeat myself?

I sent Samuel to his room to sit on his bunk bed. I needed time to cool off and decide what to do. I was also hoping his banishment to solitary confinement would allow him time to reflect on his error while I finished dinner.

After dinner, I sent him back to his bunk and said I'd be there in a few minutes. I retrieved the pieces of Apple Tree Girl that I'd collected in a baggie and marched upstairs to the boys' room. I asked Samuel to tell me what our rules were about throwing balls in the house, and he repeated them perfectly. I knew he knew. I told him there would be a consequence but said, "I want you to know something first, Samuel."

I shifted the pieces of the Hummel to my left hand and leaned closer to my beautiful, precious blue-eyed, blond-haired son and cupped his face in my right hand. "Samuel, do you see this?" I asked. His sky blue eyes widened. He nodded. "I'm really disappointed you broke something that meant a lot to me. But I want you to know, Samuel Rainey, that I love you dearly, much more than this little figurine. Do you hear me?"

I paused to let it sink in and then said, "And I want you to learn how important it is to obey in our house. Do you understand?"

With great confidence, I can assure you my response was not natural. My natural heart wanted to be really angry, to let him feel how I really felt. But in the part of my heart that wanted to please God, to do the right thing with my son—whom I did passionately love more than the silly porcelain figure—I knew what mattered most was a relationship with my son. God helped me focus on what mattered, Samuel's heart. And my heart, too.

On that day I chose God's way over mine. The relationship mattered more than the rules. He still received a consequence, a spanking given with love and prayers spoken out loud over his little body snuggled in my lap. The momentary pain would be a reminder the next time he was tempted to ignore the rules. And as always after consequences, I hugged him close and repeatedly reminded him how very much I loved him.

Relationships of love matter supremely in your home.

Nurture them well.

4 Bridge Building Lane One

Loving Unconditionally

No amount of money or success can take the place of time spent with your family.

Unknown

Driving home one night after work, I (Dennis) switched on the radio to catch the news. In an uncharacteristic moment of sincerity, the disc jockey made a statement that sliced through the fog of fatigue I felt from the day: "I hope you did something of value today. You wasted a whole day if you didn't."

His statement struck me abruptly. Maybe it was because I had just spent most of the day solving some of the problems of a growing ministry. Fortunately, that day I felt pretty good about how I had invested my time.

Or perhaps it was because of where I was heading. In ten minutes I would be home, where one lovely lady and six pairs of little eyes would want and need my attention.

Will I do something of value with them tonight?

It's just one night, and besides, I'm exhausted, I thought.

Then I pondered how one night added to another, 365 times, adds up to a year. The nights and the years seemed to be passing with an increasing velocity.

Just one night, Lord. It's just one night. And then the same angel that wrestled Jacob to the ground pinned me with a half nelson as I drove into the garage.

Okay, okay. I give. You've got me. Being a Christian parent is not always easy in a narcissistic culture.

As the kids surrounded my car like a band of banditos whooping and screaming, "Daddy, Daddy, Daddy!" I was glad on this night I had made the right choice.

After dinner I gave them three choices for what kind of memory they would like to make that night:

- play Monopoly together as a family
- read a good book together *quietly*
- wrestle on the living room floor together

Which do you think they chose?

Three little sumo wrestlers grabbed my legs as they began to drag me into the living room. Dad was pinned by the kids. Mom was tickled by Dad. And kids went flying through the air (literally) for the next hour. Our ten-month-old even got in on the action by bouncing on me, imitating the other kids.

Do my kids remember that night? I doubt it. There were no wounds. Nor did we break anything to make it memorable. But choices like this are crucial for parents. Every day we need to decide what kind of legacy we want to leave. What kind of children do we want to raise? And what kind of relationship do we need to build with them?

Love Is Life-Giving

We cannot overstate the importance of spending time with your children, building a storehouse of memories, and, above all, loving your child well. Your love is life-giving. It says to your child, "You belong to us; you are significant and secure with us." True love is even willing to die for the other. If your child knows that kind of love, she will survive and thrive in life.

The absence of love is neglect and indifference. Both lead to the most dangerous condition for all relationships: isolation. The devil of hell's strategy is to create distance between spouses and between parents and children. In isolation a child can become convinced of almost anything—lies about God, lies about you as his or her parent, and most lethal of all, lies about himself or herself as your child.

This is why you as a parent must become a tenacious bridge builder to your child.

Bridge Building 101

Tall steel-beamed bridges fascinate us as a marvel of humankind's creative engineering. Think of the Golden Gate Bridge linking San Francisco to Sausalito with a length of more than a mile and a half. Or the Mackinac Bridge in upper Michigan, nearly five miles long. But the award for the world's longest bridge goes to Danyang–Kunshan Grand Bridge in China, part of the Beijing–Shanghai high-speed railway. It crosses 102 miles!

Historically, bridges contributed significantly to the booming growth of twentieth-century United States. As they sprouted from the Atlantic to the Pacific across rivers and valleys of all sizes, they made it possible to connect people and grow communities.

> If we're walking with the Lord and abiding in the vine of Christ, His Holy Spirit gives us wisdom that we don't have and patience and grace in moments of crisis. Parents need to be saying, "God, I need You, and I need to focus on You every day. I want to stay clean and close in my relationship with you because You're the source of all that is good when it comes to parenting."
>
> STEPHEN KENDRICK

In a similar way, constructing a bridge to your child's heart—his soul and his spirit—will help you cross from your world to his and establish and nourish a relationship built on love. The bridges you build to your child's heart will give you the right of way to

- give unconditional love daily, repeatedly
- comfort in times of failure, loss, and sickness
- teach and train in character-development issues
- establish and enforce standards of behavior
- discipline him when he disobeys or misbehaves
- speak words of truth when friends reject, tempt, or criticize

- lead your child to a relationship with God and spiritual growth
- answer the thousands of questions asked seemingly every week, or with some kids every day!

It's important to do everything you can to truly love your child and keep the relational bridge—with all its lanes, entrances, and exits—maintained and strong. Naturally, we need to correct and teach our kids. It's not always easy to balance the stern, authoritative side of parenting with love and affirmation.

But it's crucial. Because *having rules without relationship usually leads to rebellion.* When you build strong relationships with your children, that love spans obstacles, like your shortcomings and weaknesses as a parent, and connects your heart to theirs.

We suggest building a bridge with three lanes going from you to your children, and we label these lanes *love, pursuit,* and *forgiveness.* Hopefully, as your relationship grows, your child will begin construction on three lanes coming back to you.

Lane One: Love Your Child Unconditionally

Some stepparents find it difficult to find feelings of love and affection for prickly stepchildren. Choosing to act in love out of gratitude for God's love for you is one key to finding your way to an authentic love for the child.

RON DEAL

Every child is a mysterious combination of personality, gifts, talents, strengths, weaknesses, predispositions, innate fears, physical uniquenesses, and limitations that arrive with her at birth or adoption. Each child is "fearfully and wonderfully made" by our heavenly Father (Psalm 139:14).

Loving is easy when children are smiling happy babies, sweetly singing preschoolers, well-behaved middle-school kids, and successful, well-liked teens. And love is always easy when your children are sleeping peacefully and safely at home. Ahhh. Even teens are easy to love when they are asleep!

But love isn't so easy when they cry all night, refuse to get in the car seat, hit their fellow students, don't do their homework, rebel against all

The Love Chapter

Paul wrote about unconditional love in his famous Love Chapter, 1 Corinthians 13. Try personalizing the phrases in this chapter to help you see the depth of God's love. When you read, "Love is patient and kind," think, "*God* is patient and kind to me."

Then substitute *your* name: "I am patient and kind to my children. . . . I am not arrogant or rude." That's quite a challenge. How do you measure up?

And when your children do something wrong, you can explain from these verses, "Your choice does not make me happy, and God is likely not pleased, either. But whether you choose right or wrong, I will always love you, and God will, too." Explain you will always believe in them, always hope for them, always suffer with them when they hurt. Let them know your love isn't perfect, but it will never end, just as God's love will never end.

When you correlate your actions with what you know to be true about God, not only are you crossing the bridge to your child's heart and soul, you are taking his hand and guiding Him to the One who will never fail in any way.

your standards, scream and yell at you, and make life miserable for everyone in the family. In the sweet early years, it's impossible to imagine your precious angels could act abusively or dangerously.

God's love for us is unconditional, and it is boundless. In Psalm 36:5 we are told, "Your steadfast love, O Lord, extends to the heavens, your faithfulness to the clouds." God calls us to love others—and especially our children—in the same way. As John 13:34 says, "A new commandment I give to you, that you love one another: just as I have loved you, you also are to love one another."

The key to loving your children well involves a word not often associated with love. That word is *commitment*. Consistent, unending love means choosing daily to love regardless of how one feels or how the object of the love behaves.

Married couples know this. And it's equally true in parenting. Commitment means

- choosing self-control when you'd rather yell at them
- choosing to tell your children you love them every day, even when you don't feel like it and they are NOT being very lovable
- choosing to thank God for your child's preferences—for a child's interest in cooking rather than basketball and a thousand other surprises you never expected

From an Unknown Dad ─────────────

My family's all grown and the kids are all gone. But if I had to do it all over again, this is what I would do. I would love my wife more in front of my children. I would laugh with my children more—at our mistakes and our joys. I would listen more, even to the littlest child. I would be more honest about my own weaknesses, never pretending perfection. I would pray differently for my family; instead of focusing on them, I'd focus on me. I would do more things together with my children. I would encourage them more and bestow more praise. I would pay more attention to little things, like deeds and words of thoughtfulness. And then, finally, if I had to do it all over again, I would share God more intimately with my family; every ordinary thing that happened in every ordinary day I would use to direct them to God.

Quoted in John MacArthur, *MacArthur New Testament Commentary: Ephesians* (Chicago: Moody Press, 1986), 318–319.

- choosing to express affection—hugs, holding hands, kisses, etc.—when your child acts disinterested, even when he pushes back or refuses to hug you in return
- choosing to thank God over and over for the gift of this child, no matter what. Remember, God does not make mistakes.

When you let your child's negative actions or behavior stop you from moving forward in love, he or she is controlling you. It is imperative that you, the parent, remain more mature, more dependent on God, more prayerful, more committed to loving well than your child. You set the tone, not your child.

Warning: Teens can be emotional mud wrestlers. They know that if they can get you into the mud puddle with them, yelling, yes, and screaming as they do, they *think* they've won!

Love says no to mud wrestling. The bridge of love must span the mud holes and messiness of children of all ages. As children grow from total dependence upon us toward independence, they will fall, crash, make wrong choices, maybe try lying or stealing or a host of other poor behaviors. Your first goal on the road to your child's heart is always love.

Spanning turbulent rivers, dark valleys, and dangerous roads

Building the bridge of love in the early years and keeping it maintained and strong during the golden years will allow you to continue to travel across it when the often stronger storms of the teen years stir up troubled waters and test the steel structure of your heart.

Situations and obstacles commonly faced by parents can include

- rebellion of all sizes, from small refusals to running away from home
- deceit and manipulation
- video game addiction
- isolation created by social media (yes, this is an oxymoron; there's virtually nothing social about it)
- drug and alcohol use
- sexual immorality
- immodesty
- pornography
- peer pressure from expected and unexpected friends
- a prodigal who lives at home (this one definitely needs a bridge, but it may get washed out by too many storms and have to be rebuilt)
- a child who makes it clear he or she doesn't want to be in your family
- a child who rejects your faith
- a child who makes a life-changing mistake

Sometimes when teenagers are going through a hard time, the best thing to do is write a note: "I know you're going through a hard time. I know you don't like me very much right now, and maybe you don't even like yourself. But I love you totally and completely, and nothing can ever change that." Now, don't look for appreciation. They probably won't mention it. But one day you will find that note folded up in the corner of their drawer.

SUSAN YATES

The temptations and dangers in your child's life grow with each passing year. In other words, you are going to be at work keeping that bridge operational over your lifetime, not for just eighteen years.

In the middle years of your child's growing up, your young teenager is secretly asking, "I know I'm not lovable, but am I still loved? Will my mom and dad still love me? Because I don't even like myself right now. And I am so filled with self-doubt and self-contempt. Will they still believe in me?"

We need to love our children with Christ's love and with a love that reaches out to pick them up, nurture them, and cherish them. That means receiving them as gifts from God even when they act like the immature children they are.

We have a little phrase at our house that our kids picked up on. We look our kids in the eyes in the middle of a heated moment, put our arms around them, and say, "Nothing you can do will make me stop loving you."

In the next chapter, we'll talk about your bridge's second and third lanes.

5 Bridge Building
Lanes Two and Three

Pursuing and Forgiving

A child is the most needy person in our society, and the greatest need is love.

D. Ross Campbell, *How to Really Love Your Child*

A well-known Christian leader had just completed a fourteen-city tour for his new book and arrived home to a packed schedule. One appointment was a lunch that had been sold at a charity auction for $500. His surprise turned to astonishment when he learned that the person who'd won the bid had spent her entire savings account to have lunch with him.

But he was stunned when he found out who the person was. It was his teenage daughter, wanting some time with her daddy.

Many parents say they would do anything for their kids. But truly loving them and spending time with them is a challenge for many. It's important to be proactive and become a tenacious bridge builder to your child.

In the previous chapter we talked about the first lane of this super highway bridge—loving your child unconditionally. Now let's discuss the construction of lanes two and three.

Lane Two: Pursue Your Child

If you know Jesus as your Savior and Lord, you know the truth of this verse: "We love because he first loved us" (1 John 4:19). Christ pursues, chases, and persists in reaching the object, the person of His affection. Love finds a way through storms of protest. Love risks spanning the great chasm to reach us. As Romans 5:8 tells us, "God shows his love for us in that while we were still sinners, Christ died for us." So parents pattern their love after His in pursuing a love relationship with their children.

Pursuit is action. It's initiative and movement. It is a commitment to be involved with your kids through every phase of youth and adolescence.

Pursuit means a refusal to quit from discouragement. Pursuing love finds a way to build a bridge in the middle of a battle, crisis, or impasse. Pursuing love acknowledges and demonstrates the value of the object of affection by relentless seeking, refusing to be deterred, sticking with your child till death do you part.

We'd suggest three practical ideas for pursuing a love relationship:

1. Pursue with a strategy to date your daughters and your sons. Dating your children simply means finding ways to spend special one-on-one time with them. Our children are different people when outside their sibling relationships. So much of what we see at home is their attempts to make a name for themselves among the crowd of family members. Even in a family of two kids, a child has an identity in the group that is not the same as when one-on-one.

It's not easy to date your children in your busy lives of work and activities, but it's essential. Set an achievable goal for the number of dates per year per child—if you have a large family, three or four dates a year may be a reasonable starting place. It doesn't have to be a flashy expensive outing. It can be something as simple as a spontaneous Coke date. It's the focused time together, with purposeful questions and words of affirmation, that makes it meaningful and builds your relationship with your child.

One of our favorite stories comes from John Trent, who tells of a man with two daughters who took his two-year-old out for a date. They went to McDonald's for breakfast, and before they started eating, he looked little Ginny in the eyes and said, "Ginny, I want you to know that I love you. I want you to know how much I really love you as a little girl and how special you are to your mom and me. We have prayed for you for years, and now that you are here, we are thrilled that you are in our family. We could not be more proud of you."

Once he had said all of this, he started to eat, but Ginny's little hand caught his hand. "More, Daddy, more." So he began to tell her why he and her mom loved her so much, how proud they were of all the things she did, how nice she was to her sister, and how so full of energy she was. He reached down again to get a bite of pancakes. For a second time she said, "Longer, Daddy, longer."[1]

That is what our kids are interested in—some quantity and quality time with us.

2. Pursue with questions that can't be answered with a grunt or "I don't know." Our second child, Benjamin, was just starting middle school, and as with other boys his age, it wasn't easy to get him to talk and open up. One evening after work, I found him at the kitchen island waiting for dinner and lobbed a softball question: "Hey, buddy, how are you doing?"

He replied, as usual, "Great, Dad."

We talked about school and stuff for a few moments, and then something prompted me to ask a more probing question. "Hey, pal, at school, are you looking at anything you ought not to be looking at?"

I will never forget his shocked look as he asked, "Uh . . . why do you ask?"

"I don't know really. I just know at school there can be all kinds of toxic stuff floating around. I just wondered if you are keeping your eyes and heart clean."

The kitchen was buzzing with activity—a pot of spaghetti boiling on the stove, younger siblings racing through, his older sister stacking plates to set the table, Barbara making a salad on the other counter. Benjamin felt both inconspicuous and in the spotlight. He looked away, shuffled his feet, and said quietly to me alone, "As a matter of fact, today something happened at lunch."

One clear quality of smart stepparents is a dedication to pursuing a relationship with their stepchildren. Like all parents, pursuit of your child is important. What's different for stepparents, however, is whether or not the child is pursuing you. Children naturally pursue their biological parents, but not always a stepparent. Wise stepparents, however, continue to pursue their stepchildren even in the face of distance or rejection. Stay stubbornly persistent in your pursuit.

RON DEAL

> **I have** learned that when I love my kids, I speak affirming words to them and they know they are valued with me. And it's easier for them to believe they are valued in the eyes of God. If Mom and Dad love them unconditionally, it's easier to believe God loves them unconditionally.
>
> ALEX KENDRICK

Looking at me as though I were omnipresent, he said that after lunch he found some friends huddled around the teacher's desk in their homeroom. They called out, "Hey, Ben, come look at these porn pics."

I played it cool, leaned toward him, and asked, "What did you do?"

He said, "I left the room."

I cheered like he'd just scored a game-winning touchdown! I fist-bumped him and with a measured degree of intensity and declared, "Yes! Way to go, son!" It was just one choice on one day, but a decision to turn away from peer pressure and pornography can be a key moment in a young man's life.

Sometimes the right question can loosen a child's lips and help you learn what's going on in their hearts and in their world. Here are some you might try. And to stir the pot, you should be ready to answer them yourself.

- What was the highlight of your day? What was the lowlight?
- What did you learn today?
- Who was kind to you today? Who were you kind to?
- Is there anything going on that you are struggling with that you'd like to talk about?
- Did God show you something new about yourself or someone else today?

When they are older, you might try some bigger questions around a campfire or on a trip together:

- What's the most courageous thing you've ever done?
- What would you say are your greatest strengths? What are your dreams and ambitions?
- If you could be any living person in the world today, other than yourself, who would it be? Why?
- If you could be any person from the past, who would it be? Why?

Great opportunities exist to ask questions while driving carpool; while driving to or from events like games, practices, or youth group; around the dinner table; at bedtime. Kids are *always* willing to talk at bedtime—they're relaxed, they have your attention, and they love to delay lights-out! Even if you are exhausted and can't wait to get time to yourself and unwind, resist the weariness and pursue them.

3. Pursue your child with affirming and inspirational words. God pursues us with words. He calls us His beloved. He tells us we belong to Him forever. And it's all written, so we can read those words over and over and over. God also spoke audibly to us in the person of Jesus.

Our kids are thirsty for positive and encouraging words from us. Develop the art of affirmation with your children (and spouse, too), both verbally and in handwritten notes.

A few ideas:

- Pray and ask God to help you see and recognize your child doing something right. It's easy to catch your kids doing something wrong, but focus on finding the good and affirm—sometimes privately and sometimes in front of the whole family. Or write a note they can keep forever.
- Express belief in them: "I believe God has a great plan for you." Many teenagers struggle with self-doubt and wonder if God really does have a plan for their lives. Your words can give them hope and courage.
- Compliment them on who they are, not just what they do.
- Affirm them by asking them what they'd like to go do next Saturday or one night this week on a date. Watch what lights up their faces.
- Read good books with your child. Studies have proven that parents who read out loud to their children of all ages (not just toddlers) build vocabulary and knowledge, inspire adventure and conversation, and bond deeply as they cuddle together sharing the journey of a story into other worlds and places. Sharing the words of great authors can take you and your child on adventures better than any theme park offers and will assist you in building great relationships.

Lane Three: Make Forgiveness a Part of Your Family's DNA

Forgiveness is the oft-traveled lane of a humble person. Forgiveness demands humility. Forgiving love releases anger, sets aside the desire to get even, and refuses to heap on guilt. Forgiving love is willing to hurt, suffer, and never be repaid for the sake of another. Forgiving love mends relationships and keeps our hearts pliable and teachable. Forgiving love is always needed when pursuing love attempts to connect with the rebellious or broken heart.

Parents are, in some ways, like God to their children. We imitate and demonstrate and model what God did for us. Over and over and over. In the process, we grow a relationship with each child, and our relationship with God grows exponentially deeper as we desperately depend on Him to enable us to truly forgive. And our children take those initial baby steps toward their own relationship with the creator God who formed them.

The gospel of Jesus Christ is the ultimate bridge. God stepped out of eternity and became a man, dwelling among us to show us what grace, mercy, and forgiveness *really* look like by paying the penalty for our sins so that we might be forgiven. Forgiveness is at the heart of the gospel.

Forgiveness ought to be in the heart of every parent. Our lives, as parents to our children, are the first explanation of forgiveness that a child hears and sees.

When I (Dennis) was a teenager, I didn't like getting up for my first-period study hall. One morning I didn't respond very well to my mom's reminder that I needed to get up and get ready for school. I took a "swing" at her—maybe better stated would be a half-hearted leave-me-alone swipe.

Fortunately . . . I missed.

Eventually I apologized (and did so again several times as an adult), and Mom forgave me. But it was chilly around the house for over a week. I was an idiot. I don't think she told my dad.

Mom's forgiveness kept our relationship alive.

Read the above sentence again. You and I are the adults. As we raise our children, we can't afford to be anything other than a forgiver.

Paul reminds us of what that means in a challenge from God in Ephesians 4:32: "Be kind to one another, tenderhearted, forgiving one another, as God in Christ forgave you."

How did God forgive you? Even though you rejected Him, ran away from Him, and lived as if you were smarter than your Creator, He never stopped loving you. So He sent Jesus Christ to suffer the punishment for your sins, and by that sacrifice He offers you forgiveness. When you trust in Christ to save you, God will forgive you no matter what you've done. Forgiveness means that God gave up the right to punish you for your sins.

In the same way, when you truly forgive your children, you give up the right to punish them for what they've done. You give up the right to be angry and withdraw from them, or lash out at them in anger. Forgiveness frees you from being imprisoned in resentment and gives you the confidence to *repeatedly journey* across the bridge toward your children to reestablish a relationship with them.

Asking Your Children for Forgiveness

A crucial element for making forgiveness part of your family is maintaining a humble heart yourself. When you sin against your children—and you will—don't hesitate to apologize and ask for their forgiveness. It's one of the most powerful things you can do as a parent—it maintains your relationship, it demonstrates how to ask for forgiveness from others, and it shows the gospel of peacemaking in action.

Counselor and author Elyse Fitzpatrick says, "I was very, very afraid of telling my children about my own sin. When they have been the focus of my sin, then I have an obligation to go to them

> The teen years are all about one thing in our opinion—relationship. If you're giving them rules and there's no relationship, we all know that equals rebellion. The natural tendency for a parent is to pull back. They want to be dropped off a block from school. Don't want you at the theater anywhere near them. So many of us just retreat. And it's like, no, *pursue*.
>
> DAVE WILSON

and ask for forgiveness, and it's shocking what that does in a relationship. Because it tears down defensiveness, and it tears down the 'We're good, you're bad' dynamic. And then it makes us fellow sinners who flee to Jesus together."

For several years I (Barbara) was part of a mom's prayer group in our school. We prayed for revival in our school and in our children's lives.

Every time I would begin to pray, the Lord always brought me back to myself. I couldn't pray for revival in our children's lives without feeling like it was an incomplete prayer—I needed spiritual renewal, as well.

Then, in the fall of 1995, I began to sense God's working in my life in an unusual way. For many years as a parent, I had struggled with feelings of anger toward my children. I was diligent in rectifying my mistakes when I

> If you have your children's hearts, you have their ears. If you lose their hearts, you lose their ears. If your children aren't listening to you, ask yourself if you've disciplined in anger or have been hypocritical. But often, you can just ask them: "Have I hurt you and not made it right?" Let them talk, and you listen. It is so important that we model not only righteousness, but repentance, as well.
>
> STEPHEN KENDRICK

made them—for example, if I yelled at the children and shouldn't have, or if I disciplined them out of anger, I would ask for their forgiveness. But now I realized that He wanted me to deal with *the attitudes of my heart that had led to the anger.* And, oh, that was difficult—to see my selfishness and admit my desperate need for Him.

On the night before Thanksgiving we all gathered in the living room. Dennis and I talked about how God had been working in our lives during the previous months. I told them I wanted to make sure nothing I had done in the past would hinder them from experiencing the fullness of God in their hearts. Then, through my tears, I confessed my sinful attitudes and anger and asked for their forgiveness.

The kids had never seen me apologize to them collectively, through tears. I think they were a little stunned. But one-by-one, each of them forgave me.

Now, looking back, that moment was a major spiritual milestone in our family because I modeled humble repentance. The truth of James 5:16, "Confess your sins to one another . . . that you may be healed," was realized as God healed my heart and gave greater openness and connections with my children.

Speaking to a Child's Soul

David Robbins, our friend and the new president of FamilyLife, tells about a conversation with his eleven-year-old son after they experienced a conflict. As they finished talking, David spoke to his son's soul when he said, "I will never stop loving you, because God has never stopped loving me. I will never stop pursuing you no matter where you go or how long it takes, because my God has never stopped pursuing me. And I will never stop forgiving you or seeking your forgiveness of me, because God has never stopped forgiving me."

25 Ways to Provoke Children to Anger

One of the more convicting exhortations to parents in Scripture is Ephesians 6:4, "Fathers, do not provoke your children to anger, but bring them up in the discipline and instruction of the Lord." Colossians 3:21 says much the same thing: "Fathers, do not provoke your children, lest they become discouraged."

Parents are human, and it's very easy to fall into unhealthy patterns of behavior. And of course, this is a problem for mothers as well as fathers.

In his book *The Heart of Anger*, author Lou Priolo lists some ways parents provoke their kids to anger:

1. Lack of marital harmony
2. Establishing and maintaining a child-centered home
3. Modeling sinful anger
4. Consistently disciplining in anger
5. Scolding
6. Being inconsistent with discipline
7. Having double standards
8. Being legalistic (making man-made rules equal to God's law or a test of spirituality)
9. Not admitting when you are wrong
10. Constantly finding fault
11. Parents reversing God-given roles
12. Not listening to the child's opinion or side of the story
13. Comparing your child to others
14. Not having time to talk
15. Not praising the child
16. Failing to keep promises
17. Chastising a child in front of others
18. Giving too much freedom
19. Not giving enough freedom
20. Making fun of the child
21. Abusing a child physically
22. Calling a child names
23. Having unrealistic expectations
24. Showing favoritism toward one child over another
25. Employing child-training methodologies that are inconsistent with God's Word

Good parenting requires building our own character in addition to the character of our children. How fortunate that God has given us a spirit "of power and love and self-control" (2 Timothy 1:7). Even when you feel powerless to change your ways, God is still able to tranform your heart if you continue to be open to His work, willing to do whatever He desires for the sake of your children.

List adapted from Lou Priolo, *The Heart of Anger: Practical Help for the Prevention and Cure of Anger in Children* (Sand Springs, OK: Grace & Truth Books, 2015), 30–51. Used by permission.

This is the picture of how we really love our children well—by reflecting to them the immeasurably deep love of God. Make sure each of your children know without a doubt that your love will never end, even at death. You will love them forever because Christ has secured eternal life for all of us and we will live forever together in that love. Nothing will build security in your child more than your relentless, God-like love.

6 Teaching Love for Others

Sibling relationships outlast marriages, survive the death of parents, resurface after quarrels that would sink any friendship. They flourish in a thousand incarnations of closeness and distance, warmth, loyalty and distrust.

Erica E. Goode, author

I f your children wrote their thoughts to God about their siblings, what would they say? Is that a scary thought? Would they express how annoying their siblings are like these kids did?

Dear God, thank you for my parents, my sister Anita, and for my grandma and grandpa. I forgive you for my brother Phil. I guess you didn't finish working on him.

Sean, 12

Dear God, I learned in school that you can make butterflies out of caterpillars. What can you do for my sister? She's ugly.

Greg, 11

Dear God, do you have an extra plague for my sister? Like you did for the Egyptians? She's real stupid.

Stanley, 8

Dear God, I heard you say to love our enemies. I am only six and do not have any yet. I hope to have some when I am seven.

Amy, 6

If you have more than one child, these quotes may sound very familiar! As parents, one of our primary assignments is to teach our children how to love other imperfect people.

We like to think of the family as a greenhouse—a place where children are taught and trained how to live in relationship with others. It's at home that we plant the seeds of treating others with love. Home is where we nourish the hearts of children to speak and act with kindness. The seedlings of respect and patience are first grown at home, not at school or church.

Parents are the first and most important gardeners and guardians of their children's relationships. If children don't learn love at home, they won't know how to love out in the world. And as some who read these pages know personally, it's difficult to grow good things in the toxic soil of an adult's heart that wasn't cultivated properly as a child.

The challenge for parents is that these lessons are forged in the fire of sibling relationships. When your children are in conflict, it's not fun to watch them take out their hurts and anger on one another.

In Romans 12 Paul writes, "Love one another with brotherly affection. Outdo one another in showing honor. . . . Repay no one evil for evil, but give thought to do what is honorable in the sight of all" (vv. 10, 17). Brotherly affection? To us it seemed like brotherly *infection*! How many nights did we suffer through our two sons arguing and wrestling in their upstairs bedroom? Their room was right above the kitchen, and the kitchen light would bounce as they wrestled. On one occasion they bounced off the door and ripped it off the hinges!

We wish we had a ten-dollar bill for every sibling skirmish we've witnessed in the Rainey household. Our children verbally sparred over life-changing issues such as these:

- who gets to sit in the front seat of the car
- who got the biggest slice of Mom's homemade apple pie
- who has had the most friends over to the house, or who last had a friend spend the night

Teaching Our Sons to Be Friends

With seven sons, there's a lot of competition in our home. Squabbles naturally happen. Boys are rough and loud and physical, and someone is always getting hurt. As a mom, I want my boys to like each other and become friends. So here are a few ways I try to accomplish that goal.

When two of our boys get into an argument, my first preference is to help them talk it through. Often the offense was unintentional or accidental. They take turns hearing the other brother out as he tries to explain his perspective.

Michael and I are both teaching them to practice listening skills. We'll ask, "What did you hear your brother say?" so that they repeat what they heard. My dad always said, "Communication isn't what is said; it's what is *heard*." We want our boys to learn to listen as well as verbalize clearly.

Sometimes we need to let them cool off first. Often when we do this, I tell them they will need to apologize for their part in the conflict (each is almost always wrong in some way). Then I say they can take care of it whenever they are ready. This is good for our older kids, who can take responsibility for making it right without our constant supervision or help. I will ask them later if they have done it, and I encourage them throughout the day to make it right.

As our oldest became teenagers and much stronger physically, the middle brothers felt more picked on. They perceived the older two were abusing their greater power. Conflicts increased.

I often made the two offending boys sit in another room (so the rest of us could go on with life) on stools facing each other until they resolved the dispute. Often one or both would stayed frustrated until they got tired of sitting there, and then they would make up and be allowed to get down.

We also make them hug for five long seconds (and we count the seconds) when the conflict is resolved. They think this is a terrible idea, of course! Though they act like they hate it, the result has almost always been laughing, tickling, and embarrassed grins by one or both boys. Even when they're teenagers, it's good for them to hug one another occasionally.

We also try to promote shared activities that build positive memories. For example, my seventeen-year-old took his eleven-year-old brother disc golfing the other day, and they had a blast. Our boys have played paintball together, built our chicken coop as a team, and dug ditches (can you tell I believe in hard work, too?). Now that they are older, they are going on mission trips together. They have massive Nerf battles in the house, play lots of games, are constantly building something, are learning to cook. . . . We are teaching them to support one another as much as they would a friend, being present for their piano recitals, sporting events, and all birthdays.

It's a lot of work, and our house is often a disaster. My dad has often encouraged me by saying, "You are majoring in the majors and minoring in the minors." I can have a clean house later. Now that our oldest is a senior in high school, I understand how quickly the time goes by, and I know it's been worth it.

Ashley (Rainey) and Michael Escue

- who made the mess and who cleaned it up
- who had permission to wear what—"She never asked to wear my blouse!"
- who got more freedom while growing up—who's spoiled and who isn't!

As we watched our six children struggle through hundreds of squabbles, conflicts, disputes, and divisions, we would wonder, *Are we being successful as parents? Is there something we're doing wrong? Are we raising a group of juvenile delinquents?*

The truth is that conflict is common to all relationships. Every parent knows that it's especially true among siblings. Children are going to struggle with one another, compete with one another, irritate one another, and have conflict.

We finally realized that God was providing multiple training opportunities for our children. As a result, we repeatedly taught them in practical ways how to honor one another, how to begin to speak well of one another, and above all, how to love one another.

Loving others inside the home is a precursor to loving others outside the home. If you are the parent of an only child, look for opportunities to foster relationships with cousins, neighbors, and friends from church and school. Keep in mind that an only child will need a different but equally purposeful approach to relationships than children in larger families.

Changing Hearts

Teaching your children to love others is a heart issue and an impossible task without divine intervention.

Your "precious little ones" are born with a sin nature, which means they are prone to selfish choices. You can teach your children to speak with respect and be nice to their friends, but unless you help them understand they have a sinful heart condition that cannot be cured by anyone but Jesus, you are only temporarily modifying external behavior. Nice behavior will not stand the test of time.

The goal is to tirelessly teach, train, and pray that God will *change their hearts.*

Training them to surrender their wills to Christ is what will ultimately bring love and peace to siblings and homes. But until their physical, mental, and emotional maturity develops, and until those choices of spiritual surrender to Jesus are made, parents need to keep teaching so that children can learn to recognize selfishness in their hearts.

Like building muscle memory in athletics, the heart can be trained to remember that Christ is the One who empowers us to love others.

Even for adults, this isn't always easy, right? Both of us vastly underestimated our own need to learn love as we raised our kids. Our hearts were very imperfect.

But this is one of the best opportunities parents have to regularly, even daily, share what God is doing in our own hearts. Psalm 78:4 challenges us to "tell to the coming generation the glorious deeds of the Lord, and his might, and the wonders he has done." We wish we had understood this during our parenting years as clearly as we do now and practiced it more. Just as you build a love relationship with your child with a three-lane bridge of love, pursuit, and forgiveness, so you will be daily modeling and teaching those concepts to your kids as they relate to siblings and friends and adults.

Fortunately, God has not left us without clear instructions that equip us to train our children in the fundamental principles of relationships. One such instruction is found in Paul's writings to the church at Rome. It is not a comprehensive teaching on love and interpersonal relationships, but it is a great place for us to begin as parents:

> Live in harmony with one another. Do not be haughty, but associate with the lowly. Never be wise in your own sight. Repay no one evil for evil, but give thought to do what is honorable in the sight of all. If possible, so far as it depends on you, live peaceably with all. Beloved, never avenge yourselves, but leave it to the wrath of God, for it is written, "Vengeance is mine, I will repay, says the Lord." To the contrary, "if your enemy is hungry, feed him; if he is thirsty, give him something to drink, for by so doing you will heap burning coals on his head." Do not be overcome by evil, but overcome evil with good.
>
> Romans 12:16–21

God gave us multiple opportunities in everyday life as parents to practice this passage ourselves and to use circumstances our children experienced to repeatedly instruct them in how to love others.

Training Children to Respect the Dignity and Value of Others

During our parenting years, we often found ourselves discussing with our children the contrasting values between the Scriptures and the world. We talked about God's view of money and possessions, about our purpose in life, and about loving others well.

We often took them straight to the Bible. For example, in the creation account we learn all human beings are created in God's image (Genesis 1:26–27). All people are image bearers, we reminded our kids; therefore, we are imbued with value and dignity. The greatest assignment God has ever given any of His creation is to reflect the goodness of His character and the greatness of His love to others.

Blended-Family Wisdom: Building Relationships

When a couple marries and forms a blended family, what each spouse wants for their family is the same: a good blend. Bonding in step-relationships is vital to blended-family success. Here are some key thoughts on fostering a good blend.

Like the mighty Mississippi River flowing over hundreds of miles, there are many "bends" to a child's life and "landscapes" of behavior. Unlike biological parents, a new stepparent does not have the benefit of flowing downriver with the child over a period of time. Stepparents jump in midstream and must learn to guide a new ship—sometimes over some rapids—while building relationships.

While a stepparent is navigating this new role, it is critical that the biological parent remain emotionally connected to the child and a strong leader. Expecting a stepparent to take a primary role in parenting too quickly can cause unnecessary rapids for everyone.

Some tips for stepparents

- Be careful with comments like "My kids never acted like this" or "Your daughter is very irresponsible." Your spouse might become defensive and guarded.
- Focus on building a relationship with each child. Start your relationship with what naturally connects you (e.g., shared interests) and grow from there. Bonding can take years with some children, particularly teens. All stepchildren, including adult stepchildren, have to find a place for you in their heart that does not come at the expense of their other biological parent. Be patient and meet them where they are.
- Articulate your desire to connect to the children. Even if they don't reciprocate, it's helpful for them to hear that you care about them.

C. S. Lewis reminds us that we are not rubbing shoulders with ordinary people, but with image bearers of the God of the universe:

> There are no ordinary people. You have never talked to a mere mortal. Nations, cultures, arts, civilizations—these are mortal, and their life is to ours as the life of a gnat. But it is immortals whom we joke with, work with, marry, snub and exploit—immortal horrors or everlasting splendors. . . . Next to the Blessed Sacrament itself, your neighbour is the holiest object presented to your senses.[1]

I (Dennis) remember a girl I went to school with from first grade through high school. I'll call her Doris. She came from a poor, uneducated family; she was not very smart and she wasn't pretty. All this, plus her tattered clothing and her personal hygiene set her up to be ridiculed by far too many of her classmates, including me. In my arrogance I thought I was better than she. And by the time we were seniors in high school, she had such an inferiority complex that she rarely looked anyone in the eyes. She kept her head down,

---

- Make sure children know you're not trying to replace their mom or dad. In fact, go out of your way to support their relationship with the parent in the other home or the memory of a deceased parent.
- A good way to enter their life is to keep up with their daily activities. Take them to soccer practice, ask them about their math test, and play with them.
- Keep pace with the child's level of openness to you. If you sense he or she is uncomfortable being around you, orchestrate group activities so someone else is involved. Move toward one-on-one activities when you can; this allows you to build a relationship that stands on its own.
- Be sensitive to children's experience of loss. Show compassion for their grief, allow them to talk about losses, and encourage ongoing connection to parents and extended family not in your home.
- The ambiguity of stepparenting can be discouraging. Successful stepparents are not detoured. They are stubbornly determined to move forward.
- The average stepfamily needs five to seven years to integrate their family and bond relationships. Be patient with the process.
- Both the biological parent and stepparent must constantly bathe this process in prayer. You need God's wisdom to know when to zig or zag—and when to back up and start again.

Ron Deal

filled with shame. Later, as I grew up and surrendered my life to Christ, I was the one who was ashamed of how I had treated her.

When Barbara was taunted and rejected in junior high—not by her entire class but by just one classmate, her best friend—it affected her for decades.

We shared both of these stories with our children to teach them we weren't perfect. We understood the pressures they felt in school and wanted to inspire them to treat others with dignity and honor.

Because God values every person and loves everyone greatly, we decided His values would become ours as a family. We chose to address heart attitudes of superiority or pride—which translated to acting or speaking disrespectfully toward anyone, inside or outside the family.

Down with put-downs

For us, the bottom line was we didn't allow our children when angry to say certain hurtful things like "I hate you," "I wish you'd never been born," or "I wish you weren't in our family." Those kinds of statements can inflict wounds of hurt that a sibling might take years to get over.

Frankly, our children have said plenty of hurtful things to each other over the years, but this level of verbal vengeance was ruled off-limits long before they reached the teen years. On a couple of occasions children have screamed hate-filled words at one another, but not without severe discipline.

But when our kids were in middle school, they became "importers"—bringing home habits of clever put-downs—those unkind, disrespectful comments that kids make to one another. I (Dennis) drew a line in the sand one day and declared that kind speech unacceptable in our home.

They quickly replied, "Oh, Dad, we can't help it. Everyone does it at school. We are around it constantly. It's just so natural!"

> One season in our family, I felt like we were all really self-centered. So we wrote out tasks and put them in a bowl: "Pay one compliment today," "Send one note today," "Make one phone call today," "Meet someone in the hall and say hello today." Every morning we each drew one task. Every night we reported what we had done. It helped each of us move from, "Here I am, people" to "There you are, people."
>
> SUSAN YATES

We knew that correcting this behavior would require a consequence to motivate them to change. We did not feel comfortable using the method of our parents' generation, washing a child's mouth out with soap. Instead we came up with something edible—a drop of Tabasco sauce. Perfectly designed for a junior-high boy's loose lips!

I said, "Okay, here's what we're going to do: You each get one free put-down. After that you get a single drop of Tabasco sauce on your tongue, and you can't spit or wash it out for sixty seconds." Guess what happened? Each child got the feared sauce treatment only one time! It was amazing how quickly their self-control appeard.

Some might consider that cruel and inhumane. Our belief is that allowing children to say whatever they wish, to whomever they want to say it whenever they wish to say it, will not create an enjoyable environment at home. The Tabasco sauce worked, and now some of our kids have used the same method with their older kids.

> **B**uilding sibling friendships is a long journey. You are not going to see results in one week, two weeks, or even three years, and that's so discouraging to parents. So first of all, have realistic expectations. It's years of inputting. Don't get discouraged.
>
> SUSAN YATES

Practical ways of teaching your kids how to respect others

If you have more than one child, we guarantee you will have plenty of opportunities to train your children in respecting each other. They'll make fun of each other, refuse to share their toys, refuse to play with each other, team up against another sibling. . . . It's constant, and it's exhausting.

It's likely that you'll need to teach them how to show respect to you as their parents. One Sunday, not long after one of our sons received his driver's license at age sixteen, we let him drive the family home from church. At one point I said, "Son, you're driving too fast."

"No, I'm not—I'm driving okay," he shot back smugly, in typical teenager fashion.

We rode farther down the road, then Barbara piped up: "You went around that last curve a little fast, didn't you?"

"Mom, I'm within the speed limit."

> **S**ome stepsiblings immediately hit it off and enjoy each other's company; others struggle to relate to someone they would never normally be friends with. Adult stepsiblings often have their own lives, families, and concerns and simply don't need to bond with new stepsiblings. Some stepsibling conflict is inevitable. You cannot make them like each other, but you can insist on kindness and basic respect. Trust that a climate of kindness will create an environment where love will happen.
>
> RON DEAL

Technically that was probably true, but he still took a thirty-five-mile-an-hour curve faster than he should have with a car loaded with a large family.

Finally, we commented on his driving a third time. And he said arrogantly and angrily, "Look, I am an experienced driver! I've been driving for five years." He was counting the times he sat on my lap, "helping" drive down a logging road as a boy. "Why are you on me like this?"

This little exchange not only bent truth and logic out of shape, but also was disrespectful. Because he had repeatedly shunned our observations about his driving, he was penalized. A two-week grounding from driving realigned his tongue, restored reason, and resulted in a sweeter attitude and more prudent driving approach—and, we might add, fewer white-knuckle moments for the parents.

One of the most important ways to teach respect is to model it when you relate to your spouse. Show respect in your tone, attitude, and facial expressions. Do the same when you speak to your children, using respectful words and a tone that affirms their worth and value. If you speak to them in anger or sarcasm, or are constantly criticizing them, they will treat others the same way.

Also, show your children how to be kind to others regardless of who they are—the plumber, a neighbor, a janitor, a checkout clerk at the supermarket. You can judge a person's character by how he or she treats a waiter during the dinner rush or an airline representative when a flight is delayed or canceled. Your children are watching how you treat every person you come into contact with.

Training Children to Resolve Conflicts

In our opinion, conflict resolution skills are among the most important relational skills you will develop in your children. Here are seven relationship qualities to teach and discuss—as well as correct and train—in your family.

1. Teach them how to really listen well (James 1:19–20).
2. Train them how to speak the truth in love—a lifelong training exercise for all of us (Ephesians 4:15–16).
3. Equip them to look out for the interests and needs of others inside and outside your family. Consider memorizing Philippians 2:2–3 as a family.
4. Train them how to ask for forgiveness and how to grant it (Ephesians 4:32). See if they can define what true forgiveness is. One working definition—which, we promise you, you will have an opportunity to

Teaching Our Kids How to Have Healthy Conflict

Our four children didn't get to choose their siblings. They don't really have a choice about growing up in this house. We're trying to interact with them around how to have a relationship with each other, and how to have healthy conflict.

Recently, our daughter was yelling at one of her brothers for taking food from her school lunch box. He had to realize he didn't have the right to raid another's lunch to get what he wanted.

The world is so hard, and we want our home to be a safe space for the kids. That means it's a safe place to be sad, angry, happy. A place where they want to be versus a place where they are being attacked by their siblings.

Because I (Samuel) am a counselor, I understand that conflict is rooted in the emotional disruption that we experience. When you take care of conflict, you have to address the emotional responses that are happening. We try to give them language and words to express verbally what their experience is. We do get pretty heated with each other and show our emotions, but we've tried to teach them that when they hurt a sibling, they need to repent, go back, and ask for forgiveness.

We have tried to help them understand that personally accepting Jesus' forgiveness means they have to make peace with others around them. It is beautiful to see them take responsibility for the things they have done to hurt or offend or harm their siblings (or us) in the process of accepting God's forgiveness.

Samuel and Stephanie Rainey

apply—is this: *Forgiveness means giving up the right to punish or get even with the other person.*

5. When your children do something wrong, educate them on why trust must be earned and reestablished. Explain why reconciliation and restoration are so important, how they are different, and how to do both. Coaching them through each step is how you train them in healthy relationships at home and with friends.

6. Teach them how to use their words to bless others.

7. Teach them how to handle their anger.

We learned to make plans for those times we knew sibling squabbling would be at a peak. When our children were little, we filled a jar with dimes or quarters and took it with us on long car trips. We told the kids that at the end of the drive, they could split the money left in the jar and spend it however they wanted. But we would take a coin out of the jar every time they misbehaved.

Almost as soon as we drove out of Little Rock, the bickering started. "Okay, that'll cost you," we said, and removed a coin. When they reacted poorly because we took the coin out, we took out another. "Way to go, kids—keep griping to us and to one another, and we're going to get rich off these dimes!"

By lunchtime they were down a couple dollars, and slowly they began to realize they were losing money. Their behavior was costing them. Even the troublemakers were trying to figure out a way to keep the peace.

What you're doing is building habits of good behavior while continually taking them back to the Scriptures to talk about the love of God, the fear of God, and how we are called to love each other with the same love that God demonstrated to us.

We'll warn you—it's exhausting to transplant this skill into your children's hearts. But then there are those moments that give you a glimpse and a hope that maybe they are learning something. Like this letter from our son Samuel, who was in junior high at the time:

Dear Mom and Dad: I am sorry about the way I have been acting these past few weeks. The pressure at school and stuff, well. I am glad you are my parents. Thanks for sticking to your guns. Well, that concludes my letter. Your loving son, Samuel.

It's worth it for that!

Blended-Family Wisdom: Typical Parental Missteps

Stepparent Missteps

- Expecting too much of yourself. Stepparents are often eager to "fill the gaps" in a child's life or quickly become an influential dad or mom. Lower your expectations of yourself and how quickly your relationship will develop.
- Being overly harsh on stepkids or your spouse's parenting. Be very careful how you offer criticism, even if you think it is constructive. Begin your observations with, "Because I care about Rachel . . ."
- Demanding love and affection without earning it. You may be helping to pay the family bills, but that doesn't entitle you to big bear hugs. Like any relationship, yours may be cordial at first. Then "like" each other. Then "love" each other.
- Perceiving hesitation from a child as rejection. This should be expected.
- Viewing the time your spouse spends with their children as a threat to you. This actually may be beneficial if your spouse is helping the children embrace you into the family.

Biological Parent Missteps

- Becoming paralyzed in your parenting. Due to guilt over the past, fear for your child's future, or sadness regarding what is happening in your home, some parents become paralyzed in setting boundaries or following through with discipline. Resist this temptation.
- Holding on to veto power. Don't hinder your spouse's influence or involvement in parenting because these are "your children." Make space for the stepparent.
- Not trusting the stepparent's heart toward your child. You may not agree with every aspect of how the stepparent relates to your child, but guard against judging him or her as uncaring. That sets you against one another and teaches your children not to respect the stepparent.
- Giving up trying to connect. Unfortunately, some parents get marginalized after divorce or alienated from their children living in another home. If this is you, don't stop trying to connect. They need you.

Ron Deal

7 The Bridge That Love Built

Teaching Love for God

Our children need Jesus because they are without God and without hope in the world. . . . Only as they know God, in and through Jesus, can they become the people that God has created them to be.

Alistair Begg

One of our most important goals as parents was introducing our children to Jesus. Knowing we will live forever, and hoping to live one day all together in God's perfect kingdom, motivated us to take our children to Him, to His presence.

We began making this introduction to God early, when our children were toddlers. We would often explain, "God loves you, and Mommy and Daddy do, too!" We prayed for them before bed at night even when they were babies. We talked about Jesus being our friend. As they grew older, we used their disobedience as opportunities to explain sin and forgiveness, introducing them to the basic concepts of a relationship with God.

One night as we put our two oldest into their bunk beds, we were talking about going to heaven. Ashley had already asked Jesus into her heart, but Benjamin, sixteen months younger, had not. As He listened to us explain that Mom, Dad, and Ashley would all go to heaven together, the light went on in his five-year-old head. He understood that he needed to make a personal decision on his own. Going to heaven wasn't automatic.

"He's in My Heart"

Marsha Kay and I have been teaching our girls since they were little that God is everywhere, and He speaks to us and He loves us. One night we went out to eat as a family, and our daughter Savannah fell and broke her arm. We raced her to the emergency room, hovering over our firstborn while nurses were getting her sedated and ready for surgery to insert some pins into her elbow for stabilization. As the nurse placed a stethoscope on Savannah's chest, she asked as only a three-year-old could, "Do you hear Jesus in there? He's in my heart." Even at an early age, she was aware of Jesus.

Ben and Marsha Kay Rainey

From the upper bunk, Benjamin stuck his head over the edge and asked, "How can I go to heaven, too?" We explained the facts again, and this time he said he was ready to pray.

Was that the moment Benjamin became a born-again child of God? Only God knows. Our responsibility as a parent is to help our children understand, to give them the opportunity to talk to God on their own, and to trust God's Spirit to lead each child to Himself.

The Bridge That Love Built

In earlier chapters we talked about building a bridge to your child by building a strong and loving relationship. This bridge metaphor is also common in materials explaining the gospel of Christ, because our sin creates an inconceivably deep chasm between God and us. It's an appropriate image of the impossibility of reaching God through our own efforts and merit.

But the love of God reached across this chasm created by our pride and selfishness. God became a man, Jesus Christ. His love did what we couldn't do for ourselves—He stepped out of eternity and became a living human being, fully God and fully man, yet without sin. He lived a perfect life so that He might die and become the perfect sacrifice for the penalty of our sins. He defeated death and rose again and is seated at the right hand of God the Father in heaven.

The bridge that love built spanned the gorge between God and us.

When we were young adults, God's love transformed each of us so profoundly that, by the time we married, our lives were focused on Him. In fact, during our first Christmas together, we decided to give God gifts from our hearts before we gave each other material gifts. Our marriage was new, and we wanted to start it right. So we each wrote a list of gifts that we wanted to give to God. We gave Him our desires for our future, our present possessions and desires for more, the hope for children, and our desires to live for Him only. We signed those papers and placed them in an envelope.

Someday, after we are gone, our children will open that envelope and find two sheets of paper, dated, signed, and labeled "Title Deed to Our Lives"— all that we gave Him that first Christmas. The two most important pieces of paper in all of our possessions. It declares whom we were living for and the object of our ultimate love.

One of our primary desires was to raise our children to know God and to know His love and forgiveness as we did. We wanted them to begin a love relationship with Him of their own.

Guiding Your Child into a Relationship with God

When we started having children, we were pretty clueless about parenting. But it made sense to us that if our relationship with God is the focus of our lives, our children should see our faith in action. Our speech, our priorities, our daily actions should reflect our faith.

This is the type of parenting style we find in Deuteronomy 6:5–9, one of our favorite passages on raising children:

> You shall love the Lord your God with all your heart and with all your soul and with all your might. And these words I am commanding you today shall be on your heart. You shall teach them diligently to your children, and shall talk of them when you sit in your house, and when you walk by the way, and when you lie down, and when you rise up.

This passage shows us that, first, parents are to *model a relationship with God in front of their kids.* You cannot pass on what it means to love God and have a relationship with Him unless you have an infectious love for Him first. You want your kids to see what it means to love God with all your heart and soul and might.

Our friend Tim Kimmel, in *The Art of Parenting Video Series*, makes this statement: "I really don't think our kids figure out a whole lot about life by what we tell them, what we teach them. I think they figure it out by what we show them, because if it isn't backed up by our life, then it's just information."

Just going through life gives you so many opportunities to model your faith—talking about different ways God showed up for you that day, asking for forgiveness when you say something in anger to a child, praying for God to provide in times of financial need, reaching out to a neighbor in need of love and comfort. . . .

> I think the greatest thing you can do for your kids spiritually is for us, the parents, to walk with God. You can't give away what you don't have.
>
> ANN WILSON

Filmmaker Stephen Kendrick says, "It is so powerful when a child comes home and sees authentic Christianity lived out at home."

He recalls his childhood and how his parents modeled their faith:

> Anytime there was a crisis, of course we would see our parents praying. If it was late at night, my mom would come and sit down next to us on a bed. I had horrible nightmares—I felt like I was being attacked by a demon or something—and she would come and open up the Scriptures and start praying boldly according to the Word over me, and then just a peace would set over me.
>
> Too often people will stumble upon their parents doing something wrong. I never stumbled upon my dad looking at pornography, but I did stumble upon him on his knees in prayer.

When children are taught only faith facts or faith platitudes by parents who aren't living an authentic walk with Christ, they see the disconnect between what we say and what we do.

A good question for every parent is, "Would you be satisfied if your children developed a walk with God like yours? If not, then what needs to change in you?"

A Way of Life

As we look at the passage of Deuteronomy 6:5–9, we also notice that *parents should teach and train about God throughout the day, as a way of life*. In a house full of children, every day presented us with opportunities to show them how the Scriptures applied to their relationships, their speech, their temptations, their challenges and triumphs, their fears and failures.

We asked our children what they remember of how we taught them about God. Rebecca, now a mom of six, recalled how at dinner we occasionally shared about someone we had met that day who had a great story of God's redeeming love. Deborah remembered her father's prayers every day when he dropped them off at school (see sidebar).

Each day gives you opportunities to let your children know something you are learning about God. Tell how He has corrected you, answered a prayer, or reminded you to give thanks for someone or in all things. Consider sharing stories about special experiences of trusting God in the past. When you share what God is doing in your life, you let your children into the interior of your heart and soul, and they get a glimpse of what the real walk with God looks like. It's not just something we teach as parents; it's something that we practice as we follow Christ.

Our friend Susan Yates tells a great story about her early years as a mom, when she was so tired she called late afternoon the "arsenic hours." (We called those hours "The Valley of the Shadow of Death"!) She would often ask her oldest child, Allison, to sit on the front steps with her, and would say, "I'm going to be such a bad mommy in the next two hours. Will you please pray for me?"

Allison would put her hand on her mom's shoulders and pray, "Dear Jesus, make Mommy patience."

Susan recalls, "She ministered to me, but even more important, she saw Mommy needed Jesus. And that enabled Allison to feel the freedom as she was growing up to go straight to the Lord with her needs. She realized that Mommy knows Mommy is not perfect. Mommy needs Jesus."

In a home environment like this, faith becomes a lifelong topic of conversation. You will likely have opportunities to point your children to Christ in hundreds of different situations.

An Epic Introduction

As children learn about Him, you have the opportunity to explain the gospel. As a parent, you have the primary responsibility and awesome privilege of making the most important introduction that you will ever make. This

A Prayer of Fatherly Love

Most days we got to ride to school with Dad. He would drive with one hand on the wheel, one hand on his coffee cup, and another one on his electric shaver. Other times he also juggled a handful of cereal, which he would shake in his hand, then toss into his mouth. Don't ask me how he did it, with his invisible octopus arms, always depositing us at school alive.

The conversations on those short rides to school impacted me in enormous ways. There was always time for conversation in the car (whether I wanted it or not). There was prayer, too. Always.

Dad's prayer always ended with the same words: "Protect them from evil, harm, and temptation."

Now that I'm a parent to two elementary-age girls, those words are more powerful to me. My girls and I pray every day on the way to school. The girls alternate who leads the prayer, even at the ages of seven and nine. We have done this since they were babies and I was the only one praying.

I want them to know God is with them at all times, that they simply can speak from the heart when they need to, whether it is out of worry or gratefulness. All I can do as a parent is equip them with truth and prayer.

If Jason and I are to raise our children to follow God, we need to model trust and surrender before them. So I pray with them, just like my dad did, breathing truth into their very well-being, because the world is not going to do it for me.

Understanding that Jason and I are the link between our girls and God is enough to keep me repeating this prayer—that God would protect my children and keep them from evil, harm, and temptation.

Dad said it all in that prayer. A prayer of fatherly love.

Deborah (Rainey) and Jason Petrik

introduction will truly change your child's life forever—introducing him or her to almighty God, the Alpha and Omega, the one who loves them and has a plan for their lives.

What a privilege you have to make this introduction!

You can't force your children to repent and come to Christ. The new birth is God's work. Your job is to encourage their interest, answer their questions, be available to explain what it means to be a follower of Christ, and model what it looks like to follow Christ.

What do your children need to understand in order to become children of God?

First, they need to understand that *they are sinners*. The great English preacher Charles Haddon Spurgeon was asked at what age a young child can believe in Christ. He answered, "A child who knowingly sins can savingly believe."

Next, children need to know that *Jesus Christ died for their sins*. Teach them that Jesus is God's bridge. But knowing this intellectually does not mean they are forgiven.

In order to receive God's gift of forgiveness and eternal life, your children need to *place their faith in Him* as their Savior and ask Him to be the Lord of their lives. They must trust Christ for His death for their sins and invite Jesus into their hearts.

Ultimately, God in His great mercy and grace does the real work of salvation, moving within their hearts. He opens the door, builds the bridge. He just uses you in the process. Remembering this is God's work takes the pressure off you.

> **W**e've tried to teach our kids how to repent rather than just change their actions. We ask, "Does that please the Lord?" "No, it doesn't." "Let's pray right now and ask God to forgive you, because he tells us, 'If we confess our sins, he is faithful to forgive us.'" Our hope and desire is to help them see we don't just want them to be a good kid, we want them to love Jesus.
>
> ERIC RIVERA

Make Your Home a Spiritual Greenhouse

In addition to talking about God as a way of life, it helps to develop a plan for some more purposeful activities designed to teach your children about walking with God. Here are seven big ideas.

1. Pray with your children. When prayer becomes a way of life in your family, it teaches your children that

- prayer at its essence is faith that recognizes that God exists
- prayer acknowledges that God hears
- prayer believes that God cares
- prayer means surrendering our wills to the loving authority of God our Father

Let your children see, hear, and experience both of you praying as a way of life (Philippians 4:6–7), and pray with them often.

Pray over them—for blessing, protection, guidance.

Give thanks for them—for who they are, not just for things they've done.

At meals, give thanks for God's provision, and pray for people you know who are in need.

Pray with them about problems they are facing with their siblings or at school.

As they grow older, pray about standing strong against temptation, about representing Christ with their peers.

And don't forget to share and write down answers to prayer! We wish we'd chronicled more of God's handiwork in our family's life.

2. Read the Bible to your kids. Consider asking God to guide you in creative ways to read stories from the Bible and make it interesting for your children.

Many of my (Barbara's) favorite times with the kids involved reading Bible stories before I put them down for a nap or at bedtime. I did this almost every day of their preschool years.

You might read one of the Psalms before prayer at dinner and use it in your prayer. Or have fun reading and acting out stories from Scripture on a family night. Our kids acted out the stoning of Stephen (no, they didn't have real stones!), the Easter story, and of course the Christmas story, too. Playacting involves all the senses in learning, so let your kids be imaginative as they pretend to be Bible characters for an audience of Mom and Dad.

We also suggest using *The Jesus Storybook Bible*, by Sally Lloyd-Jones, for children ages four through eight. It combines Bible stories with beautiful illustrations.

3. Collect spiritual milestones and answers to prayer. Get a journal or notebook and keep it in the kitchen or near where you eat together to record what God is doing on behalf of you, your family, and your children. As you ask about your children's days and they tell you stories that show they were really listening to God, write them down. If you've been praying for a new friend, Dad's new job, or Grandpa's health, record any and all answers in your journal.

These spiritual milestones show the ways God has been at work. They are His fingerprints on your family. "He has made His wonders to be remembered" (Psalm 111:4 NASB). Write them down. You'll be surprised how many you collect over the years, and how meaningful they will be when you read through them in the future.

4. Read (or listen to) books and stories that invite imagination about God and His love. Our favorite was listening to The Chronicles of Narnia book series by C. S. Lewis during long car trips. We also listened over and over to *Adventures in Odyssey* stories from Focus on the Family. The "theater of the mind" can stir imagination and creativity. It's a great way to keep kids off screens and engage their minds.

I (Barbara) also enjoyed reading to the children about men and women who knew God and walked with Him. I wanted them to have faith heroes outside of our family. The books in my Growing Together series, which I wrote after my children were grown, each tell seven stories about the heroic faith of men and women and youth who trusted God for great things. (Visit EverThineHome.com to learn more.)

5. Take your kids to church regularly. We made the decision to make church attendance a weekly priority. It signaled to our kids that learning about God and being with His people was important in our family.

And don't just be a "consumer" at church. Get involved. We taught several Sunday school classes and helped lead small groups. A highlight was teaching the sixth-grade class and having all six of our kids go through the class. They never realized it, but we taught that class for them! It allowed us to teach our kids a Christian worldview regarding many of the life issues they would soon face in adolescence.

If your current church doesn't teach the Bible, consider finding one that does. Life is too short to spend fifty to a hundred hours or more a year at a church that isn't alive spiritually, that doesn't take great delight in learning about God from the Bible.

6. Invite heroes in the faith to have dinner with your family. Loving God means we are obedient to do what He commands us to do. We invited some great warriors for Christ to have dinner with our family to tell stories of how they walked by faith with God. We loved having our kids hear faith

> The truth is every one of our kids will fail. They will fail and stumble at some point. And I guess our job as parents is to point them to the grace giver, who is Jesus. And to have consequences, but also offer love and grace at the same time.
>
> ANN WILSON

stories from someone they thought was "cooler" than Mom and Dad! Courageous followers of Christ infect others to become courageous in their faith, too.

7. Encourage your kids to go on mission trips—and go together if you can. We are strong believers in moving kids out of their privileged lifestyle in America and into third-world mission experiences (international trips or inner-city trips). It helped them see Christianity with cross-cultural eyes and gave them a vision for reaching people around the world with the gospel. It also helped them return home with greater gratitude for the immense privileges they have in the US.

Our Imperfect Family

Writing on a topic like this, it's easy to give the impression that we were flawless parents in passing on our faith. Yet there are so many things we lament, things we didn't do as well as we had planned:

- We wish we had read the Bible more often as a family.
- We didn't memorize nearly enough Scripture as a family.
- We wish we had read more books together as a family—biographies, missionary stories, and other great books that light a child's imagination.
- We wish we'd found a way to have had more friends of ours into our home to share their stories of faith with our kids. (We have known some incredible men and women of faith.)
- We wish we had been more intentional about pointing out God's creative genius in nature—we walked by thousands of opportunities.
- We wish we had done a better job of making Jesus the focus of our family holidays. To help other families in this area, Barbara has created Christmas ornaments that highlight the names of Jesus, cross-focused Easter items, and other resources to make the holidays focused on Jesus. They are being used by hundreds of thousands of families. Check them out at EverThineHome.com.
- We wish we'd kept a better documented record of God's provisions for our family.

There are so many things we could have done better. But if there's one thing we managed to do, it was staying involved in their lives and maintaining a constant spiritual dialogue. It was a continued discussion of how God was working in all our lives—our failures and successes—and how they could walk with God in everyday life. It was pointing out specific Bible verses that applied to their circumstances, praying with them over issues they faced, and always pointing them to the God who loves them. All in the hope that the day would come when they walked with God on their own.

Meaningful Moments

A favorite memory is from my senior year in high school when I met my dad for breakfast every Friday morning. We would study Proverbs together. I love the intentional time Dad took to teach me and lead me through Scripture, challenging me to dig deeper into the Bible, to know more about myself, and ultimately to know more about the Lord. It was a pivotal time, right before college, and he made sure I knew what I believed, who I was, and *whose* I was (I belonged to God) in a subtle but meaningful way.

My parents are incredibly intentional, and most mornings we would read a devotion while eating breakfast or making our lunch for school. Since our family was so big, it was difficult to have dinner all together, but Mom and Dad made sure we had at least two nights a week when we would sit down as a family and eat together. Most of those nights would be loud and fun, and Dad would read from William Bennett's *The Book of Virtues*. I'm sure we rolled our eyes and thought it was silly, but it stands out because they weren't being passive parents.

I imagine that if they were parenting today, they would snatch up all the phones and put them in a basket somewhere for the evening and make sure we were all talking to each other without disruption. We would probably throw a huge fit about it, but as my mom recently said, "If you let your child's negative actions or behavior stop you from moving forward in love, he is controlling you." I appreciate that my parents didn't let our attitudes or negative responses control the family. They pushed through and made our moments meaningful when we were all together.

Laura (Rainey) and Josh Dries

Section Three

Building Character

We have grasped the mystery of the atom and rejected the Sermon on the Mount. . . . The world has achieved brilliance without wisdom, power without conscience. Ours is a world of nuclear giants and ethical infants.

General Omar Bradley

Samuel Taylor Coleridge, the famous British poet of the early 1800s, was arguing with his friend about raising children. Coleridge believed instruction was necessary for a child's character development, while his friend felt it was "very unfair to influence a child's mind" with moral teaching.

Coleridge took his friend to a section of his land and told him this was his botanical garden. "How so?" answered the friend. "It is covered with weeds."

"Oh," Coleridge replied, "that is only because it has not yet come to its age of discretion and choice. The weeds, you see, have taken the liberty to grow, and I thought it unfair in me to prejudice the soil towards roses and strawberries."[1]

Every child left to choose his or her own way, we believe, will become like Coleridge's patch of tangled weeds. Your children will not naturally choose right; they will choose wrong. They will always choose their own way unless taught otherwise.

Nearly one hundred years ago, the Minnesota Crime Commission did a fascinating study about crime. Its conclusion includes some startling words about the nature of humans:

> Every baby starts life as a little savage. He is completely selfish and self-centered. He wants what he wants when he wants it: his bottle, his mother's attention, his playmate's toy, his uncle's watch, or whatever. Deny him these and he seethes with rage and aggressiveness which would be murderous were he not so helpless. He's dirty; he has no morals, no knowledge, no developed skills. This means that all children . . . are born delinquent. If permitted to continue in their self-centered world of infancy, given free rein to their impulsive actions to satisfy each want, every child would grow up a criminal, a thief, a killer, a rapist.[2]

Can you imagine a government commission using words like this today? You may think this sounds too harsh, but we do not. The Bible makes it very clear: "No one seeks for God. . . . No one does good, not even one. . . . All have sinned and fall short of the glory of God" (Romans 3:11–12, 23).

We have the opportunity to build godly character in our children. Training your children's character begins early. You are their personal trainer. It is your responsibility to teach standards, develop conscience, and nurture convictions. You are on a journey with your children—coaching, correcting, and calling them to a higher good.

Made in God's Image

What differentiates and elevates God's people above all else in creation is that *we have souls*. Men and women are made in God's image; animals are not. Only humans can admire and enjoy beauty, pray to our Creator, and be transformed within. Your dog takes no pleasure in a sunset, a symphony, or a ballet. It cannot entreat its Creator. It is incapable of being born again, for it has no soul, no heart that will live forever.

What makes parenting so frightening, as well as a noble privilege, is the knowledge that our words, actions, and decisions can and will mold and shape this tiny living being's eternal soul!

Yet this same responsibility is pregnant with potential for incredible joy and satisfaction. What will be the end game of your parenting? It is you, Mom and Dad, who will have the greatest influence on each of your children, for good or bad.

You can't change your children's innate personalities, physical characteristics, or mental capacities. You will not determine the length of their days. But you can help shape their character.

What Is Character?

Character is an invisible collection of traits that informs our thinking, resulting in good, healthy choices or bad, unhealthy choices. This complex of attributes governs and guides each person's moral and ethical choices or responses in any given situation.

We like to think of character as our response to authority and life's circumstances. Henry Cloud and John Townsend offer another helpful definition: "Character is the sum of our abilities to deal with life as God designed us to."[3]

Character is what you think about when considering the essence of how a person lives his life—how he fulfills his responsibilities, how he responds to life's circumstances, how he treats other people. When we describe someone as honest or humble or considerate, we are speaking about his character. The same is true for those we call foolish, greedy, or cruel.

Those are all character traits.

Interestingly, there are only a few uses of the word *character* in the entire Bible. One describes God: "The unchangeable character of his purpose . . . in which it is impossible for God to lie" (Hebrews 6:17–18). God's character does not change—it is impossible for Him to be anything other than truthful.

The Gospel of John describes Satan in opposite terms: "He was a murderer from the beginning, and does not stand in truth," Jesus said. "He speaks out of his own character, for he is a liar and the father of lies" (John 8:44).

A third passage using the word *character* is Romans 5:3–4, which tells us, "Suffering produces endurance, and endurance produces character, and character produces hope." The apostle Paul wrote these words to encourage the church in Rome that their suffering *was changing their character*.

God's character is unchangeable. Satan's character is unchangeable. But the character of a human being is malleable.

This is great news for parents! Your character is still moldable, as are your children's. You can still grow and develop, and they can, too! The question for us and for our children is whose character we will choose to imitate.

One last thought: Although the word *character* appears only a few times in the Bible, it is interesting that the Bible is the ultimate book for developing character. From Genesis to Revelation, God speaks about how to be wise and not a fool. And that is the essence of character.

Developing a Plan

Character training begins when your children are tiny babies, and it continues until you release your arrows when they are adults. Parenting is an incredible privilege, but it is also never-ending training. And training is often draining!

That's why you need to develop a plan, which is what this section is about. We will discuss some of the essentials of character development, and we'll show you how God develops our character—and how you can use similar methods for training your children. And we'll talk about how discipline fits into your character plan.

Are you ready? This is the challenge of a lifetime. . . .

8 A Plan for Building Character

Right is right, even if nobody does it. Wrong is wrong even if everybody is wrong about it.

G. K. Chesterton

A friend invited me (Dennis) and our two sons, Benjamin and Samuel, fourteen and twelve at the time, to join him on a fishing trip three hundred miles north of Winnipeg, Canada. The lodge where we stayed was made out of beautiful yellow pine logs, and the dining room was decorated with replica trophies of northern pike.

A northern pike is a long, slender fish, a fierce carnivorous predator with an average weight of three to seven pounds and average length of twenty-four to thirty inches. The lodge had an impressive display of more than two dozen monster northern pike, each between forty and fifty inches long, mounted on the walls.

Also on one wall was a plaque with the names of those who had caught a trophy pike forty-two inches or longer and weighing more than twenty pounds. Ben and Samuel scanned the list and expressed hope that their names would be enshrined on that plaque.

Over the next four days we caught a lot of fish, but the trophy "monster" pike eluded us. And as the sun began setting late in the afternoon on day five, our hopes were plummeting, as well. Suddenly Samuel's pole bent double.

The three of us instantly knew he had a whopper on the line. The fish made several lengthy runs, but Samuel was wearing him out, slowly pulling the giant toward the boat.

When Samuel pulled the fish alongside the boat, I could see it was indeed Mr. Big, the pike we were hoping for. I kneeled next to the edge of the aluminum boat, getting ready to bring the big boy in with a net, when suddenly Samuel exclaimed, "He broke my line!" As I thrust the net deep into the water, I said, "No! The fish is right here!" And with that I muscled the huge, exhausted pike into the net and hauled it into the boat.

Samuel stood there in astonishment with his fishing rod in hand and the line broken, dangling in the air. Cheers went up, like we'd won the Super Bowl. Then we worked quickly to measure and weigh the fish, for this was a catch-and-release lake. It looked as though Samuel's name was going on the wall!

We laid the fish on the floor of the boat and measured it . . . and to our astonishment, the tape read forty-one and three-quarter inches. We couldn't believe it. No matter what angle we tried, Mr. Big was a quarter inch short—still remarkable, but too short for Samuel to be enshrined on the wall of records. We let the fish go, and as it swam away, there was a sense of both great accomplishment and sadness in Samuel.

We motored back to the lodge to tell the tale to half a dozen other men. When they asked what the fish measured, Samuel said, "Forty-one and three-quarters." They congratulated Samuel on his catch and empathized with his disappointment.

Later after dinner, the owner of the lodge came to me and said, "I have to tell you, Samuel Rainey is more of a man than a lot of those names on the wall. Many of their fish measured a whole lot less than Samuel's, but they stretched it. Your son didn't, and I am in awe of his character at his age."

Was Samuel's character fully formed at the age of twelve? Of course not. But for years Barbara and I had trained our kids to be truthful no matter the cost. For Samuel this was an important test of whether he took that training to heart. The apostle Paul wrote that he took "pains to have a clear conscience toward both God and man" (Acts 24:16). Samuel chose a clear conscience over compromised glory.

It brings great joy to the heart of a parent when you see your children making right choices.

Building character in your kids is a constant, never-ending part of life for a parent. But developing a plan will keep you on track. The famous baseball player Yogi Berra, who had a habit of creating humorous and twisted phrases, once said, "If you don't know where you're going, you'll end up someplace else." Funny, yet true for parenting.

Before we examine a process for building character in your children, here are four foundational questions to ask yourselves:

1. What Will Form the Bedrock for Our Character Training?

As we mentioned before, our overall goal in parenting is to pass a living faith on to our children. As you work toward that goal, you will find that the Bible remains the greatest source of truth and wisdom for training your children.

Over the years we developed a list of skills, habits, and character traits that we wanted to teach our children. Here is our top-ten list of character traits:

- **Love:** Love for God, love for others.
- **Respect:** Respect for God and His Word, and respect for other people, even those with whom we disagree, as they are also made in God's image.
- **Wisdom:** Discernment to know whom to trust or not trust, what to believe and not believe, how to act or respond appropriately in any given situation, godly skill in everyday living.
- **Faithfulness:** Being dependable, hardworking, trustworthy.
- **Truthfulness:** Speaking, writing, and treating others without deception or manipulation.
- **Humility:** Not thinking too highly or too condemningly (lowly) of oneself; living in light of the truth that God sees and hears all and knows the depths of our hearts; treating others as more important than ourselves.
- **Teachability:** A willingness to learn and admit mistakes and failure through life. We really emphasized this one trait because to stop being teachable—whether us or the child—means to stop growing.
- **Generosity:** A willingness to serve with kindness, to give of one's life, gifts, skills, and talents for the sake of God's kingdom on earth.
- **Gratefulness:** Practicing thanksgiving as a way of life in good times and hard times.
- **Excellence:** As children of the King, remembering whom we belong to, whom we represent, whom our lives must please. Knowing we are

ultimately accountable to God means our work and our lives must be worthy of the King.

Keeping this list before us as goals kept us headed in the right direction.

The more you learn what God values in the Bible, the more you will notice the contrast with the values you hear from others. For example, Western culture emphasizes personal autonomy. Today it celebrates sexual freedom and diversity and tends to silence and ridicule those who hold conservative values on marriage. As we raised our children, we had to decide which value system would be ours. Who was our audience? Whom must we please?

To restate the obvious, we did not parent perfectly. We did not accomplish every single goal on our list. But we did have a plan. Imparting our values was our primary goal. We were intentional and purposeful and kept our focus on God's value system as our own.

2. Will We Be Friends or Parents?

God commands children to "obey your parents in the Lord, for this is right" (Ephesians 6:1). It is at home where a child learns to submit to authority, to obey, and to feel safe in a rhythm set by his or her parents. A healthy, secure parent-child authority relationship is a prerequisite for developing character in your child's life.

For some parents, the idea of parental authority seems harsh, unloving, and unkind. Even heavy-handed. Having heard about or known families with strict authoritarian parents, they may believe being their children's friend is the better alternative.

But creating order in our children's lives—even simple things like when they sleep at night and when they eat, work, and play in the daytime—begins the understanding that they are not the center of the universe, they are not in control. Benjamin Franklin wrote, "He who cannot obey cannot command."[1] The word *obey* means "to stand under." Just as we teach our children how to walk, we must also teach them to know how to *stand under the authority of another*. A child who never learns how to follow instructions will never be safe or effective in school, in relationships, in the workplace, or in life in general.

Following the rules of the road keeps us safe in our cars. Laws, rules, and instructions create order and stability. Romans 13:1 says, "Let every person be subject to the governing authorities. For there is no authority except from God, and those that exist have been instituted by God." The same is true at home.

Also consider that you are the first taste your children have of God's character and authority. You are older and wiser; your children need you to order their world for their safety, sustenance, health, and growth. All the normal actions of parents—feeding them, clothing them, soothing them when they are hurt—instruct little ones that authority is good for them. And they begin to learn God is good. When moms or dads don't rush to their kids' rescue at every whimper or complaint, the children learn to wait on their loving parents to do what is best for them. The seed of learning to trust God and His timing is planted.

You are the parents; you are their first human authority. And with that authority must coexist generous quantities of love, encouragement, security, and forgiveness. Homes characterized by fear and legalism are not safe, secure homes and do not honor God.

Your moral and spiritual authority in your child's life has been given to you by God. The relational bridge that you are building with your child is absolutely essential if you are to transport the heavy loads of truth that will shape and transform her heart and help her to be wise, knowing how to choose right and not wrong. Ask God for favor as you keep building that bridge and keep doing everything within your power to pursue a healthy love- and grace-based relationship with your child.

Three cautions regarding authority

1. Beware of misusing your authority. Certain personalities can become high control and dictatorial, and the wise parent recognizes this as a weakness if this propensity is real in your life. Children don't respond well to rules without relationships.

When God became flesh and dwelt among us, the apostle John said, "We beheld His glory . . . full of grace and truth" (John 1:14 NKJV). That's a good model for us as parents—a healthy balance of grace and truth. Together parents must find healthy and effective ways of holding one another accountable to practice benevolent authority—always seeking the best for their child.

> **O**ne reason kids need parents is because it's important for them to understand they need authority in their lives. We all live under authority, and the sooner they can understand that, understand *they* aren't the authority, the better. That's a safe place for them, and it allows for God's authority to be something they appreciate and love and accept. We get to give them that picture of God Himself.
>
> ERIKAH RIVERA

2. Beware of permissiveness. The opposite of dictatorial authority is permissive authority, which sets no limits or boundaries or schedules. Often, parents feel this is the way to be the most loving. It's the use of authority to give children what they want, be the generous benefactors, be "friends" to their kids.

True love, however, does not indulge children with everything they want—that creates children who lack the skills of self-control or self-denial. Nor does real love overprotect children by cushioning their failures so they don't feel the pain of losing or of poor execution. Failure is one of the best teachers you will ever employ as a parent.

3. Beware of manipulating them. Build clear boundaries and establish consequences, but do not use emotion to manipulate children into behaving as you desire through guilt or condemnation. Years ago we knew a man who apparently thought he could motivate his children by ridicule, anger, guilt, and shame. I (Dennis) remember when this father told me, "I've got some advice on parenting that you can put in your book."

Oh boy, this should be good, I thought.

"Don't have kids."

Ouch! His sons were standing right there listening. I felt terrible for those two young men—not only did they hear his rejection and lack of love, but they felt shame because the father had made this statement to someone outside their family. They grew up to be angry young men.

3. Will Our Children Trust Us?

Trust is an outgrowth of your relationship. If you promise to go fishing with your son or daughter or promise to discipline one of them, then you need to follow through. If you say something is wrong or dangerous, your child needs to trust that you are telling the truth and that you follow your own advice.

Why? Because that's exactly what God is trying to do with us, His children. All His communication can be summed up with the words of Isaiah 30:20–21: "Your eyes shall see your Teacher. And your ears shall hear a word behind you, saying, 'This is the way, walk in it.'"

Children need to trust you when you set standards, when you order their world for their good and for their protection. When our kids were very

We're Raising Adults

We've tried to create an environment in our home where taking responsibility is the norm. Own your mistakes, and take responsibility. When our kids make sinful and selfish choices, they learn that there is a consequence. And when they grow up and live on their own, if they screw up in something, our hope is they'll know how to recognize it and deal with it. And they will know their poor choice didn't end the world.

When there is a need for a consequence, we try to make it applicable to the offense. A child once spilled a glass of water on our computer after we'd told him several times not to have any liquids near him when he was using it. His consequence was to pay for a new laptop. The $750 bill was a lot for a ten-year-old! To earn the money, he did extra work around the house that we would have paid for a professional to do. The biggest job he did was to dig a fifty-yard drainage ditch in our backyard. It took him five weeks to dig it, and that's how he earned the majority of the money.

Also, our kids work hard for things rather than just receiving them from us. If they want a smartphone, they have to save their money and buy it. Our daughter saw a friend at school dropping her phone face down on the floor. She asked what was going on, and the friend said, "I'm trying to break my phone so my parents will upgrade it." Parents give their kids expensive phones, and then complain that the kids don't appreciate anything.

We've realized we are raising adults who will someday be married and have children of their own. We're raising them to go out on their own and be productive members of society and followers of Christ. Our kids are learning how to cook and clean; they know what a mortgage is.

We've been pretty intentional. We're seeing the fruits and benefits, because all our kids are hard workers.

Samuel and Stephanie Rainey

young, our post–World War II yellow bungalow did not have a fenced yard. Even though I (Barbara) watched my children carefully, I knew there was a chance one of them could get out of my sight and toddle naïvely into the street. So early on I began telling them what a street was and that it was dangerous for children.

I remember walking each child, at the appropriate age, to the end of the driveway for this important lesson. I didn't explain the dangers of traffic and the possibility of broken bones and surgery. They were too young for logic—they wouldn't understand. I needed them to believe me by faith and trust me.

So with my finger I drew an imaginary line at the end of the driveway, looked my little one in the eye, and said as I touched the asphalt on the other side of the line, "This is the street. The street is a no-no. Mommy says you cannot go in the street. Do you understand?"

Then I prepared to follow that little instructional session with some discipline, because I knew they would test me to see if I meant what I said. And each one did. As they got older, we continued to educate them on street, sidewalk, and crossway safety, and with greater maturity they learned to understand the wisdom of those boundaries.

4. What If We Fail?

Every parent starts with high hopes and in time begins to absorb the immensity of both the length and depth of the task. And then fear creeps in, accusing us of failures, making us second-guess our decisions, and terrifying us with possibilities of failing with our children. Parents love their children passionately and want the very best for them. The possibility of not succeeding can feel overwhelming.

The best news of all is that you aren't parenting alone if you are tackling this adventure in partnership with God Himself. A wise friend once said, "Only God can take your teaching and put it in a child's heart." Only He can cause your instruction to grow. Only He can change hearts. And heart growth is the ultimate goal of parenting, not behavior modification.

Some of the most important prayers of your lifetime will be coming before almighty God pleading for Him to do what you can't. Prayer is one of the most important advantages you employ as your raise your children.

Here's what you need to remember:

- God loves your children even more than you do.
- He will help you build character in your children's lives.
- He loves it when we've come to the end of ourselves and cry out to Him on behalf of our children.
- God loves the prayers of a helpless parent.

The Five-Dollar Bill

One night during the years our oldest four were teenagers, I (Dennis) stopped at the ATM on the way home and withdrew sixty dollars in five-dollar bills. Once home I deposited my keys and money clip with the crisp new bills on my desk, where one of my sons was doing homework.

Later that evening, after my son had gone to bed, something told me to count the five-dollar bills. One was missing. I had not intentionally baited him. Emptying my pockets at my desk every evening was purely habit.

> **S**ometimes as a parent, I want my anger to cause my children to repent and change. But as I think more about God, I hope my children know that God does not withdraw His grace, His favor, or His love when they mess up. I may not do it well as a parent, but I want to move in that direction. I'm not going to withdraw my love and affection from them.
>
> JUDY MOK

I asked Barbara if she'd taken the money, and she hadn't, so I went in my son's room and asked, "Did you take a five-dollar bill out of my money clip that was lying on the desk where you were studying?"

"No, Dad, I wouldn't have done that. That was your money."

I suspected he was lying (after all, I had taken money from my dad when I was a boy), but I didn't have any evidence—it was possible another child had taken it. So I said, "Well, I want you to know I'm choosing to believe you. And I want to pray for you, too."

Kneeling beside his bed, I put my hands on him and prayed, "Lord, I thank you for this son of mine. Father, I'm going to trust that he didn't take the money. But if he did, Father, I pray that you trouble him, and that you disturb his sleep."

Nothing happened that night or the next, but God was at work. On the third night, my son came in and confessed. "Dad, remember that five-dollar bill you're missing? I took it. And what's more, I've been taking a lot of money out of your money clip. I need to come clean."

Barbara and I look back on that event as a spiritual watershed in this boy's life. The Lord dealt with him, and he responded appropriately.

God really does answer the prayers of the helpless parent. And you know what? We got our screened-in porch painted at no cost. Loved that part!

9 How God Builds Character in Us

> I have no greater joy than to hear that my children are walking in the truth.
>
> 3 John v. 4

Years ago I (Dennis) was meeting with a group of Christian leaders, and we were asked to vote on a particular issue. I was seated next to a very close friend who had a strong opinion that was opposite from mine. During the debate that ensued, I kept silent about my convictions.

Finally we were asked to stand to indicate a yes vote. I watched my friend stand and thought, *I'm against this, but how can I stay seated when one of my best friends is standing and is one who will be impacted by this decision?* I looked around the room as other men stood, and I did what every pre-adolescent or teenager and, yes, adults, too, is tempted to do: I stood. Only two men voted against the proposal. I still remember them because of their courage and convictions.

Rainey, you're a hypocrite, I thought. *You have just succumbed to peer pressure.*

God taught me some very important lessons that day. I was concerned about raising my children to resist peer pressure, but I realized I was still susceptible to peer pressure myself. I also understood at a deeper level the courage it takes to stand for my convictions. At a key moment, I feared man more than I trusted God.

Have you given in to peer pressure as an adult, too? Experiencing our own weaknesses, our own failures, is good motivation to strengthen our resolve so that we can model before our kids what we hope to teach them. Seeing our own need to continue growing as parents is a very healthy place from which to lead our children. We aren't yet mature. Knowing this need is a protection against foolishness and arrogance.

Our Father in heaven, as Jesus instructed us to address God, is actively working to grow our character to be like His. He set the bar impossibly high when He told His people, "Be holy, for I am holy." *Be like me*, God said! It's truly laughable, but gratefully, He doesn't expect us to do it in our own strength.

Instead, it is God who does the work of building, developing, correcting, and refining our personal character each day as we walk with Him. His ways with us provide the best model to imitate as we seek to replicate His fatherly work in our children. What follows are six ways God calls to our hearts, *"Be like Me."*

God Pursues Us with Transforming Love

Christmas is God's story. It's the advent of Love to inhabit our world, to walk with us in our space, to absorb the gravity of our multitude messes. Emmanuel. God *with* us. With crystal clarity Jesus explained that those who saw Him also saw the Father. They are One.

The manger, likely chiseled out of rock, became the stepping-stone upon which Jesus transformed the cross into the Way, His outstretched arms, a bridge of flesh between Himself, the Father, and us.

God initiates. God pursues. God comes after a relationship with us again and again and again. He is not easily dissuaded, as are we, for His love is pure and holy while ours is fractured and stained. He has plans for our welfare, for a future and a hope (Jeremiah 29:11). His love endures forever (Psalm 136:26), and nothing will separate us from His love or His presence (Romans 8:37–39).

Does that feel like your love for your children? Are you intentionally pursuing a love relationship with them? Learn from Him and seek to imitate His love.

God Gives Us People—First Our Parents—to Guide and Train Us in Wise Living

Many people influence us over the course of our lifetimes, but the names at the top of every list are always Mom and Dad, for good or for bad.

Baby Jesus had a mom and a dad just like the rest of us. And they weren't perfect people, either. God put His Son into a family with parents to guide, teach, train, and comfort Him. Jesus' parents took Him to temple; they taught Him to make His bed, to cook and wash the dishes, and to relate to others.

Another young man, Timothy, learned his faith from his grandmother and mother (2 Timothy 1:5). Paul, his mentor, also wrote, "From childhood you [Timothy] have been acquainted with the sacred writings, which are able to make you wise for salvation through faith in Christ Jesus" (2 Timothy 3:15).

I (Barbara) love that these women, Mary, Lois, and Eunice, diligently taught, trained, and nurtured Jesus and Timothy in the faith, and God was so pleased that He recorded their names to encourage us moms that He sees, notices our work, and remembers.

Take courage. It's endlessly repetitive work. Keep teaching your children all these basics of life, including how to know God. You don't have to be perfect parents. Be faithful and eager to grow, admit mistakes, and don't give up!

God Gave Us His Handbook to Teach Us, Correct Us, and Show Us How to Live

Second Timothy 3:16–17 is the key verse for this entire book. "All Scripture is breathed out by God and profitable for teaching, for reproof, for correction, and for training in righteousness, that the man of God may be complete, equipped for every good work."

These words summarize the steps God takes with us individually as our heavenly parent to show us the way and help us stay on His path.

First, His Word exists to introduce us to Him, to explain who He is, what He's like, and the way He wants us to live. Second, His Word shines a light on our mistakes so that we can see and make midcourse corrections when we've run off the road. Third, He helps us get back on the road by showing us how to repent, ask for forgiveness, restore relationships, and not lose heart in well-doing. Fourth, like a parent with his hands on a child's shoulders, He whispers, "This way," points us back in the right direction, and says, "Keep going."

Though the words below are ancient, they are living, eternal, and relevant today. The Ten Commandments have formed the foundation blocks of governments, including our own, through the ages, and they are a solid starting place for parenting, too.

1. You shall have no other Gods but me.
2. You shall not make for yourself any idol, nor bow down to it or worship it.
3. You shall not misuse the name of the Lord your God.
4. You shall remember and keep the Sabbath day holy.
5. Respect your father and mother.
6. You must not commit murder.
7. You must not commit adultery.
8. You must not steal.
9. You must not give false evidence against your neighbor.
10. You must not be envious of your neighbor's goods. You shall not be envious of his house nor his wife, nor anything that belongs to your neighbor.

Take them beyond dos and don'ts. For instance, restraining a child from hurting another by throwing a rock or hitting or biting is the first step toward murder prevention, commandment six. Dramatic? Perhaps. But uncontrolled hurtful passions have motivated too many school shootings and other murders. Teach your child not to steal, and you are building a trustworthy adult. Jealousy can lead to all kinds of evil, so training in contentment creates a heart of faith in God's good giving or withholding.

Another good rule is the one we call the Golden Rule: "Whatever you wish that others would do to you, do also to them" (Matthew 7:12). Not only did Jesus teach this to us, but He demonstrated perfectly how we are to love, forgive, and treat others with respect. The life of Jesus Christ is the supreme portrait in all of human history of pure character and wisdom—how to do life God's way.

Do you regard these old words inscribed by God's finger on stone as archaic, or do you recognize the unalterable truth they represent? How you view them will impact how your child views them and the God who spoke them.

God Tells Us We Will Answer to Him for Our Actions

Parenting often left me (Barbara) feeling like a judge in a courtroom, albeit without an imposing robe and gavel. Maybe that would have helped! "Slow down. . . . Let your brother talk. . . . You'll get your turn. . . . Is that the whole story? . . . Now it's your turn. . . . Oh, really? . . . Plaintiff, is that true? . . . What do you say in response? . . ." And on it goes. Without fingerprints and DNA, I rarely heard the whole truth and nothing but the truth.

Children recognize their parents as authorities because of their position and stature—whether the parents want that position or not. They will come to you with their problems more than you'd like sometimes. I was a poor arbiter. Thankfully, when I go to God, He knows all the facts!

Not only do we know God is bigger and a whole lot smarter, but He tells us we will have to answer to Him one day, just as our kids answer to us for their choices. This is the fear of God. A misunderstood part of God's love is His desire for authentic transparent relationships with us. He will stay after us until we recognize the sin we are hiding. Like my kids, who were prone to telling only the part of the story that bolstered their argument in my kitchen court, so are we prone to hide things from God. Hiding kills relationship. Just ask Adam and Eve.

Knowing and believing that God sees all and knows all is a powerful motivator for making right choices. Psalm 111:10 tells us, "The fear of the Lord is the beginning of wisdom; all those who practice it have a good understanding." Proverbs 19:23 says, "The fear of the Lord leads to life, and whoever has it rests satisfied; he will not be visited by harm." At the Rainey household, we like to say that the fear of God leads to a good night's sleep.

Do you live aware that God sees all? Do you consider what God might think of your choices? If you want your children to evaluate their choices, it starts with you. *There is a God, and it's not us.* Respect Him. Fear Him. And teach your children to have a healthy fear of Him, too.

God Uses Suffering to Build Character

One of my (Barbara's) favorite music artists, Laura Story, wrote a song called "Blessings," in which she ponders the idea that "blessings come through raindrops" and "healing comes through tears"—that our greatest trials are often "mercies in disguise."[1]

One of the hardest lessons in all of life is learning to recognize and be at peace with God's upside-down kingdom, His not-at-all-like-we-would-do-it ways to conform us to His image. But in the rearview mirror of life, don't you see some of the hardest places were where you learned the most? Yes, there are still painful times that have yet to be turned into good, but we all know the way God works is true. God uses pain to mold character in each of us, including your children.

In the middle of hardships, we long for relief, for the comfort of what we consider normal. But God tells us as plainly as any other instruction that it is beneficial even in the middle of it. Paul even audaciously says in Romans 5:3–5, "We *rejoice* in our sufferings, knowing that suffering produces endurance, and endurance produces character, and character produces hope" (emphasis added). Rejoicing while suffering does not come naturally, but eventually, by faith, we can give thanks.

How do you respond to hard times, difficult relationships, setbacks at work, an economic downturn, rejections, being misunderstood, illnesses, and more? What are your children seeing in you? What are they hearing from you?

A little perspective always helps. When you think your life is too hard, go spend some time with Joni Eareckson Tada on her website (www.joniand friends.org). Take your kids to her page. Listen to her give thanks to God for her fifty-plus years strapped to a wheelchair as a quadriplegic. Maybe our lot isn't so bad after all.

Believe this truth for yourself, teach it to your children, but quote it gently when others are hurting. "And we know that for those who love God all things work together for good, for those who are called according to his purpose" (Romans 8:28). Hardships give you the opportunity to trust God in all circumstances. It is a miraculous wonder that God can transform hard things into positive good—opening doors we wouldn't have seen, taking us places we wouldn't have gone, and in it all producing character, endurance, and hope in our hearts.

God Gives Us the Holy Spirit to Teach, Guide, and Help Us Every Moment

One of the best things you can do for your children is to let them see firsthand God's present-tense work in your life. One Christmas when we had but three or four little ones, we piled everyone into car seats and headed to the closest tree lot, the beginning of what we intended to be a fun tradition.

After buying the perfect tree—who doesn't look for the ideal tree?—we drove home to discover our tree wouldn't fit in our stand. So I (Dennis), working on our elevated front porch, got my power saw out and began to slice away at the end of the tree to carve it down to shape. Looked pretty good to me.

The larger context of this story is that I am not one of those men who can fix much of anything around the house. I'm in the bottom 2 percent of being able to work with my hands. Mechanical aptitude is not my strength.

So guess what happened when I finally got the bottom of the tree to fit into the stand? The little prongs at the bottom of the stand wouldn't connect with the tree to stabilize it. So the tree just kept falling, the trunk flopping like it was a swimming pool noodle.

Plan B commenced. Out to the garage I stalked, got a piece of wood and some nails. Barbara followed, because she knows anytime I start doing something with my hands, she needs to protect me from myself. I was perturbed, but I was confident I had the solution. I would stabilize the tree by nailing a small block of wood to the trunk bottom. Then I would stand the tree up and Christmas would be merry and bright.

My first nail somehow bounced off the porch. The second went into a ninety-degree convulsion. Then the next two nails followed suit. And when the fifth nail bent, I threw the hammer across the porch.

I stormed off the porch with the tree—pine needles flying everywhere—and pitched it into the back of our car. I slammed the car in reverse and peeled out of the driveway, and as I took off, I noticed little Benjamin, my five-year-old son, learning against the porch, his eyes very big. He probably thought I was about to cancel Christmas.

I took the tree back to the lot and found a kind man who fixed our tree. And somewhere on my way home the Lord got my attention. The Holy Spirit whispered, "You know, you're acting like a fool."

"Yes, Lord. I agree. Forgive me." When I pulled into the driveway, guess who was still standing on the front porch, eyes still as big as saucers?

After hauling the tree up the porch steps, I got down on one knee with little Benjamin so I could talk with him face-to-face, eye-to-eye. I said, "Benjamin, your daddy was kind of mad, wasn't he?"

He looked back and said, "Yeah, you sure were, Dad."

"Benjamin, I'm sorry. I didn't let Christ be on the throne of my life. Will you forgive me?"

I'll never forget his response. He put his little arm up, patted me on the shoulder, and said, "It's okay, Dad. Everybody makes mistakes."

Your kids are going to make mistakes as you attempt to train them to be wise and not a fool. Our friends Tim and Darcy Kimmel call it "grace-based parenting." Perhaps occasionally you might want to consider patting them on the shoulder, giving them some grace (like you've been given), and saying, "It's okay, everybody makes mistakes." And then giving them a hug.

A little grace and a hug go a long way.

10 Building Character in Your Children

Children are not casual guests in our home. They have been loaned to us temporarily for the purpose of loving them and instilling a foundation of values on which their future lives will be built.

James Dobson, *How to Raise Children That Love the Lord*

One Sunday afternoon when I (Dennis) was a teenager, I had what my mom would have called a harebrained and wild idea. I decided to drive from my hometown, Ozark, Missouri, to the then sleepy town of Branson thirty miles south. What made this a true adventure was that the road, Highway 65, was under construction. This brand-new route, slicing through the Ozark Mountains, had merely been bulldozed. It was all dirt, not yet paved or even graveled.

My vehicle of choice was my parents' old 1956 Chrysler, heavier than a small aircraft carrier. That was my first mistake—I should have taken an amphibious tank.

Actually, that was my second mistake. My first was not asking my dad what he thought about my adventure. Obviously, I didn't really want to know. Typical teen thinking.

As I drove off the first and only finished section of the concrete highway, passed the "Under Construction, Do Not Enter" sign, and drove onto the bulldozed roadbed, it all seemed quite doable. It was a fine Sunday afternoon, nobody was working, and the roadbed was dry. Over the next fifteen to twenty miles, I dodged boulders and passed all kinds of earth-moving equipment. I knew I just had to be nearing Branson, but since this trail wasn't on any map and no signs had been installed, I had no idea where I was.

I topped a massive hill, and as I began my descent, I saw two obstacles: At the bottom of the gorge was what appeared to be a small, harmless, gravel-bottom stream, Bear Creek. The second obstacle looked more ominous—a massive limestone hill rising on the opposite side that had not yet been carved out by dynamite and bulldozers to form a road.

So what did I do? I decided that I could cross Bear Creek in my two-wheel-drive Chrysler. Hey, it was only fifteen feet wide and a foot deep. What could go wrong?

I put the pedal to the metal and gunned it! The Chrysler made it to the middle of the creek . . . and sunk into the gravel up to its hubcaps. I was stuck in the middle of nowhere . . . in Bear Creek. No cell phone, no one in sight.

I hiked up the limestone bluff. Not a living thing in view. Back down in the valley, I wandered for a couple of hours before finding a small farmhouse with a kind overalls-clad owner who agreed to help me. He fired up his tractor, and we rode back to the creek. He pulled my car out of the mud and pointed me to a real road in the right direction to Branson. Ultimately, I achieved my goal, but not as I had planned.

Bear Creek is legendary in our family. Ask any of our children, and they'll laugh and tell you the story again.

The Right Road

My foolish journey to Branson illustrates the process of how God builds character in us. Your mission impossible is to train your children to travel on the path that God has laid out, the *right* road . . . not like the one I drove that was under construction.

As we wrote in the previous chapter, God's work follows a pattern, a road He has constructed for us to walk. The steps in this verse are also the basis of a plan you can follow with your kids: "All Scripture is breathed out by God and profitable for teaching, for reproof, for correction, and for training in righteousness, that the man of God may be complete, equipped for every good work" (2 Timothy 3:16–17).

Affirm Right Choices

When you're a parent, you have to address a lot of negative issues in the lives of your children. When you get the chance to cheer them for making good choices, go all out!

We made some firm decisions about what types of films and television shows our kids were allowed to watch. When she was ten, Rebecca was at a sleepover, and she called to ask about a movie they were getting ready to watch. She had been told that if friends were about to watch something rated PG-13, she should call us for permission. In this case she said, "Dad, I don't think I need to be watching this."

We told her no so that she could use us as a scapegoat. But it still cost her with her friends, because they had to choose another movie. So we made a big deal out of that one when she got home. We were proud of her for being accountable to us and for being willing to stand up to her friends.

The progression of those four words—*teach*, *reprove*, *correct*, and *train*—is exactly what I experienced on Bear Creek. I got off the path, got stuck, and needed correction to get back on the right road and pointed in the right direction. Detours will cost your kids, just like mine cost me, but good lessons are learned through mistakes. It's all part of the journey.

Building Character through Personal Instruction and Teaching

The best way to teach a teenager to drive a car is with both verbal instruction and practical hands-on driving in a really big parking lot. It wouldn't work to hand a driving manual to a teenager but never let him or her sit behind the wheel and drive. Teaching must be followed by "Let's practice."

In the same way, teaching your kids the truth of God's Word isn't for someone else to do on Sunday mornings. It is to be a way of life if you have a real relationship God. In fact, God told His people,

You shall teach [the commandments] diligently to your children, and shall talk of them when you sit in your house, and when you walk by the way, and when you lie down, and when you rise. . . . You shall write them on the doorposts of your house and on your gates.

Deuteronomy 6:7–9

God means for this instruction to be a way of life, woven into the fiber of your everyday life. A good friend of ours, Voddie Baucham Jr., assures parents that "God has given you everything you need to do this. You don't have to be a seminary-trained theologian to read the Bible and talk about what it means. Besides, God would not have given you the responsibility unless He knew you could handle it."[1]

Here are some tips to help you make God's Word front and center in your home:

You are the first and best teacher

Words matter. And it's not an accident that God said He intends for His Word to "be in your heart." Not just your lips, not giving lectures, but a living

Supporting Your Kid's Good Choices

Our thirteen-year-old had a big dance performance coming up. She came to us only a few days ahead and told us that she was feeling uncomfortable in the fishnet leggings that her dance troupe was going to wear. She felt they were too immodest. At first, we tried to convince her that it was no big deal, that it was too late to change, that she likely would feel just fine when the day came. But she kept coming back to us and expressing her uncertainty.

As we talked, we realized we needed to back our daughter and make sure she felt supported in her decisions. And we certainly did not want her to ignore her conscience!

We knew there could be consequences. Everyone had already purchased these leggings. We might ruffle some feathers and risk offending the dance instructor who took great pride in planning age-appropriate dances.

We met personally with her instructor and explained how our daughter was feeling. Was there an alternative? We also volunteered to pay for the tights that would now go unused.

As it turned out, the instructor was fully supportive of our daughter's decision, and a couple other parents and dancers also immediately agreed.

We ended up with a great teaching moment. Our daughter knows she can come to us with anything, and we'll listen to her, support her, and tackle it with her, no matter the cost.

Ben and Marsha Kay Rainey

part of you. Albert Einstein once said, "Setting an example is not the main means of influencing another, it is the *only* means."[2]

You can talk about the Bible, you can teach the Bible, you can have kids memorize verses from the Bible. But if you aren't living a life of obedience to the God of the Bible, your children are seeing mixed signals.

A brilliant professor once told me a story about taking his family to a fair. As they drove in and were about to pay admission, he noticed a sign that said children twelve and under were free. One of his daughters had just turned thirteen, and before he pulled up he whispered to her in the back seat, "Scoot down in the seat and look small."

When his car reached the front of the line, he told the person at the window, "Two adults and two children." He paid for the fees and drove on, and then he heard a voice from the back: "Daddy, you know I'm thirteen."

Clearly, *brilliant* doesn't mean wise or without fault. Convicted that he had set a very poor example for his daughter, the professor put the car in reverse, backed up to the window, confessed his lie to the cashier, and paid the difference. And his two daughters saw genuine humility and repentance modeled. I'm quite sure they never forgot it.

Barbara and I both have confessed multiple faults and mistakes to our kids. It does not feel good; it is embarrassing. But it is a part of God's living message through us to them.

My dad taught me much about integrity and character, although I don't ever remember a single lecture. My dad simply lived it. His much-too-early death at sixty-six years of age drew over five hundred people, a third of our community, to honor him at his funeral. He lived his entire life in that town and had no secrets. A man I didn't know told me that day, "You know, I never heard anyone say a negative word about Hook Rainey." Hook was my dad's nickname. He was a tall lefty and had a wicked curve ball in his prime. It was the only thing wicked about my dad.

Take advantage of teachable moments

Everyday life is full of opportune moments for teaching. Conversations about bullying, attitudes toward teachers or neighbors, people who are hard to like, siblings who constantly get in each others' stuff, and a thousand other realities present themselves daily. A lot more than any one parent has time to address. But if you are asking God regularly, even daily, for wisdom to see the

> It's one thing to explain, "Here's why you should be thankful. Here's why you should be kind. God wants you to; go do it." It's another thing to actually lead kids toward transformation. We want to change them from the inside out. That's how we have to look at our kids. Our goal isn't behavior modification, isn't just morality. Morality is an outcome, but the goal we're looking for is transformation— spiritual formation, not just information.
>
> PHIL VISCHER

best opportunities, to notice when your child is especially teachable, He will guide you and help you recognize these moments.

When she was ten, our daughter Deborah lost a friend from school in a car accident. She was understandably quite sad at the dinner table that night. Her normal understanding that people her age don't die was shaken to the core. She didn't have a lot to say, but we listened to what she did say, respected the somber circumstance by keeping dinnertime more quiet than normal, and prayed as a family for this child's family. After dinner we encouraged Deborah, who has always been good with words, to reach out to his parents by writing them a letter. Here's what she wrote:

I'm sorry for what happened to Edward. Edward was a sweet boy. He always came to school with a nice grin on his face. He always wanted to play with me. He is a good friend for me. I couldn't believe what happened. I wanted to cry. I did. . . . I want to write this verse from the Bible. "Even though I walk through the valley of the shadow of death, I will fear no evil, for you are with me; your rod and your staff, they comfort me," Psalm 23. May God comfort you. Love, Deborah Rainey.

Stay a step ahead

The best drivers are always driving defensively, anticipating what's ahead on the road, looking around the next curve. But in parenting, anticipating what's next in a child's life helps you to play offense. Think back to your life at that age. What was it like for you?

Take the time to observe what's happening with students a few years older than your child. What issues are they facing? Ask those parents. They'll happily share what they see. Then begin to talk with your children about these issues and encourage them to trust God with their choices.

Healthy Co-Parenting

Co-parents are parents raising their children in two separate homes, usually because of divorce or a dissolved relationship. This is a stressful life for children, so your relationship and cooperation with a co-parent will play a key role not only in the children's happiness but also in building their character.

An ideal co-parenting relationship is one of mutual respect and cooperation because of your mutual commitment to the child's well-being. Each parent may hold different expectations for the child (food choices, bedtimes, etc.), but hopefully, they are minimal and not rooted in contrasting worldviews (e.g., godly versus secular values).

When talking with a co-parent, it's important to separate personal from parental matters. Historical relationship conflicts should be put aside when discussing parental matters. If not, your decisions will be sabotaged by negative emotions tied to the past.

Tips for co-parents

- Work hard to respect the boundaries and rights of the other home.
- If you can't be friendly, maintain a business-like attitude; look for ways to help both of you succeed, and be willing to make sacrifices to keep the relationship in working order.
- Have regular "business" meetings and use technology (texting, online co-parenting calendars, etc.) to communicate. Guard against too frequent communication so both homes keep a sense of autonomy.
- Understand that your children are like citizens of two countries, and should be loyal to each. As you meet with a co-parent, be an ambassador on your children's behalf.
- Do not make your children spies in the other country.
- Don't bad-mouth the other home or the parents therein. Show decency and respect.
- Make your custody/visitation plan work. You may not love the plan, but do your best to support it for the sake of your child.
- If you have a difficult former spouse, do everything in your power to maintain peace, but recognize that he or she can make life very difficult for your child and you. If necessary, seek help as you strive to "overcome evil with good" (Romans 12:14–21).

Ron Deal

Adapted from *The Smart Stepfamily* (2014) by Ron L. Deal, Bethany House Publishers, a division of Baker Publishing Group. Used with permission. All rights to this material are reserved.

As our children approached adolescence, we would take each child off for a special weekend to have fun and to talk about the issues they were about to face as teens. With the girls, I (Barbara) would book a room at a nice hotel or bed-and-breakfast. We would listen to recorded material and read selections from books that discussed the process of growing up and becoming a woman. We would talk about the changes that were about to occur physically and emotionally. Dennis did the same with our sons.

To help you pull off a weekend getaway like this, Dennis and I, along with FamilyLife, have created a great resource called Passport2Purity. You can order it from our online store at FamilyLife.com. It has everything you need for your weekend getaway.

Building Character through Reproof and Correction

Isaiah 53:6 describes the nature of every child ever born: "All we like sheep have gone astray; we have turned—every one—to his own way." Going astray is natural. Our from-birth predisposition is to do life our own way, selfishly for our own benefit.

Reproof can feel like a harsh word, but it simply means to admonish or reprimand. It means to point out the error to your child. It's not berating or shaming. Out of love, you want your child to know his choice isn't good or healthy but can bring harm to him or others.

C. S. Lewis remarked, "A man does not call a line crooked unless he has some idea of a straight line."[3] Your child needs help identifying he is in the ditch (which is crooked) and help getting out and back on the road (which is straight). *Reproving a child means bringing him to a point of admission that what he is doing is not right.*

Just as when I was stuck in Bear Creek, he needs you to come alongside him and pull him out. He needs the correction, and he needs you to point him in the right direction. Most of the time in parenting, these two steps of the process usually occur at virtually the same time. When your child gets off the highway, you point out the error (reproof), and then you show him how to get back on the road (correction) almost in one smooth motion.

If one of your children, for example, insults a sibling, point out the wrong and then show how he or she could have spoken with love and respect.

This stage often requires lots of time and patience. A little child may need help in picking up toys. You tell her to pick them up, but she doesn't do it right or gets distracted. You may need to take her little hand in yours and start picking up the toys together. Our kids hated that, but it got them involved.

It's not easy to keep up with all a child needs to learn. I (Barbara) cut all our kids' hair for a number of years. When one of our boys was a teen, he decided he wanted a real haircut. He made an appointment but then didn't bother to show up. He didn't understand how barbers were hurt financially when people didn't keep their appointments. That was our mistake; we hadn't explained how the appointment system worked.

Inspect What You Expect

Before Dennis and I left for a date one Sunday night, we told Deborah and Laura to do their homework and read a book if they finished early; they were not to watch television. The instruction was abundantly clear.

As we drove home and neared the driveway a couple hours later, something told us to go into stealth mode. We turned off our headlights as we approached the house, silently got out of the car, and walked up to a window where, sure enough, we could see the girls' faces bathed in the blue glow of the TV.

While I stayed outside in front of the window to watch, Dennis walked around to the back door and entered noisily, calling, "We're home, girls." They immediately jumped up, turned off the TV, and opened books.

"How are you girls doing?" Dennis asked casually. "What have you been doing since we left?"

"We've been doing homework."

"Been watching any TV?"

"Oh no, Dad. We haven't watched any TV."

"Really? Turn and wave at your mom outside the window. We've been watching you watch TV for a couple minutes."

Busted! Not only had they disobeyed our clear directive, but they had been caught lying. As a result, we had a good conversation about being able to count on them and trust them. We then grounded them from all media—music, television, computer—for a month. It was so peaceful, we almost hoped they'd disobey us again!

Wise parents will inspect what they expect. Make sure children pick up toys as instructed, turn off their smartphones when they go to bed, and make it in before curfew. Check their texts, limit time on screens, check on them late at night. And be sure to applaud them when they do a job well and stay within your boundaries.

Correction may mean forcing two children to work out a problem in their relationship. Our two oldest, Ashley and Benjamin, were arguing about something, so we said, "You need to go take a walk together and just talk this through." It may mean bringing two siblings together and telling them to face each other, say they love each other, and then hug. Kids hate that! But it begins to melt the difficulty that is between them.

And correction will often involve some form of discipline. We define discipline as bringing a measured amount of pain in order to correct a wrongdoing. In the early years, sometimes the pain is in the form of a time-out, a chore to complete, or perhaps even a spanking.

We'll say more about discipline in the next two chapters, but an important point to make here is that discipline is often necessary to tame a child's will. The question with your children is, Who is in charge?

Building Character by Continually Training Your Children the Right Way to Live

Character training doesn't always involve reproof and correction. You will train your children in working hard, completing a job well, avoiding temptation, managing time, and many other elements of mature, responsible adulthood.

A husband once came up to Dennis at a Weekend to Remember marriage conference and said he was a Green Beret. He said, "As Green Berets, we train in what to do in every conceivable circumstance over and over and over again. So in times of battle we know what to do. It's just second nature to us." That is a picture of what a parent does with his kids.

Let's say you need to prepare your child for the peer pressure of first grade. (Yes, peer pressure starts way before adolescence!) Around the dinner table, you may want to role play. "What should you do when a group of kids wants to take you off to do something you shouldn't be doing? What should you do if your friend wants to copy your paper?" Discuss possibilities and help them think ahead.

As they get older, talk about new situations they will face: "What do you do when you get in a car with some friends and find out they have been drinking or doing drugs? What are you going to do?" Our kids knew that if they found themselves in that situation, they were to get out of the car and call us, no matter where they were or what time it was.

Training in right living (righteousness) also means sharing your convictions and how you came to embrace them. Let's say we're talking about deciding what films to watch. You can talk about your convictions about what you will allow yourself to see, what you won't see, and why. Dennis and I and another friend saw a film in college that I've never forgotten—*Rosemary's Baby*. We told our kids we regretted seeing some movies because images you allow into your mind sometimes never go away.

We also trained our kids in the importance of accountability. Some kids are naturally accountable, while some resist accountability. Before a prom night, we talked through the schedule of where they would be, when they would be there, whom they would be with, and when they would home. Our kids would sometimes say, "You don't trust us!" But the reality was we didn't trust some of their peers, nor others who would be on the road early in the morning.

We'd say, "We are your parents, and we want to know where you are going to be. You will do the same with your kids."

And they do.

My wife and I do something called conspiracy parenting. If a child tells a lie, we're going to teach him God's Word about that. We may discipline him for telling the lie, but that night I'm going tell a story about two twins, one who told a lie and one who didn't, and the consequences and rewards from that. Then we may download songs about telling the truth, or memorize Scriptures about it.

STEPHEN KENDRICK

Stealing a Toy

Let's show how this process of character-building works by focusing on an incident from our early years of parenting. We wanted to teach our children that they should not steal from others—they should be content with what they have and not desire the possessions of other people.

One of our sons, who was about five at the time, came home from playing at our next-door neighbor's house, tightly clutching a little toy car in his hand. I was in the kitchen making dinner and saw him try to hide it as he walked past me. For a few seconds I talked to myself: *Maybe it was a mistake;*

he didn't mean to take it. Or was it truly intentional? I decided it was an opportunity to teach.

I got down on his level and we talked. I explained that taking something that doesn't belong to us is called stealing. "God tells us not to steal from others, and we don't do that in our family. Now we need to go to David's house, return the car, and apologize. Okay?"

I explained what he needed to say to the mother and his friend, and that I would help him. Together, we walked hand in hand across our front yard to our neighbor's home. When they opened the front door, I said, "My son has something to say to you and David." Bending over, I coached my little man on his lines, which he repeated clearly and ended by asking for forgiveness, which they granted, and then he returned the toy car.

When we got home, I told him I loved him and that I was proud of how well he did apologizing. I then gave him a spanking for stealing, since it is a big no-no in God's Word. I held him as he cried, and I hugged him and repeated several times how much I loved him. Although we had to address stealing with this child again some years later, the prompt discipline at that

Behavior Modification versus Heart Change

One common goal of character training is to help your children move from discipline imposed by parents to true self-discipline. Children can learn to say no to temptations, to control their tongues, and to resist telling lies. At first they do it to please their parents, but as they mature, they can use that experience and impose their own discipline.

But you can't stop there. It's not enough to help them develop a habit of right behavior. That's just behavior modification—they are following your rules to please you and to avoid punishment. This doesn't address their heart issues of selfishness and sin. Only God can deal with that.

In *The Art of Parenting Video Series*, Bryan Loritts says he often uses Deuteronomy 5:29 to pray for his kids, that they would have a heart to fear God and keep His commandments, "that it might go well with them and with their descendants forever!" He'll pray, "God, get to their hearts. I don't want to have kids who just outwardly comply. God, would you get to their hearts and release into subsequent generations kids who fear and obey and walk with you."

The real goal isn't to teach moral or biblical behavior. It is pointing your children to the God who can transform them from within.

age firmly and concretely established in his young understanding that stealing is wrong.

Parenting is full of lessons like this—year after year of taking kids through the process of instruction, reproof, correction, and training in righteousness. Ultimately, it's about continually pointing to God and showing children how to trust Him and His Word no matter what they experience or how they feel.

Your children's character will define their lives—it will affect their commitments to marriage, family, and career. It will govern their choices and determine what legacy they will leave to their children.

And we guarantee that these years of training are worth it. Few things in life are as satisfying as watching your children grow up to have children and raise them to love and fear God, too.

11 Using Discipline to Build Character

Who thought up the word *discipline* in the first place?

Rebecca Rainey, age 12

Jane Hambleton called herself the "meanest mom on the planet."

When she bought her son a car, she set two rules: No alcohol, and always keep the doors locked. After finding alcohol in the car, she decided to sell it. She placed an ad in the local newspaper, and the story it created made its way to media across the country, including *Good Morning, America.*

OLDS 1999 Intrigue for sale. Totally uncool parents who obviously don't love teenage son, selling his car. Only driven for three weeks before snoopy mom who needs to get a life found booze under front seat. . . . Call meanest mom on the planet.

Jane received more than seventy calls—emergency room workers, nurses, school counselors, other parents, and more all wanted to congratulate her. No one called to say, "You are really strict, lady."

The only critic was her son, who she said was "very, very unhappy" with the ad and claimed the alcohol was left by a passenger. Jane said she believed her son but decided mercy wasn't the best policy in this case.[1]

As soon as I (Barbara) read this, I became a fan of Jane. Being a "mean mom" suddenly felt like a badge of honor! Jane didn't let her son manipulate her. She stuck to her rules and loved her son well. Her choices give us renewed courage.

As you build character in your children, at times you will feel that the meanest thing you'll ever do is disciplining them. Actually, it's the exact opposite.

Even though your children will try to make you feel like the meanest parent, correcting and giving discipline is the most *loving* thing, the most *courageous* thing, perhaps the most *effective* thing you will ever do for your children.

Making discipline decisions raised more self-doubt for us as parents than just about anything else. And we suspect it is or will be for you, too.

Where on Earth Did Discipline Come From?

The Bible's opening pages tell a very instructive story about discipline. This short narrative formed the basis of our confidence as we made a multitude of decisions regarding correction and discipline with our children.

As you know, Genesis begins with the story of Adam and Eve, created in God's image, placed in a pure and perfect environment, beneficiaries of a perfect relationship with their Father, the almighty God.

The Father loved them so much that He gave them everything to enjoy freely, with only one restriction: To Adam God said, "You may surely eat of every tree of the garden, but of the tree of the knowledge of good and evil you shall not eat, for in the day that you eat of it you shall surely die" (Genesis 2:16–17). One no-no and one clearly stated consequence. And we all know what happened.

God's response was clear and gives parents a model to follow.

- First, God went after His children. He called for them, went looking for them, expressed His desire for them.
- He intentionally gave them each a specific, measured amount of physical pain. Not too much, not too little, though we recipients often feel it's too much.
- He gave them emotional pain, or loss, when He sent them out of the garden.

- He was not angry with them, but sad and disappointed, for it was also a loss for God Himself.
- He gave them hope of restoration, a promised return to things as they had been.

All humans are pain-averse. No one enjoys hurting. But pain is a gift that protects us from harm. If we know what it feels like to get burned by a hot pan on the stove, the memory of that pain will motivate us to protect our hands with oven mitts. As adults, we can imagine the pain and suffering from falling off a rock ledge or driving recklessly, so we monitor our behavior to remain safe and pain-free.

Disciplining a child with a measured amount of pain appropriate for the offense creates an association to help him or her want to obey and avoid the pain or loss again. Children are dependent upon us for this kind of protective instruction and reinforcement until they are mature enough to logically and with reason make safe decisions.

Giving a measured amount of pain in love to correct and train a child around a heart issue, attitude, or behavior is following God's example. The type and amount of pain depends on the age of the child, the severity of the disobedience, and the context of what's happening in the child's life.

In his book *The Problem of Pain*, C. S. Lewis wrote, "Pain insists upon being attended to. God whispers to us in our pleasures, speaks in our

Polar Extreme Parents

What if you and your spouse are at different ends of the spectrum when it comes to discipline? One is too permissive, the other is too strict. The fun-and-games daddy or permissive mommy can make the other parent look like the bad guy.

Every parent has a leaning toward being too strict or too lenient. Pray together as a couple, and seek to better understand one another and migrate toward the middle. Learn how you both can benefit from one another and realize that God has a purpose in putting you two together. Talk about ways both of you can take responsibility for discipline and not leave it to the other parent.

We've warned that rules without a relationship result in rebellion. Likewise, a fun-and-games family with no boundaries can become chaotic and dangerous. The easiest thing to do about discipline is nothing. Don't ignore issues and think you are winning your child's heart by not bringing pain into his or her life.

conscience, but shouts in our pain: it is His megaphone to rouse a deaf world."[2]

Sometimes your children seem deaf to your instruction. Discipline is one of your most important tools for building character in your children. Sometimes it is the only thing that can gain the attention of a self-centered heart. Yet it's also one of the hardest tools to use, because it brings pain to a parent's heart, as well.

The Benefits of Discipline

When Eve gave birth to her firstborn, she undoubtedly felt like it was more than she could bear. Adam experienced the consequence of pain in his work, likely feeling it, too, was unbearable.

At times as a parent you will wonder if you are doing what is right. We aren't perfect, so we will make mistakes in discipline, either overdoing it or overlooking an offense we should have corrected with purpose.

Author Meg Meeker, a doctor of pediatric medicine and a contributor to *The Art of Parenting Video Series*, says, "I've seen many parents who don't want to discipline because they feel that saying no to their children is cruel. They see the word no as oppressive, restrictive, which of course it is, and it creates conflict in their relationship with their children. And a lot of parents bail on discipline because they don't want conflict."

But can something like discipline that feels wrong be right? Absolutely. This is one of the themes of Scripture—that discipline is redemptive. It saves. It results in transformation and the development of character. Ironically, the measured amount of pain in discipline can prevent a much greater amount of pain as your children grow up. Children who learn to trust their parents are more likely as teens to believe Mom and Dad's warnings about the dangers of drugs and alcohol and other perils.

> **P**arents who refuse to discipline their kids, feeling it's mean to the child, are doing just the opposite. They're being cruel to their child. How cruel is it to teach a child it is okay to live with no self-discipline? You're setting a child up to be a young adult who's going to fail in every aspect of life.
>
> DR. MEG MEEKER

The book of Proverbs often speaks of discipline as a way of gaining what every parent wants for their children—wisdom. Proverbs 19:20 (NASB) says, "Listen to counsel and accept discipline, that you may be wise the rest of your days."

This theme is continued in the New Testament. Hebrews 12, for example, compares a parent's discipline of a child to God's discipline for us as His children, and talks about the benefits of discipline:

> God is treating you as sons. For what son is there whom his father does not discipline? . . . For they disciplined us for a short time as it seemed best to them, but [God] disciplines us for our good, that we may share his holiness.
>
> Hebrews 12:7, 10

The words of Hebrews 12:11 (Rainey paraphrase) remind both parents and children, "Discipline is never welcomed; in fact, sometimes it results in crying and wailing. But afterward, if a child has gotten the point, it can sure result in all kinds of peace and quiet—and dutiful obedience, with chores getting done on time with excellence."

Here's a quick list of discipline's benefits that, we hope, will give you courage to be the parent:

- Discipline brings wisdom—godly skill in everyday living.
- Discipline instructs children that there are boundaries, limits, rules, and guardrails in life that are important for their safety, their flourishing, and their happy enjoyment of life.
- Discipline teaches your children that they can't live life their own way. They are accountable to a higher authority (you and God), and they must learn how to surrender to that authority.
- Discipline heads off foolish behavior and prevents children from ruining their lives.
- Discipline communicates love to a child.

We know a family whose parents had not practiced any discipline with their children. The poor mom was being overrun by the little outlaws, and with no fear of pain, they ignored Dad's attempts for control, too. After going through our parenting curriculum, the parents realized they were actually harming their children by giving them all that freedom with no boundaries.

Mom and Dad called a family meeting to inform the kiddos that a new sheriff would be ruling in town, Deputy Discipline. He began showing up with a few simple but painful disciplines. Three weeks into the new order, one daughter came to her mom and said, "I think I need a discipline. . . ." None of our kids ever asked for a discipline! But her request acknowledged the presence of a new stability and calm in their home that she valued and wanted to return.

In addition to the benefits we listed above,

- Discipline is a form of discipleship; children learn how to live life.
- Discipline prevents the parents from being shamed (Proverbs 29:15).
- Discipline may keep a child from hell. At issue is the child's will and his or her surrender to Jesus Christ. It sounds harsh, but hell is a real place that no parent wants to see his or her child be condemned to (Proverbs 23:13–14).

Speak Life into Your Kids

It was the spring of our son's senior year. He was eighteen and headed to the university in the fall. One night he walked into our bedroom. In an instant I saw him clearly as he was in that moment—a young man with so much potential ahead of him. So I decided to voice that and said, "I believe in you, son. When I look at you, I think, *He has good leadership gifts; he's such an influencer; when he walks into a room, he radiates joy and life.* I want you to know that I'm going to miss you."

He replied, "Oh, Mom, whatever," and he walked out of the room. About ten minutes later he walked back in and had tears in his eyes. He said, "Mom, I'm not that great."

I said, "No, you are."

"No, I messed up bad last weekend. I'm not who you think I am."

We sat and talked for a long time. I realized, when we speak life into our kids, as I had, it makes them want to become how you see them. But when we speak hopelessness or are constantly criticizing their flaws, I think it's easy for teenagers to become hopeless and feel like they'll never live up to the standard their parents have. And I feel like we hold such life in the power of our tongues.

Ann Wilson

It's important to realize that, when executed with love, clarity, and control, discipline is your friend; it can help you straighten some of the crooked bends in your arrow so that it is stronger and can fly straight. As Alistair Begg says, "No discipline is pleasant at the time, says Hebrews, but later it yields the peaceable fruit of righteousness. And part of the challenge of the parents is actually believing that. That what we're doing now is vital to that end."

Types of Discipline for Wrong Choices

Earlier we wrote that discipline is giving a measured amount of pain to train and correct a child around a heart issue, attitude, or behavior. It is difficult to think of intentionally inflicting pain upon our children. We know from experience that pain is something we don't like. It causes discomfort and distress to both child and parent.

But pain can also attract our attention. It can save us. Our body may feel different, and we may suspect something is wrong, but we often don't act until we feel acute pain.

So it is with our children. Pain may be the only thing that attracts their attention and forces them to listen to wisdom.

As we raised our children, we did spank them in their early years—carefully, lovingly, and under control. We believe in it; we believe it's biblical. (We discuss spanking more fully in the next chapter.)

But we used many other forms of discipline:

- Time-out in the child's room. (This is emotional pain—the loss of relationship for a period of time.) Removing a child from his or her audience (parents and the rest of family), and the attention the behavior begets, is a way to say, "This tactic isn't going to work." Time-outs are especially effective for children who thrive on relationships and hate missing out.
- Restriction from a privilege or the use of something they really love for a period of time. Screen time and devices are the easy candidates, but removing a favorite clothing item or the privilege of sitting in the front seat of the car also works.
- Suffering the natural consequences. Sometimes parents just need to let children experience the natural effects of certain choices. We have a friend whose teenage son refused to take the family garbage can to the street,

and as a result, the garbage truck didn't pick it up. That young man was surprised to find he had a new companion in his room for the next week—the garbage can and all its rotting contents! A child who leaves the milk out all night, allowing it to spoil, pays for the new gallon and doesn't get the favorite cereal for breakfast. You get the idea.

- Grounding, or confining to the house. For certain ages, this is like going to prison, but it sends a significant and important message. Missing out on a sleepover, a ball game, a birthday party, a trip to the mall with friends—all great measured amounts of pain.

- Extra chores. God made work to be hard, not easy, so we tagged on extra chores or work, especially in the upper-elementary through teen years, as a way to give measured pain. It was also a benefit to us. I (Barbara) loved the extra help I got from kids who needed to work off their disobedience. To help us in the moment, we took a small wooden box, labeled it "Extra chores—for those who care so little and do their very least," and filled it with more than three dozen slips of paper, each listing a chore like mopping the kitchen floor, cleaning all the toilets in the house, or sweeping our driveway (which was quite long).

- Hard labor. Painting fences or a porch, digging a ditch, hauling soil or rocks, etc., worked great when our teenage boys needed to remember that avoiding pain is a great reason to respect Mom and Dad's curfew. Hard labor is good for teenage boys. Lamentations 3:27 says, "It is good for a man that he bear the yoke in his youth."

Each child is different, and each is motivated by different types of pain. For one child, time-out may feel like torture, but an introverted child may love

> When we take a child to the doctor, sometimes the doctor puts a sharp metal object in the child's arm that causes temporary pain—the kid may yelp or cry. But we inflict this pain on purpose, because it's a vaccination that prevents a harmful, painful disease later on. A little bit of pain now prevents the greater pain down the road. And that's what discipline is.
>
> ALEX KENDRICK

that alone time. Some children may not consider grounding to be terrible punishment. The key is learning what motivates each child, what causes each the appropriate level of pain.

Recently we were having dinner with our adult children, and the topic of the chore box came up. We had been quite pleased with ourselves all these years, until we found out that our sweet children had gone through all the slips of paper when we weren't looking and removed the nastiest chores!

What Do You Discipline For?

Remember that discipline is for correcting the heart, dealing with a bad attitude, and training a child to repent. It's important for parents to talk through what types of discipline you will use, and then match them to different levels of behavior.

We agreed on certain things being automatic for a discipline:

- Pride, willful disobedience, or defiant rebellion against authority.
- Being sassy or disrespectful with Mom or Dad.
- A young child throwing a fit. We would not classify a momentary outburst of anger as a fit, unless it reached a pitch that broke glass or caused hearing damage. You'll know it's a fit when your child throws himself or herself on the floor out of protest or rebellion, continues the tantrum when you've asked him or her to stop, or attracts a small crowd to watch the drama.
- Passive rebellion against authority. This is more difficult to spot because the child will just ignore your request or claim not having heard it.
- Stealing. Sometimes, you'll have to ask God to help you catch a child in the act or help you find the evidence.
- Lying. Invent a lie-detector test for parents of teens, and you'll be rich.
- Hitting, biting, or any kind of physical expression that attempts to hurt another person.

This list was inspired by Proverbs 6:16–19, where God lists seven things He hates: haughty eyes, hands that shed innocent blood, a heart that devises wicked plans, feet that run rapidly to evil, false witness, deceit, and spreading strife. We decided that if God hates it—which is pretty strong language—then we should not tolerate that behavior, either.

One of the challenges is distinguishing between clear rebellion against authority and just plain naïve childishness. Sometimes it's just a child behaving as a child. Much of childish behavior is unpleasant to adults and needs to be ignored. If, however, the childishness endangers the child or anyone else, it's very important to address it with clarity and in a timely manner.

Here's an example of a situation that required discipline. I (Barbara) was in the kitchen one morning, helping our girls make their lunches, when I witnessed a mild crisis because we had no potato chips. Imagine that!

I told this daughter I was sorry we were out, and I suggested some other options, to no avail. She whined, "There's *nothing* in this house to eat. *Nothing* for my lunch!"

In fact, there was enough food in the house to feed a platoon of marines. I tried again to help with alternatives. "We've got yogurt, fruit. . . ." But we didn't have the one thing *she wanted*.

Finally, I warned her, "You need to gain control of your attitude. I'm going to the store this afternoon. I'll have potato chips tomorrow, but not today."

> **D**uring the toddler years, you've got to figure out what to discipline for and what not to discipline for. You discipline for deliberate acts of the will. If a child is defying you, testing your will against theirs, you discipline. But you don't discipline for normal childish behavior. Your son jumps over a couch, breaks a chair, drops his milk—don't scream at him that he's a horrible child. That's normal boy stuff.
>
> DR. MEG MEEKER

Then the demand went over the top: "You need to come to school and *buy* my lunch!" she said.

On the spot, I decided to ground her from the phone for a week. Her disrespect and demanding attitude were inappropriate.

This is the kind of petty and selfish attitude you will sometimes encounter, especially with teens. Usually, it needs correcting. Swiftly. Even if our daughter wasn't feeling well that day or was worried about a test, feelings don't justify selfish choices that are disrespectful, arrogant communication with parents. Rewarding such behavior by going to buy chips just to make her happy was out of the question. Resist the temptation to give in to some irrational demand just to calm the waters and ease the migraine headache. Don't cave.

The Flip Side of Discipline: Rewards and Affirmation

Martin Luther has been quoted as saying, "Spare the rod and spoil the child—that is true. But, beside the rod, keep an apple to give him when he has done well."[3] We believed strongly in affirming our children, especially when they went through the adolescent years. Your teenagers may look grown up, but don't believe all that you see.

The teen years can be hard for your kids. They are filled with self-doubt. Identity issues abound: *Who am I? Where do I belong? Am I good at doing anything?*

Here's where we recommend the prayer of the *hopeful* parent. Ask God to help you catch your kids when they respond with kindness, helpfulness, love, generosity, or compassion. Ask God to let you know when you just need to hug them. I remember one day when I (Barbara) spontaneously hugged Ben when he was seventeen. I let go . . . he didn't. So I hugged him some more. Ask God for opportunities and practical ways of expressing hope and encouragement to your teens.

- Praise and hug your teen for making a right choice in the face of peer pressure or temptation. Brag on one of them in front of the entire family at the dinner table, or in front of grandparents or a friend.
- Dads need to kiss their sons and daughters. Even an adult child needs to feel "Daddy's scratchy face" on his or her cheeks, accompanied with "I love you." At men's conferences, I (Dennis) have been approached by men who say, "My dad never hugged me as a boy growing up. Could you hug me?"
- Affirm your kids in front of their peers. And affirming their peers in front of your child is also very important.
- Increase privileges for doing chores with excellence and without having to be reminded.
- A date or a trip with Mom or Dad can be a reward.
- Offer a bonus—a *cash bonus*!

Please hear us on this one: The need for you to continually express belief in your child cannot be overstated. Discipline should be held in tension with generous amounts of affirmation and affection.

How We Discipline Our Children

We have a variety of discipline options in our repertoire. But all of them give some kind of pain or some kind of loss that hurts. Pain is a motivator for all of us, even adults. No one enjoys it, and we all order our worlds to avoid its sting.

Recently, we were spending the evening with some families. After dinner, the adults decided to send the kids upstairs to watch a movie. We asked our oldest to take our toddler with her. She started to obey, but then realized she was behind the other kids and was about to miss the opening seconds of the movie, one of her favorites. So she set her baby sister on the floor and ran upstairs.

Our toddler started crying because she'd been abandoned. It was obvious her big sister had not followed directions, so we pulled her from the screen and asked her three questions: "What were you asked to do?" . . . "What did you choose to do?" . . . "What should you have done?"

Her consequence was missing the first ten minutes of the movie.

Kids have momentary lapses in judgment and thinking. They get easily distracted, so training must be accompanied by vigilance.

One of our rules is that there are no toys at the dinner table. We want to teach our children to participate in conversations as a family.

One day our four-year-old brought toys to the table and refused to put them down. We asked the same questions we had asked our oldest earlier: "What were you asked to do?" . . . "What did you choose to do?" . . . "What should you have done?" Then we ended with, "We are really sorry for you, buddy. We asked you to put your toys away, and you chose not to. So you can't get ice cream tonight when we all go to Sweet Cow."

And, yes, we do spank our children, but always in a carefully orchestrated manner. We always review the same three questions. We always make sure the child understands it was his or her choice that led to our decision to spank.

Our spanking is firm enough to give a measured amount of pain appropriate to their age, but it's not out of control. We never take out our anger on them. It is a tool we use, among many others, to teach that poor choices have painful consequences.

After we spank, we hug for a long time and often lean back in the chair and snuggle. We ask them to tell us how they feel. We let them say they are angry or sad, and we talk about why they feel that way. We want to reinforce their very real emotions. We usually end by telling them, "We know you can make a good choice next time, and we know you want to."

Training and correction take a lot of time. It's a sacrifice for parents to set aside what they are doing to attend to a child. Ignoring them is far easier, but consistency builds security in children. If our kids know without question there will be a consequence for not obeying, they are much less likely to make a poor choice. And the result is less disobedience in the long run.

Rebecca (Rainey) and Jake Mutz

12 What about Spanking?

Fathers, do not provoke your children to anger, but bring them up in the discipline and instruction of the Lord.

Ephesians 6:4

One hot summer day a friend asked me (Dennis) if I'd go crawdad fishing with him at a pond across town. It was the perfect gig for a couple of ten-year-old boys. You'd put a little piece of worm on a hook and the crawdad would grab hold of that worm and wouldn't let go, if you reeled him in slowly enough.

Mom gave me permission, with one clear order—to be home by four. It turns out that was just about the time the crawdads were biting. So I ignored Mom's curfew.

That was my first mistake.

When I finally arrived home after five, Mom was gone, likely searching for me. Walking in the back door, I noticed a freshly cut forsythia branch, which in our family was the notorious switch. I knew the switch was for me, so I grabbed it and carefully broke it in half a dozen places, but left the skin in place, so the branch looked perfectly intact. Then I propped the branch against the wall, thinking Mom would never notice.

That was my second mistake.

When Mom came in the back door, I knew judgment day was upon me. There was no question she loved me, and her discipline was an extension of that love. She made it clear that I had disobeyed and then reached for the switch, which became a noodle in her hand.

That's when I realized my third mistake: Our forsythia bush had many additional worthy offerings.

That was the last spanking I received from my parents. Obviously, it was memorable.

God is our Father. He created us and wants a relationship with us. It's why He disciplines us. He wants to correct our hearts and reestablish our relationship with Him. He knows that we are fallible. He knows that if we wander from His love and protective care, we will get hurt and suffer. Because of His great love, He is not afraid to bring discomfort to our lives to bring us back to Him. It's a heart issue. It's about restoration. It's about a relationship.

He is not disciplining us just because we made a mistake. He is disciplining us to bring us back to Him. There's a consequence to doing life our own way. He is willing to inflict discomfort and pain to bring us back to His love.

As parents who want to build character in our children, we often need to discipline our children for the same reasons. Discipline, as we wrote in the last chapter, is *giving a measured amount of pain to train and correct a child around a heart issue, attitude, or behavior.*

> **S**olomon, the wisest man who ever lived apart from Jesus, was so clear about how spanking can be a huge blessing. He said, "Foolishness is bound up in the heart of a child; the rod of correction will drive it far from him." Spanking is not the only means of discipline, but when done in a loving way, in a balanced way, it can be a very effective means.
>
> STEPHEN KENDRICK

Strong Feelings about Spanking

In our culture, the one type of discipline that does not feel loving for many parents is spanking.

Feelings run Grand Canyon deep on this issue. About two-thirds of Americans say they approve of spanking, and half of parents say they sometimes spank their children.[1] But some psychologists label any form of corporal punishment as abuse. They cite research that, they say, shows spanking is ineffective in changing behavior, encourages anger and aggression, and can lead to juvenile delinquency and crime.[2]

We are aware of differing opinions on this issue in the community of faith. Some believe corporal punishment shouldn't be used at all. They cite parents who, using the Bible as justification, embrace an excessive use of corporal punishment, using it too frequently and harshly. And in many situations that may be true.

To those who oppose spanking, we want you to know that we respect you and your perspective. We aren't trying to pick a fight, nor are we trying to say there is one way and one way only to develop character. We are trying to help a generation of parents be effective in raising children to honor God, respect others, and become good citizens. If you've read this far, you know that we are basing our perspective and blueprints on the teachings of Scripture. If you don't agree on this topic of spanking, let's agree to disagree and press on respectfully.

Before we dive in, here are some caveats:

- We would never agree with any parent—Christian or not—who disciplines physically or emotionally when angry or out of control. Spanking is *never* physical retaliation! Words and actions matter. They communicate far more than we often know. If out-of-control anger has happened in your family, or if it occurs in the future, we strongly suggest you repent and ask your children to forgive you. If it repeatedly happens, we urge you to become accountable to another mature believer for your behavior.
- We are also very aware that some of you grew up in homes where spanking was used in an abusive manner, overly used to the point of physical or emotional harm. We want you to know that we are genuinely sorry you suffered this way. Neither of us grew up in an abusive home, but we know many who did. That is not how God wants parents to treat their children (Ephesians 6:4). We abhor the abuse of children, whether physical, emotional, spiritual, or sexual. God hates it, and we believe those of us who represent Him have been far too passive about addressing these issues in our culture and in the church. We suggest that, if you

came from an abusive home, you and your spouse may need to agree that it's best for you to use a different form of discipline.

- One further thought: We want you to know that we do not base our approach to parenting on research polls, even though they can be helpful. Just because the majority believes something is right does not make it so. But we believe the Bible does speak to this issue. We will not present an exhaustive biblical case for the practice of corporal punishment, but we will attempt to present the biblical evidence briefly and help you focus on how you might use this approach sparingly in love with your children so that it is effective and never abusive.

> It is not advisable for newly adopted parents, foster parents, or stepparents to spank. It is a child's trust in you as a loving parent that gives merit to the corrective message of spanking. It is unwise if you have an undefined and fragile relationship.
>
> RON DEAL

Our goal is to respectfully call all parents to protect, love, and encourage their children as they help to shape godly character in them.

What Does the Bible Say?

One of the most loved and comforting psalms is Psalm 23, the first Bible passage many children memorize. "Your rod and your staff, they comfort me" speaks of a kind, loving shepherd who tends to every need of His flock.

Moses carried a tall rod of wood as his scepter, the visual representation of his authority from God for His people. And Proverbs uses the word *rod* in reference to disciplining a child. These Scriptures remind us that parents are all three of these in their children's lives: shepherd of their hearts, authority for their best interests, and the guide and trainer of their characters.

It is interesting to note that the specific concept of giving a measured amount of physical pain is found in the book of wisdom, Proverbs:

> He who witholds his rod hates his son, but he who loves him disciplines him diligently.
>
> Proverbs 13:24 NASB

Foolishness is bound up in the heart of a child; the rod of discipline will remove it far from him.

Proverbs 22:15 NASB

The rod and reproof give wisdom, but a child who gets his own way brings shame to his mother.

Proverbs 29:15 NASB

Spanking was never our primary form of discipline, though we used it more in the preschool years than after. We reserved it for serious offenses—usually willful disobedience like lying, stealing, physically hurting someone (typically, these are all tried at least once before kindergarten), significant disrespectful attitudes or clear acts of defiance toward us, and second attempts to lie, steal, etc. (usually seen in elementary or middle-school years). Again, this list came from Proverbs 6, the list of behaviors and heart attitudes God hates.

One of the benefits of having a large family was that after child two, we began to see a pattern of repeating behaviors. For example, every one of our children told their first calculated lie after their third birthday. So by child three or four, we began to expect it to happen. And it always did. Children younger than three don't have the cognitive ability to formulate a false story or to deny the truth.

Because God hates lying, we decided we wanted to nip any lying in the bud with our kids. The first time we discovered a deliberate lie, we took the time to explain what a lie is, that it's wrong to lie, that we don't tolerate lies in our family, and that the consequence for lying is a spanking. "Do you understand?" we always asked. And little one always said yes with all seriousness. We didn't spank for this first lie because we wanted them to understand both the offense and the consequence.

Inevitably, each child tested us to be sure we meant it. And we had to prove that we did mean it. So we reminded the child what we'd said, asked if he or she remembered, sat the child in our lap, and told the child how much we loved him or her. Then we gave a spanking on the upper thigh. There were always tears and lots of hugs and reminders of our love. We always prayed that God would help the child choose to tell the truth. And after that first spanking, we rarely had another issue with lying until our kids were in upper elementary, were a little smarter, and decided to try again. Because we acted on what we said, our children believed us and had greater respect for our promises.

We didn't, however, spank for childishness. When our daughter Ashley was about two, she took Barbara's lipstick and colored on our white bedspread. The bedspread then served as an ink-pad for her hands and feet, as she walked all over the room, leaving a pink trail even into the bathroom on the mirror and walls. She was not being defiant; she was just being a child.

Make a plan with your spouse about when you will spank. We kept a note card taped on the inside of a cabinet door in the kitchen to remind us of our options. In the heat of the moment, it's always good to be reminded that spanking may not be the appropriate form of discipline. As we mentioned earlier, sometimes we sent children to their room or removed privileges or a treasured possession for a short period. Sometimes the discipline was forcing a child to apologize to a sibling for the behavior—that itself was enough pain!

When we've talked to parents about spanking, invariably they ask, "How old is too old to spank?" We don't know if there is a prescribed one-size-fits-all age to no longer spank, but generally somewhere between ages seven and ten was when we stopped using this method of discipline.

> **think** it's cruel to nag a child instead of dealing with disobedience. So many parents say, "Don't do that. . . . I said, don't do that. . . . I'm going to count to three, and if you do it again, you're going to come sit by me. . . . One, two, three! . . . Okay, I'll give you another chance, but don't do that." Those children may be the ones who say, "Just give me a little swat on the rear, and let's end this!"
>
> DARCY KIMMEL

By that time, frankly, there are far more effective methods of creating pain for disobedience. You will know—and God will guide you if you ask—when the child needs a different form of discipline. Every child is different, and it's important to tailor your approach to each one.

The Love Sandwich

When done properly, spanking can be an effective tool for building character. Like a sandwich, with two slices of bread containing all kinds of ingredients, so does one or both parents hugging a child before and after a discipline envelope the child in reassuring love.

When we spanked our children, we'd begin by sitting the child on one of our laps, giving a big hug, and letting the child know we were doing this because we loved them and wanted to train them in how to be wise.

We always clearly explained why we were spanking. We always asked, "Do you understand why I'm spanking you today?" and then let the child explain what he or she chose to do that was disobedient or against the rules. If they didn't get it right, we helped them say it correctly—"I lied about taking my sister's book"—because it is practice in confessing sins to God, as we are commanded to do in 1 John 1:9.

The number of swats corresponded to the age—a two-year-old received two swats, a three-year-old earned three. Three was the maximum, even for elementary school ages.

And we always ended the time with a second "slice of bread"—a hug and a verbal affirmation of our love. Then we'd pray, thanking God for the child and asking God to help the child learn from his or her mistakes. As the kids got older, we'd ask them to pray, too. This helped them articulate to God what they had done, more training in their relationship with God.

Again, parents should only spank while in full control of their emotions. On occasion, we would send a child to his or her room while we cooled down and thought through our options. Sometimes, if you discipline right at the moment of disobedience, you're still angry. When you spank out of anger, Eric Rivera says, "you're showing a lack of self-control and self-discipline—the very thing, probably, that you're disciplining your child for."

And we always spanked in private. Never in public. Never in front of the other kids.

We also did it promptly when they were under age five. As they got older, we often made them wait in their room, both for our benefit and for them to think about their "crime." "When the sentence for a crime is not quickly

Should I Discipline a Child in Public?

This is a common dilemma for many parents. Say a child throws a tantrum during a shopping trip because the parent denies something she wants. The child probably needs a discipline, but not a spanking in public. As inconvenient as it was, at times I (Barbara) left my cart in the store and took the children to my car to correct the situation and regain control before resuming my shopping.

Or say you are at a friend's home for dinner, and a child misbehaves. In situations like that, we would pick the child up and go to another part of the house to talk. If discipline was necessary and we knew the family well, we might do it then and there. But if it was a family we didn't know very well, we waited until we got home.

carried out, people's hearts are filled with schemes to do wrong" (Ecclesiastes 8:11 NIV).

We used a wooden spoon that would not harm our children. Again, our goal was to give a measured amount of pain, a good sting they would remember, enough pain to make them cry. For a season, I (Barbara) strategically placed the spoon on the dashboard of my car as a reminder. You may think that's cruel and unjust, but when you are a mom of six under the age of ten, sometimes you need a little visual reminder to keep kids civilized. And sometimes all you have to do is start to reach for it!

Finally, if the offense involved another person, like hitting a sibling or or lying to us—we always made our children verbalize the offending choice, apologize to the other person, and ask for forgiveness. We always coached them on what to say. This verbalization is crucial in helping them take responsibility for their behavior choices and teaches conflict resolution.

Even when the children were too old for spanking, the basic process continued as we used other types of discipline: Assure them of our love, explain why we're disciplining them, pray with them, and have them apologize and ask for forgiveness.

The Infamous Missing 1942D Wheat Penny

We close this controversial subject with another classic moment in our family. One of our children had a small coin collection that was kept in a bedside drawer. In the collection was a rare 1942D wheat penny, named for the stalks of wheat etched on one side of the coin.

One evening we came into the bedroom and found one of the younger children looking at all the coins. We cautioned this child to be careful with another family member's property, to which the child agreed.

A few days later, the owner of the coin collection was reviewing the rare finds and was shocked to discover that the 1942D wheat penny was missing. We carefully looked in the drawer, on the floor, under the bed . . . but this coin, probably worth thirty-five cents, was AWOL.

We talked with the child who had been looking at the coins earlier, and the child denied knowing anything about it. Then we talked about the disappearance at dinner with everyone present. One-by-one, they all professed no knowledge of the coin.

Later that evening, the child who seemed to be the prime suspect in our investigation went into my office, opened a drawer in my desk that holds a bowl of my pocket change, and miraculously found the 1942D penny! Like a treasure hunter who had struck gold, the child held it up for us to see, clearly intent on proving innocence. We didn't buy this luck.

I (Dennis) looked at the penny and the child, and then I asked the child to go upstairs and sit on the couch in our bedroom. The eight-year-old's joy instantly melted. That couch was our "judgment seat."

We suspected this child had lied to us in the past, but we never had proof. So we had prayed and asked God if He would orchestrate the circumstances for us to catch this child before a pattern of lying was engrained in the heart. Presto, prayer answered in the form of the missing 1942D wheat penny.

After sitting on the couch and doing some thinking, realizing there was no way out, the child finally repented and admitted to having taken the coin. We went through the spanking process we have described, appropriate for the child's age, complete with love, tears, and prayer. It was this child's last spanking ever.

We remember that moment well. Before our child had admitted to stealing the penny and then lying about it, I (Barbara) looked into my husband's eyes with a look that said, "Are we sure about this? What if the story really is the truth?"

We both sensed this child was the guilty one. The Holy Spirit helps parents. We had prayed for an opportunity to reinforce the primacy of truth telling, and in that moment we needed to trust that God was leading us. And He was.

In summary, we believe spanking was important, especially in the preschool years when you cannot yet reason with children. We believe it should be used

Prayer of the Helpless Parent

There were so many situations when we didn't know what the truth was, who was right, and who was wrong. We needed help with a child who seemed aimless, a child who ran away, a child who was too much of a people pleaser, choosing a prom dress, and a thousand other perplexities we never imagined we'd face. Early on we learned to come to God with our bewilderment when we had no idea what to do.

The prayer of the helpless parent finds support in a favorite Old Testament story. There was a king of Israel, a good man, who found his nation surrounded by an impossibly large enemy army. Instead of making an alliance with another king, one who did not know God, King Jehoshaphat turned to God. Though he was personally afraid, he pleaded with God for help. "We are powerless against this great horde that is coming against us," he prayed. "We do not know what to do, but our eyes are on you" (2 Chronicles 20:12).

A perfect description for how parents feel, don't you agree? If you will cast yourself on God's mercy and grace, asking Him for wisdom and to show you what to do, He will guide you. And He may surprise you with circumstances only He could orchestrate.

God loves to help parents, for He loves your kids more than you do!

for only very specific behaviors or actions that you as a couple have discussed ahead of time. And we believe the frequency should decrease dramatically as you properly instruct, correct, and reinforce those attitudes and behaviors.

Children grow up with a selfish and foolish heart, and it's easy for parents to grow weary of addressing character issues day after day, year after year.

That's why one of our favorite verses as parents was Galatians 6:9: "Let us not grow weary of doing good, for in due season we will reap, if we do not give up." As we've said throughout this book, God will help you raise your children. Depend on Him for wisdom and for the strength to persevere. We have seen firsthand the long-term results of our efforts, as our kids have grown up and are now relying on God as they raise their own children.

13 Smartphones for Smart Families

by David Eaton and the Axis team

Technology is changing so fast today that parents are challenged with questions like, "When should I get a smartphone for my kid?" and "How can I control screen time in my family?"

After hosting a daily radio program, FamilyLife Today, for over a quarter century, I've had the privilege of featuring over a thousand guests on every imaginable and some unimaginable subjects. As we were writing this book, we decided we'd ask one of these guests, David Eaton, to write this chapter about developing your child's character with regard to technology and how your child engages in it. David heads up Axis, one of the most effective and relevant organizations already in this arena.

So what you are about to receive is the essence of more than ten years of work in the digital and social media marketplace. David and his team work with more than 80,000 families each year, helping parents navigate this ever-changing frontier with their children. I asked David and his team of twenty-somethings to create "uranium" for you. I said, "I want you to help parents be radioactive and know how to protect their kids and use this challenging area to build character."

This is better than uranium . . . it's PLUTONIUM! Enjoy!

Dennis and Barbara

I am raising my daughter like it is the 1950s," a flustered mom emphasized to me down the barrel of her pointed index finger.

Clearly, she was not happy. And in our experience, it is never fun to be caught between a momma bear and her cub—even if her cub is seventeen years old.

One of our Axis traveling teams had just finished speaking to a group of two hundred Christian high school students. We were teaching about smartphones, teen culture, and the Christian worldview, and this momma bear was not pleased that we had played a song by Taylor Swift—even though we were asking the students to examine Taylor's lyrics.

So what's the big deal?

She didn't want her daughter to know *who* Taylor Swift was, much less have her *hear* Tay Tay's music. After all, she was trying to raise her daughter like it was the 1950s, and the last time we checked, Taylor Swift was born a little later than that.

However . . . it's *not* the 1950s, and God has not given us our children to raise in the 1950s.

We get to raise them now.

Time Machines

But honestly, we completely understand why she was upset. It seems like things are changing faster than anyone can keep up. At Axis, we have a team of twenty-six people (with an average age of twenty-four) who wake up every morning and come to work thinking about and creating resources around teen culture. Yet sometimes even we feel behind!

Who would have thought that "broccoli" would mean weed, or that the eggplant emoji would be slang for male anatomy? Who could have guessed that the phrase "Netflix and chill" would be a euphemism for a casual sexual hookup or that "mia" would be shorthand for bulimia. And of course, LGBT-TQQIAAP[1] feels like it can't grow any longer, but it might.

Modern Swiss Army Knife

And then there's the glorious smartphone, the rectangular modern-day Swiss Army knife that's in the pockets of preteens and teens everywhere. It seems that the smartphone could be the engine accelerating the good and bad shifts in teen culture. As one dad put it, "I always feel three apps behind my kids." And we know from interacting with thousands of parents that the smartphone is the number one battleground over which parents and teens fight.

The times, they are a-changin', and if we take any amount of time to think about the shifts in teen culture and technology, it gets overwhelming fast. It will make even the best of us want to retreat into our time machines and head back to the 1950s.

Okay, maybe we just tried to overwhelm you a little.

But let us assure you. All is not lost. Actually, there are incredible opportunities for you to invest in your children and help rewire the way they interact with technology and the messages it transfers.

And it doesn't involve throwing all tech off a cliff and retreating. Or sounding the alarm and launching into a fear-based thermonuclear war against the rectangles in your life. The opportunity lies in *reframing the conversation* through "smartphone discipleship." This is a way to affirm a deeper way of being human, and it connects your *wisdom* with your students' *wonder*.

What follows are four conversations to have with your preteens and teens about technology and, specifically, the smartphone. These might be four of the most important conversations you'll have as a parent.

Conversation One: Very Good, Cursed, and Redeemed

Dr. Sherry Turkle, author and founding director of the MIT Initiative on Technology and Self, once said, "Computers are not good or bad; they are powerful."[2] That's a weighty statement, especially in a time when most teenagers use their smartphones as their primary computers.

We agreed with this statement for over a year (whoops!), but then one day we stopped and started to rethink it. Does the Bible actually say that the world God made, including the technology created from it, is not "good or bad" and that it is neutral?

Actually, in Genesis it says the exact opposite.

God weaves the world together and then declares that it is "very good." Part of that goodness includes the command God gave man and woman to cultivate the earth. In essence, we are living out the image of God imprinted on us when we create. In our view, technology—like any tool we've created—is simply one way humans have cultivated the "very good" cosmos.

But the story doesn't end there.

As we all know, this very good world has been subjected to the curse since Adam and Eve chose to rebel against God. Thus, cultivation—and therefore all technology—is affected by the curse. So rather than being neutral, technology is both very good and cursed.

And of course, the story doesn't end there, either.

God is committed to His creation, and through the death, burial, and resurrection (and way, truth, and life) of Jesus, God is redeeming that creation. The best part is that we are invited into that mission with Him.

Think about that for a second.

We are joining God again, this time in redeeming what has been lost.

So here's the first important conversation to have with your student: How is a smartphone (or anything!) very good, how is it cursed, and how can we as a family redeem it?

This positioning is huge. You are no longer the bad guy, and you are no longer making the cool new piece of technology evil. Instead, you are inviting that technology into a bigger story, into the story of God. And while doing that, you are humbly submitting that form of technology under the rule of God.

Remember to have this conversation: How is a smartphone very good, how is it cursed, and how can we as a family redeem it?

Conversation Two: What Is It For?

When it comes to technology, we will quickly confess: We like it. It's fun, interesting, and powerful. Of course, it can be massively distracting and, in some cases, flat-out dangerous.

The second conversation to have about any form of technology is this: What is it for? Although it seems like a deceivingly simple question, how you and your children answer the question of purpose ultimately determines how you ought to use that technology.

So what is a smartphone for? Maybe your family would say that it's connecting us with the ones we love the most. Okay, great! Now fast-forward to dinnertime. Your family is at a restaurant, and Dad is checking email,

Mom is on Pinterest, and daughter is keeping her Snapstreak going. Whoops. #NailedIt

How about Netflix? What is it for? Sure, it's an incredible library of long-form TV shows with a few movies thrown in. What a fun way to learn and be entertained by great storytelling! But the Oompa Loompas see TV differently:

> IT ROTS THE SENSE IN THE HEAD!
> IT KILLS IMAGINATION DEAD!
> IT CLOGS AND CLUTTERS UP THE MIND!
> IT MAKES A CHILD SO DULL AND BLIND!
> HE CAN NO LONGER UNDERSTAND
> A FANTASY, A FAIRYLAND!
> HIS BRAIN BECOMES AS SOFT AS CHEESE!
> HIS POWERS OF THINKING RUST AND FREEZE!
> HE *CANNOT* THINK—HE ONLY *SEES*!
> —Roald Dahl, *Charlie and the Chocolate Factory*[3]

That's a lot of ALL CAPS from the Oompas, but we think the message is clear.

Understanding the intended purpose and subsequently the actual outcome needs to be an ongoing conversation. If the diet we're on is causing us to be unhealthy, we should correct course. If the smartphone that's supposed to connect us actually pulls us apart, it's time to go back to the drawing board.

Remember to have this conversation: What is it for?

Conversation Three: We Are on a Journey with a Destination

When I was in high school, I was eager to turn sixteen so I could drive. To my advantage, my parents were equally eager to stop being my personal Uber. So as a family we began the process of getting my driver's license.

Getting a license can be a pretty intimidating process. You need to take a course, then pass a test (that most people fail the first time), then you apply to receive your permit. In some states, you need to have your permit for a year before you can get your license. And while you have your permit, you take lessons from a professional driving instructor and log hours while driving supervised, both during the day and at night. Finally, you take a driving test with your state's department of motor vehicles.

Oh, and while doing this, you are purchasing a vehicle, applying for insurance, learning how to drive a stick shift, figuring out how to change a flat with the hidden spare, etc., etc., etc.

We think a similar mindset needs to be taken with smartphones. In the same way that you don't hand your kids the keys to a car, without any training, and simply say, "Good luck," you shouldn't hand them a smartphone and say, "What could go wrong?"

Their lives, your life, and others' lives hang in the balance physically, legally, and spiritually. In short, we advise against giving your children a phone if you are not ready to have a conversation with them about it multiple times a week for multiple years.

Also, when you're teaching them how to drive, the goal is for them to drive on their own without you in the passenger seat forever. The same is true for smartphones: You don't want to be skimming all their texts for the rest of your life. Ain't nobody got time for that.

Which brings us to the third conversation in smartphone discipleship. Your family is on a journey together of enjoying, leveraging, and self-regulating your phones. And there is a destination! This is when your children have demonstrated integrity and have learned how to self-regulate their phones—and therefore no longer have limits imposed by you; they impose their own limits! Usually this happens in their junior or senior year of high school.

Every journey has milestones. Here are some of the key milestones on the "Smartphone Ed" journey:

Goal: heart and destination

Always start with your child's heart in mind and with the end of the journey in sight. Your goal is to mentor your child so that his or her heart loves righteousness. This goes so much deeper than behavior management. You want your child to be able to use a phone with wisdom and joy, and without your oversight. You want your teenager to be independent and able to self-regulate.

Ownership: stewardship and leasing

If God owns everything, He owns all phones. As a parent, you are responsible to God as the ultimate steward of your child's phone. A great way to help steward your children's hearts and phones is by making a family contract that they sign in order to "lease" their phones from you. There are a lot of great contracts online that you can use for inspiration. Also, consider having your child contribute financially to the costs involved with the phone.

Privacy: a privilege

Make your mantra this: We are better in community than in isolation. We recommend that you have access to the phone at any time and have access to all login information and settings. This sounds harsh, but your child does not have a right to phone privacy. Explain that privacy is earned through demonstrating integrity, and that even adults often relinquish this right to others in order to steer clear of temptation or misuse of their phones. Remember: We are better in community than in isolation, so make sure you are modeling this to your kids!

If worse comes to worst and you must take your child's phone away (or in extreme situations consider doing what two total ninja parents we know do and have all your kids share one phone), always remember that to the next generation, a phone is an extension of their identity. Taking it away is literally taking away part of who they are and their access to community. Never take it away lightly, and when you do, clearly explain what needs to happen before you to give it back.

Capacity: incremental responsibility

Phones are amazing and can accomplish thousands of functions. Upon first leasing your children a phone, we recommend you severely limit the phone's functionality! Be warned, this may be a point of contention, but it's a great opportunity to refer to the contract you had them sign. Remind them that as they learn to wisely use their phones, over time they will have fewer and fewer restrictions.

Okay, here we go. When they first get a phone:

- The **App Store** should never be left on and should be restricted. Any app on the phone will require your approval to download and update. You should know what each app is for, in-app purchases should be turned off, and apps should not be allowed to be deleted without permission. Also, check all apps, especially ones buried multiple folders deep. Over time, you will want to and should give them the keys to the App Store, but don't let them delete apps.

- **Texting/email** should not be allowed unless you have access to all messages on a mirrored and separate device. Here's the principle behind this: seeing themselves being seen. Eventually, you'll get bored and can stop skimming their messages because you trust them. Trust the Holy Spirit to prompt you to check your kids' messages when something is awry.

- **Social media** is not allowed (unreal, we know) until trust and open communication are proven. Our reasoning is that there's really no way to monitor social media. If you do at some point choose to allow your child to have a social media account, proceed with caution and be aware of the mental and emotional health problems that can be caused or triggered by social media. We highly recommend that parents join whatever social media platform their kids are on. It's beneficial for you to experience it and have the credibility to host the "What is it for?" conversation. Keep in mind that if you have given them your trust regarding social media, asking them before you "follow" them will reiterate your faith in them. Also take some time to study and learn social media etiquette and dos and don'ts. We'd hate for you to "heart" your own Instagram post.

- **Internet browsers** need to be filtered and have built-in accountability reporting. There are obvious sexual risks involved with full access to the internet, not to mention sexual predators. Think of a filter like a wall. A wall helps, but if you're clever, you can always find a way around it. Your long-term goal should be to help your kids understand what triggers them so they can willingly build their own wall. The best wall is not actually a filter, but a community of friends and mentors to whom they are accountable.

P.S. None of this will work if you are not first modeling it. #Goals

Boundaries: to be fully present

One story stands out to us as to why boundaries are important. We asked a thirteen-year-old teen what her plans were for the evening. She responded, "I'm going to go home and watch my parents stare at their phones."

Steve Jobs wanted to design Apple devices without an off switch. But sometimes the only way to be fully present and connect is to shut our phones off. Here are some of the things we've seen great families do to limit the incessant beckoning of their phones.

First, they limit which apps are actually on their phones and how each app's notifications work. Some dads refuse to have email on their phones because it causes them to work at home when they should be enjoying their families. Some moms turn off notifications for social media and even texting because they know they check them enough already.

Second, families agree to a technology curfew for all devices in the evening and the morning. A helpful curfew is no devices from eight p.m. to eight a.m. We recommend setting a gentle alarm that goes off at eight p.m. every night to remind you of the curfew. Make *it* the bad guy.

Third, some families limit or even forbid devices in the bedroom, especially at night. Instead, they buy everyone alarm clocks and charge all of their devices in a common area while everyone sleeps. This helps the devices stay charged during the day, helps everyone sleep better at night, and helps the family avoid temptations.

Finally, great families decide on time limits for devices, and then they keep track. This very good device can become cursed pretty quickly when it distracts us from creating and only encourages us to mindlessly consume.

Blaise Pascal critiques,

> The only thing which consoles us for our miseries is distraction, and yet this is the greatest of our miseries. For it is this which principally hinders us from reflecting upon ourselves, and which makes us insensibly ruin ourselves. Without this we should be in a state of weariness, and this weariness would spur us to seek a more solid means of escaping from it. But distraction amuses us, and leads us unconsciously to death.[4]

A disturbing surprise: your greatest competition

We're sure we missed some milestones, but after ten years in the teen/technology space, we think the above list is a great place to start. However, we want to give you a final warning. When we speak to parents, we ask, "When you parent, what is your greatest competition?" You may be surprised by the answer. A parent's greatest competition is . . . other parents.

Here's what we mean. Just as your student experiences peer pressure, you will experience pressure from other parents regarding smartphones and discipleship. You're going to have to call some tough shots and graciously disagree with how other parents set boundaries for their own kids. Know that this is normal, and don't be discouraged. Always stay humble, be teachable, and stick to your convictions.

Remember to have this conversation: We are on a journey with a destination.

Conversation Four: You Can Tell Me Anything

I'd been stumped.

We had just finished a rather energetic discussion about the limits a teen's parents were placing on her phone when she quipped, "The stricter the parent, the sneakier the child."

What a zinger! (Maybe this is why we love working with the next generation so much. They are clever and thoughtful and keep us sharp.)

We loved this comment, and we have had a lot of discussions about it at Axis. It's like a magic trick with words. At first her statement feels true, then it feels false, then you eventually realize there are some hidden assumptions behind her declaration.

Theology of goodness

Here's the sleight of hand. This teen was assuming, unbeknownst to her, that her parents didn't have her best interest at heart and, ultimately, that God didn't have her best interest at heart.

So instead of pointing our index fingers at our daughters and saying, "You're being sneaky," we need to ask a deeper question. Do you believe that God's path is good? Do you believe that it leads to life, flourishing, joy, and meaning? G. K. Chesterton posits, "The more I considered Christianity, the more I found that while it had established a rule and order, the chief aim of that order was to give room for good things to run wild."[5]

And if their index fingers are pointed back at us, and they say with hot tears on their cheeks, "You are being too strict!" it might be good to self-reflect: *Do my kids know I have their best interests at heart? Do they know I am safe, quick to forgive, and eager to reconcile?*

And here's the real mind-grenade to reflect upon: Are you raising a sin concealer or a sin confessor (thanks to Bob Lepine, cohost of *FamilyLife Today*, for those terms)? The only way to know the answer to this question is to ask yourself, *Do I model confession and forgiveness to my children?*

This all contributes to the fourth conversation that you need to reinforce consistently: You can tell me anything.

The "I'm Not Shocked" Face

You need to consistently tell your children that you love them, that you want what's best for them, and that they can tell you anything. If you don't, it will be virtually impossible to have tough conversations with them in which they are honest.

There will be some awkward conversations you'll wish you could avoid, but if they don't hear the truth from you, who's going to tell them? Here's a parenting secret from a couple of genius parents: Use your "I'm not shocked" face whenever you hear something shocking from your child and whenever you need to talk with them about something tough.

Tough Conversations

Ready to practice your "I'm not shocked" face? Here are some awkward topics you need to consistently bring up with your smartphone-wielding pre-teens and teens:

- **Pornography.** We hate to say this, but your children will more than likely see porn, and the average age of exposure keeps getting younger. They need to know that they can talk with you about this, they need to know what to do when they come across it, and they need you to help them define a beautiful view of sexuality.
- **Sexting.** What may surprise you is that sexting has become a normal part of dating. If you have a daughter, there's a good chance she will be solicited for nude pictures. What really shocked us is that many girls who are not asked for nudes want boys to ask them. (Are you practicing your "I'm not shocked" face?!) Ultimately, they want to be wanted, and this is how culture is telling them to measure their value. Encourage your children to never send suggestive pictures of themselves, to never pass along suggestive images, and to tell you immediately when they receive them. Let them know that they can blame you in order to scare their friends into not sending them nudes.
- **Sneaky apps.** Folks, it's getting worse before it gets better. There are some apps that are designed specifically to deceive parents. Notoriously,

the Calculator% app looks like a calculator and works like a calculator, but entering a secret numerical password reveals a hidden folder in which children can hide pictures from their parents. Yep, now's another good time to practice your "I'm not shocked" face.

- **Fake social media accounts.** Don't be surprised if your son or daughter has multiple accounts on the same social media platform. One is for parents (and grandma, too!), and the other is a place to have unmonitored conversations with friends. Ask your children if they have a Finstagram (i.e., a fake Instagram).

- **Friends' phones.** Finally, you've had enough of (fill in the blank) app. Your son has crossed the line too many times, so you're going to take his phone away for a long, long time. Or maybe you're frustrated that your time machine won't take you back to the 1950s, so you vow to never let your kid have a smartphone. There's one small problem with both of these situations: Your child will still have access to a phone, either by borrowing a friend's current phone or by receiving an old phone from a friend who upgrades. On a friend's phone, your kid can manage social media (Snapstreaks, duh!) and have access to porn, sexts, and all the depths of the internet.[6]

Overwhelmed? Sure, you can go to Goodwill and buy a rotary phone and a VCR, but we encourage you to take a different path in which you courageously pursue your children's hearts. Frequently remind them of your unshakable love and that you've got their backs. Since day one you've had their best interests at heart, and no matter what they're up against, they can come to you for a listening ear, for support, and even to confess their mistakes.

Remember to have this conversation: You can tell me anything.

The Most Important Conversation

One of the saddest byproducts of the corrosion of culture is the breakdown of the family. For example, a woman in her early thirties told us, "I've had only one real conversation with my dad."

One. Real. Conversation.

Are you serious?!

When she said this, we were dumbfounded. If the rising generation is having only one real conversation with their parents, no wonder the gospel is being lost in translation!

There is a beautiful twist to this story. This woman was not finished. After saying she has had only one real conversation with her dad, she paused, and with a sweet smile said, "We've never stopped having that one conversation."

Wow! She has had a thirty-year conversation with her dad. From the looks of it, her dad is planning on having that "one conversation" with her the rest of their lives.

Your child may have an eighteen-month conversation with a youth pastor, a four-year conversation with a favorite coach, or even a ten-year conversation with your pastor. But with you, the parent, he or she can have a sixty-year conversation. No one will *ever* be more influential than you. It's sociologically true, it's historically true, it's intuitive, and, of course, it's biblical.

Snapchat Missionary

So be a missionary to your kid. By the grace of God and the guidance of the Holy Spirit, seek to reach into their world, just like Jesus did for all of humanity.

This may mean limiting your freedom for a season to join them in a technology fast, or it may mean giving up your phone privacy to lead by example and show that you have nothing to hide. It could also mean downloading Snapchat (or whatever their go-to app is) simply to understand what they love about it. One thing is certain: According to two great parents we know, you need to plan on spending thirty minutes a week studying your teens' world so that you can better connect with them.

If you feel three apps behind your kids or just want an easier way to stay up to date on teen culture, check out *The Culture Translator* at Axis.org. Parents love it! This weekly email for parents and grandparents will help you join the conversation that culture is already directing with your preteens and teens. It takes three minutes to read and provides a short summary of what is influencing your kids this week. It is free at Axis.org and will help you deepen the "one conversation"!

Being a missionary will always mean empathizing and being curious enough to try to understand your kids' reality—a reality where bullying not only happens in person, but also online 24/7; where male/female has never been a given, but an ambiguous spectrum; where one's identity feels like it's dependent on "likes"; and where sexting is an expected part of dating.

You have what it takes, and we believe in you! Hold fast to your heart connection with your child and hold fast to the "one conversation."

Section Four

What Is Identity?

The Lord looks down from heaven; he sees all the children of man; from where he sits enthroned he looks out on all the inhabitants of the earth, he who fashions the hearts of them all and observes all their deeds.

Psalm 33:13–15

D r. Henry Faulds was a Scottish medical missionary serving in Japan in the late 1800s. He had been studying fingerprints and had concluded that every person had a unique pattern in the ridges on their fingers. In fact, after a theft of surgical alcohol from his hospital, he was able to trace the fingerprints he found to identify the thief—one of his employees.

Faulds was a pioneer in forensic fingerprinting, though it took another couple decades for the practice to fully take hold in law enforcement.[1]

If we believe the Bible to be true, we should not be surprised someone discovered these distinct markers of God's creation. Scripture makes it clear that God has made every person unique and for a purpose. We intuitively know this to be true.

And so we teach our children this important lesson: There is no one like you! God doesn't make copies. Even identical twins are not perfect replicas of one another.

Just as every snowflake is unique, the identity of each child is distinctively engineered by God with a distinctive blend of gifts, talents, intellect, and purpose. As Psalm 139 tells us,

> For you formed my inward parts; you knitted me together in my mother's womb. I am fearfully and wonderfully made. . . . Your eyes saw my unformed substance; in your book were written, every one of them, the days that were formed for me, when as yet there was none of them.
>
> Psalm 139:13–14, 16

One of our tasks as parents is to recognize how a plethora of different factors shape the identity of our children. For example:

- place of birth: nationality; rural or urban; raised in multifamily housing, in a single-family home, on a farm, or other
- family of origin: raised by biological, adoptive, foster, or stepparents; parental beliefs, values, strengths, weaknesses; siblings, birth order,

Blended-Family Wisdom: A Child's Identity

At the same time a child in a blended family is working through developmental issues related to spiritual, emotional, and sexual identity, he or she is trying to answer questions related to the changing family identity.

The fundamental task of being a stepfamily is deciding how you will be family to one another. People who are unrelated by birth try to become related by marriage. Children and adults have different last names, social-cultural histories, experiences, values, and traditions. For a child, learning "Who am I?" is one thing; learning "Who are we?" is another.

A parent and stepparent should be mindful of this journey for children and give them plenty of space as they work through where people—new and old—fit into their hearts. Don't force labels, especially terms of endearment (e.g., "Call me Mom"), and respect a child's meaningful relationships with those in the other home. And never press your timing for a quickly established shared family identity on the child, or you may find it harder to obtain. Value the relationships your family has today—make the most of them instead of being discouraged because you don't have more—while trusting that tomorrow will deepen your family identity.

Ron Deal

and extended family influences; ethnicity; circumstances of family life; wealthy, middle-class, or impoverished household; education and access to learning opportunities

- physical DNA/genetics: appearance (height, eye color, hair color, etc.), gender
- innate gifts and abilities: intelligence, talents (musical, artistic, athletic, etc.); emotional makeup; personality and behavioral style
- world forces: both the literal world environment and the child's own immediate world environment

All these factors both shape and help children understand who they are. But we want to focus on three factors that profoundly influence their identity. Here's a simple definition: "My identity tells me who I am as a unique person on earth and what my purpose in life is."

All children will eventually ask themselves questions that will begin the formation of their identity. They may or may not verbalize these to you as Mom or Dad, but you can know they are asking these questions because you at one time asked them yourself:

- Emotional identity: Am I loved, cared for, and valued?
- Sexual identity: Am I a boy or a girl, and what does that mean?
- Spiritual identity: Who is God? Does He love me? Who am I spiritually? Does God have a plan for me?

Ultimately, this final question trumps all the others. Because as life happens, as your children make decisions both good and bad, as they suffer rejections, as they battle physical illness or limitations, as they encounter influences that will shape them, their baby faith will have opportunities to grow as you encourage, pray, and remind them of God's unchanging truth about them.

14 Emotional Identity

If children live with criticism, they learn to condemn. . . .
If children live with fear, they learn to be apprehensive. . . .
If children live with ridicule, they learn to feel shy. . . .
If children live with encouragement, they learn confidence. . . .
If children live with acceptance, they learn to love.

Dorothy Law Nolte, *Children Learn What They Live*

The room was small, dark, and silent. Stepping inside we saw three walls lined with baby cribs, each occupied by a tiny baby. In the back corner a disengaged caretaker lifted her eyes in our direction. The babies were alone. Unattended. Silent.

Our daughter Laura and I (Barbara) were part of an overseas mission team working for a week in an orphanage, home to hundreds of abandoned babies and children, most with physical disabilities or medical conditions their parents were unable to provide for.

Most of the nonmedical members of our team were assigned to assist an American doctor from our group. But another woman, Lynn, and I asked if we could go to the baby room and just take care of babies all day, every day. For the next week we gave our hearts to these babies, snuggling them close while giving them bottles instead of letting the feeding happen as it normally did—with the bottle propped up on a rolled rag, much of the milk escaping the baby's mouth and soaking into the bedding.

The smallest baby drew my heart instantly. I was amazed to discover she was six weeks old, as she weighed barely five pounds, having been born premature. Lethargic and sleepy, she seemed so vulnerable and alone. I held her as often as the workers would let me. Lynn and I named some of these little ones that week since we couldn't speak their native language. For my preemie I chose the name Sarah. I prayed for her little life during the day when I was with her and at night back in our hotel.

When we arrived at the baby room one morning midweek, I went straight to Sarah and bent over her crib. Even in the dim lighting she looked blue. I put my hand on her tiny chest and discovered it was barely moving.

I ran to find our American doctor, who began the process of reviving her, and then raced her to a hospital, where she completely recovered. Her near death was the result of neglect. Sarah's needs, physical and emotional, had been ignored.

Quite miraculously, baby Sarah was adopted months later by one of the doctors on our medical team. She is now a thriving, healthy teenager.

One of my most distressing times as a therapist was working with a nine-year-old firstborn child who was experiencing debilitating headaches that consumed his life. In tears he would tell me of the emotional pain his parents' fighting caused him; he couldn't escape the anguish their conflict created in him. When I tried to intervene with his parents, they told me the subject was moot because the marriage was ending. Needless to say, the headaches continued.

JIM KELLER

Emotional Stability Is the Foundation

Without a personally invested parent to feed her body and love her soul, little Sarah failed to thrive and almost died.

Erica Komisar, a psychoanalyst and author of the parenting book *Being There*,[1] says, "Mothers are biologically necessary for babies. . . . Babies are much more neurologically fragile than we've ever understood."[2] She explains that "mothers are the central nervous system to babies. . . . Every

> **E**ven when a child has totally failed and turned his back, he wants to know: Do you still love me? Do you still approve of me? Do you still accept me? And the answer is yes, no matter what you've done, because that's how God sees us.
>
> ANN WILSON

time a mother comforts a baby in distress, she is regulating that baby's emotions from the outside in."[3] In fact, this continues for the first three years of life.

Emotional security is the foundation upon which all facets of identity are eventually built. How we feel about ourselves—whether we are loved or unloved, competent or incompetent, free or enslaved, empowered or shamed—will impact our emotional foundation. Emotional health also strongly supports the development of a child's character, natural gifts, intelligence, and relationships.

It's All about Our Hearts

We commonly talk about the center of our lives in terms of our heart. Our literal heart beats constantly and keeps us alive. But we also have a nonphysical heart in which resides our emotions, our thinking, and our decision-making or will.

Jesus spoke often of our hearts:

- Matthew 14:27: "Jesus spoke to them, saying, 'Take heart; it is I. Do not be afraid'" (emotion).
- Matthew 9:4: "Jesus, knowing their thoughts, said, 'Why do you think evil in your hearts?'" (thinking).
- Matthew 19:8: "He said to them, 'Because of your hardness of heart Moses allowed you to divorce your wives" (will).

In fact, God speaks of our hearts hundreds of times, from the first to last pages of the Bible, describing the hearts of His people. Two verses summarize this most important part of our in-His-image likeness, our hearts.

"For the Lord sees not as man sees: man looks on the outward appearance, but *the Lord looks on the heart*" (1 Samuel 16:7, emphasis added). God supremely values the choices we make internally in that hidden space inside each of us called the heart.

"You shall *love the lord you God with all your heart* and with all your soul and with all your mind" (Matthew 22:37, emphasis added). God supremely values where we place our affections, our emotions, which also spring from our hearts.

For a child to feel secure and stable, to become emotionally healthy as an adult, is to know he is loved and cared for by those who have the power to do good to him. In the formative growing-up years, this responsibility begins with and rests on parents. But as children become teens and then young adults, they need to begin looking for and experiencing their security and love needs in God Himself.

> It is my hope that my children will be able to say to God, "I will praise you, for I am fearfully and wonderfully made. Marvelous are your works, and my soul knows it well."
>
> STEPHEN KENDRICK

Emotional Identity Begins at Home with Mom and Dad

Our oldest daughter, Ashley, and her husband, Michael, have cared for over two dozen foster children in their home over the past eight years. We have observed what happens when children don't receive the emotional nurturing they require. One little boy came to their home at five months of age. He'd been so neglected that his head was misshapen from constantly lying in bed with his head turned on one side to face the door, hoping his mom or dad would come get him. Though he showed remarkable improvement after a year in Ashley and Michael's home, he was still developmentally delayed and resistant to affection.

God can redeem, and we trust and pray for this little man and so many like him that in time they will open their hearts to the unending love of God and be made new. Only He can bring emotional healing and restoration. But until that day, these children and hundreds of thousands of others like them are suffering emotional trauma.

From birth, children pick up on the emotions of their parents, responding to warm welcoming hugs, kisses, and love lavishly given, or responding in bewilderment and fear, building early defense mechanisms to protect from a lack of parental love and presence. To be honest, most of us have probably been shaped in an environment marked by both types of emotional influences.

I (Barbara) grew up in a family that was secure and stable, and I knew I was loved. I never feared my parents would divorce or leave us. They cared for us, provided for us, and taught us many valuable lessons about life.

What my head knew was true I did not always *feel*. My parents both grew up in families who experienced significant losses—the death of a child, the relentless hurtful attitude and comments of a mean father-in-law, the dissolution of a marriage, and difficult life struggles during the Depression and World War II. As I look back, it's remarkable that my parents raised me and my brothers as well as they did.

I remember I often felt insecure about myself by the time I was nearing my teen years. I also remember working hard to please my parents. I wanted to make sure my dad had no reason to be angry with me. I became stoic and subdued, never getting angry, but not expressing much happiness, either. I did not laugh often, and I rarely cried. All those emotions were a part of me, but were hidden deep within.

As a teenager, I didn't know who I was or how I fit in. I became increasingly shy, timid, reserved, and self-protective. As a nineteen-year-old college student, I understood the gospel for the first time, and my sense of self and purpose changed dramatically.

When I became a parent myself, I worked hard to foster closeness and openness with my children. I snuggled with them on the couch reading books, even in their teens. I welcomed happy and hopeful creativity in spite of the messes they left in their wake. It was fairly easy in those early years.

But as our children got older, I saw that I was often reacting to or retreating from them out of fear because I didn't know how to nurture emotional health in teenagers. I still had toddlers when my oldest two became teenagers. I recognized how easy it was for me to kiss the little ones, stroke their faces, and cuddle them. But it was

> So when we keep the priorities in line—God first, then marriage is the priority as the first earthly relationship, and right after that is the kids—it actually gives kids security. They may not recognize that initially, but it will give them security to know their parents love each other and them through thick and thin. They know, *I will be loved.*
>
> ALEX KENDRICK

much harder for me to be affectionate with my thirteen-year-old daughter and twelve-year-old son.

Ashley, our firstborn, noticed and made little snide comments about how I was spoiling the younger ones, giving them too much attention. I remember thinking at first, *It's okay that I am not as close to the older ones. That's just who I am. Besides, Dennis is very good with our teens.* I figured I could concentrate on the younger kids, he could concentrate on the older ones, and everything would be just fine.

Eventually, I understood our daughter's criticisms were her way of letting me know that she still desired my affection and nurturing. I made a commitment to myself and asked the Lord to help me strengthen my emotional connection with my teenagers. I remember going into Ashley's room to hug her real tight, even though it felt awkward to me because I had not received similar affection when I was a teenager.

I also realized that by meeting her needs emotionally at home, I was helping to protect her from getting her emotional and security needs met from others, especially boys. It was like a light went on and I understood, *If she does not get love and security from me and her dad, then she is going to have a vacuum in her heart that she will seek to fill in unhealthy relationships.*

A good question to ask yourself is, "Do my children *feel* love from me, or do they just *know* that I love them?" There is a big difference. They need to feel loved and cared for in a real, emotional, intimate way that only comes from affectionate touching and physical closeness.

Teach Your Children How to Identify and Name Their Emotions

When I (Barbara) was forty, I had corrective heart surgery. A couple days before I went to the hospital, we asked our two youngest to clean up their room. When we came back an hour or so later to put them to bed, we noticed that Deborah had stuffed everything under her bed, which wasn't the way she usually cleaned up her things. We asked how she was feeling, and she said, "I'm scared."

"What are you scared about?"

She timidly said, "I am sad."

"Do you know what are you sad about?"

Then she began to cry and said, "I'm afraid Mommy is going to die."

We hadn't talked about the risk of this surgery with our children because we wanted to help guard their fears. In spite of our caution, our seven-year-old picked up on our tension and uncertainty. To help her respond well, we felt it was important for her to understand how she was feeling. Children need training and practice in naming their emotions and understanding where they come from.

With some children you will need to work especially hard to help them identify feelings. Several of our firstborn grandchildren are naturally reserved, highly intelligent kids who value rules and factual thinking. Ashley decided her firstborn son, Samuel, needed to learn to recognize and name his emotions. She announced to him and his brother, James, a natural feeler, that she would start asking them every night to describe one high and one low experience from the day and name the emotions they felt.

Samuel said he didn't want to do it. It sounded hard. James enthusiastically said, "Oh, this is going to be easy. I got this!" What a dramatic difference in our God-created emotional makeup as people! We are not all alike.

After a while, Samuel found it reasonably easy to identify some positive basic emotions, like happy. But naming the unpleasant emotions was more challenging. One day Samuel tried to summarize his day as normal, but Ashley told him normal wasn't an emotion and to try again.

This daily exercise lasted only a few weeks, but even in that short time Samuel learned to look within and describe his experiences at school with "feeling words." Ashley told me she was intentionally preparing both boys for a future as husbands and fathers who will need this emotional understanding to lead well.

The Emotions of Our Hearts Are a Reflection of God Himself

Since we are made in God's image, like Him, are our emotions like His? From what God has revealed about Himself in the Bible, we can say yes, ours are like His.

- He loves. "God is love" (1 John 4:8).
- He gives from His love. "For God so loved the world, that he gave his only Son" (John 3:16).
- He feels delight. "The Lord took delight in doing you good" (Deuteronomy 28:63).

- He laughs, is happy. "He who sits in heaven laughs" (Psalm 2:4).
- He feels kindness. ". . . according to His kind intention" (Ephesians 1:9 NASB).
- He enjoys and gives pleasure. "At your right hand are pleasures forevermore" (Psalm 16:11).
- He feels gladness. "You make him glad with the joy of your presence" (Psalm 21:6).
- He feels compassion. "He had compassion for them" (Matthew 9:36).
- He feels grief. He was "grieved at their hardness of heart" (Mark 3:5).
- He feels deep sadness and loss. "Our sorrows He carried" (Isaiah 53:4 NASB).
- He feels anger. "I was angry with my people" (Isaiah 47:6).
- He feels regret. "I regret that I have made Saul king" (1 Samuel 15:11).
- He longs. "How often I have longed to gather your children together" (Matthew 23:37 NIV).
- He hurts. "He was . . . a man of sorrows" (Isaiah 53:3).

In His perfection, God's emotions are always pure. His anger is always righteous. His love is never compromised. His creative work is always for good, always in the right time, always in line with the higher goal of His purposes and plans.

Human emotional expressions are never totally pure, righteous, or good. Our complete brokenness and depravity compromise our every intention. It is why we so desperately need the power of God's Spirit within us to make our marriages work and to raise our children in a somewhat healthy way.

Importantly, our emotions are neutral. They are neither good nor bad, but it is the expression of them that taints them positively or negatively.

Train Your Children to Know Healthy, Nonhurtful Ways to Express Their Emotions

Our goal as parents is to teach our children to feel and name their emotions, to help them learn to identify what is driving them, what is shaping their decisions and reactions. Then we teach, instruct, train, and praise them when they express those emotions in healthy, unoffensive, nonhurtful ways.

Helping Each Child Bloom

One of the keys to establishing a loving and secure environment in your home is cherishing each child for who he or she is. Each of your children is different—and each is different from you.

Filmmaker Alex Kendrick has six children. "All our children come to us equipped with certain things that God gives them—a personality, a certain bent, certain interests," he says. "It is interesting, of all my six kids, each one came different, with a different temperament. And I love that, because I see the nature of God in all of it. They don't come into this world as blank slates."

Alex's brother Stephen says, "Our children don't just grow up differently, they show up differently. The Lord has already prewired them, not only with their gender, but with the skill sets and bents toward certain things. So part of parenting is just an ongoing discovery, seeing how God's prewired them, what He's done in them. We need to be watering the seeds that God has planted inside of them. One child may be bent toward electronics and mechanical and engineering kinds of things, so let's nurture those, let's fan those, let's put that kid in courses and provide opportunities to bloom the way that God has planted him or her."

Tellingly, God never corrects our emotions in His Word. What He does correct is the way we express those emotions. He tells us, for example, to, "Be angry, and do not sin" (Psalm 4:4; Ephesians 4:26).

Elijah was afraid, ran away, and found a cave in which to hide. There he pouted in the dark feeling sorry for himself. "I alone am left" (1 Kings 19:10 NASB). God didn't correct his emotion of fear or self-pity, but He did address his heart of unbelief by calling Elijah back to faith with the voice of a "gentle blowing" (verse 12 NASB).

In another Old Testament story, Sarah laughed at the incredible notion that she could have a baby at the age of ninety. God heard her laugh and didn't criticize her feelings of shock and disbelief, but He did correct her lie when she said she didn't laugh, "No, but you did laugh" (Genesis 18:15).

With eight broken, sinful people living in our four-bedroom house, we had lots of emotions of every kind. Anger was one emotion everyone struggled with, so one night we had a family discussion about it. We asked our children, "How do you feel when you are angry?" On a poster board we wrote down their answers, which included phrases like "exasperated," "like screaming," "verbal vomit," and "like tearing things up."

Then we asked, "What kinds of things make you angry as a child or a teen?" On another column of the poster board we listed their answers:

- "When I'm left out or excluded by a family member."
- "When I get hurt."
- "When people make fun of me."
- "When people are being a pest or picking on me."
- "When people use my stuff without asking."
- "When people don't pay attention to what I'm saying."

We talked a little about why we shouldn't hurt others when we feel angry, and suggested alternatives. The evening dissolved quickly after that, and our anger problems were not solved with one conversation. We simply wanted to help our children understand that anger is a normal emotional response to being hurt or afraid. We wanted them to hear us say, "It is not wrong to feel angry, but let's try to think about and learn constructive ways to *express* our anger in our family."

We spent countless hours correcting our children when they expressed anger, disappointment, or fear in inappropriate and hurtful ways. Thousands of times we said things like, "You may not hit your brother when you are angry at him," "You may not scream at your sister," "You may not break something when you feel overlooked," and more. Slowly they learned, not perfectly, but with lots of baby steps they grew, learning more appropriate ways to express their feelings without being hurtful.

Your goal is not just correcting behavior, but also growing, training, nurturing the kind of hearts that seek to understand and act wisely. Help your kids understand the heart behind their behavior and then learn to express those foundational feelings to one another. Your kids will likely have each other all of their lives; they need to learn how to keep those relationships healthy. Other friends will come and many won't last, but family and siblings are forever.

And don't forget to reinforce respect for your authority as parents. Recently, we had a conversation with several couples one evening while on the FamilyLife Love Like You Mean It cruise. During the laughter-filled banter, our son-in-law shared about the time he got in the face of his two oldest sons and sternly and firmly told them they had to stop talking disrespectfully to their mother, his wife. He told them the consequences would not be pleasant if they didn't learn self-control over their mouths. They knew he meant it!

A Case of Mistaken Identity

Identity. It is what claims us, defines us, and shapes us above all else. Indeed, it answers our deepest questions: Who am I? Where do I belong? Whom do I belong to? What do I stand for? What is my uniqueness in this world?

It is one thing to be loved, but another to be understood. And our mighty God knew from the beginning we would err in sin, fall short of His glory, and forget who we belong to and where our identity can be found. And He chose to claim us, redeem us, and pour light into our darkness.

Growing up adopted, I found myself in constant search of desiring to know who I was and to whom I belonged. My identity felt lost, without an anchor. My inner core was broken and incapable of letting what truth I knew of God's calling patch those holes in my heart and row me to the safety of shore.

I can blame it on adoption. I could blame it on all the unfairness I felt growing up, whether it was real or not. But it was *my* reality for much of my growing-up years.

In my early twenties, God began to shift my idea of identity. And it was beautiful. He became the anchor I longed for, the stability my soul hoped for. Beginning to learn the truth God spoke over me and finally hearing it began to change everything.

Since my childhood, I have longed to know my biological roots. For well over a decade I actively searched for genetic links but repeatedly met with closed doors. Finally, God revealed to me that my identity was in Him. My name was written in His book. He sought me out despite my own anguish. He met me in my sorrow, and I grieved the losses of my biological heritage. And He gave me peace.

I knew my God created me for a purpose according to His plan. I also knew Satan does not want me to succeed, to live, to choose life, or to protect and advocate for it. The enemy of my soul wants to rob me of my joy, steal my identity, and spit in my face for all that I believe in.

But God doesn't look at me and condemn me for my sin. He doesn't call me by my sin. He redeems me by Jesus' blood on the cross and calls me to His throne as His child.

One day my journey will all make sense. One day my questions will be answered by the One who knows every detail. One day the beauty of His plan will be clear, and I will worship Him for it all.

(For more of my story, subscribe to my mom's blog at EverThineHome.com.)

Deborah (Rainey) Petrik

Make Your Home a Safe Place

Children want and need feedback, especially as they get older, from their parents. You are their measuring line. You are their report card. You are their most important cheerleaders who must celebrate every good decision. Don't just correct them, but eagerly and enthusiastically rejoice with every right attitude, reinforcing all the good they choose to embrace on their own, reminding them as you do this positive reinforcement that God sees and is pleased, and that pleasing Him is to be their ultimate goal, now as children and one day on their own as adults.

Children want to be heard and understood, not lectured. If you are attentive and engaged emotionally on every level, your child will grow up feeling loved, secure, and whole.

Make your home a safe place for self-expression, for processing the hardships of life, for learning emotional boundaries. And always daily reaffirm your love and acceptance of each child even and especially when he or she makes mistakes. Model God's unconditional grace-filled love in your home.

15 Spiritual Identity

The God who made you is the God who has the authority to define you.

Alex Kendrick

"You, Charlie Brown, are a foul ball in the line drive of life."

Lucy

As a senior in high school, I set a school record because I was known as Hook Rainey's son.

In order to raise money for the senior prom, our class decided to sell magazine subscriptions. I started out in our town of 1,300 people going door to door, with virtually no sales. I wasn't especially patient, so I changed strategies and left town to knock on the doors of folks who farmed the surrounding countryside.

At my first stop, I explained my mission to the woman who answered the door. It was a chilly reception, until I happened to mention that I was Hook Rainey's son. Presto! "Oh, your dad is a fine man. We've bought heating fuel from your dad for years. Come right on in, son. Would you like some cookies and milk?"

After enjoying her hospitality and chocolate-chip cookies, I left with an order for three magazine subscriptions. And I realized my success was all about my dad, not me. My dad had lived his entire life within three miles of where he was born. He earned a good living and an even better reputation by selling fuel and being a trusted businessman.

For the next two weeks, my sales pitch began with, "I'm Hook Rainey's son." Using my dad's identity netted me several hundred subscriptions. I earned a herd of stuffed animals and a tape recorder (do you know what that is?), and I set the school record in fund-raising for the senior prom.

Secretly, I knew I wasn't that good of a salesman. I just leveraged my dad's good name and my identity as his son to capture sales and win the prizes.

> **V**ery young kids really just need to know about God's love. "God made you, He made you special and unique, and He loves you." And repeat that about ten thousand times.
>
> PHIL VISCHER

So it is with your children.

Just as I leveraged my dad's good name and reputation, so your children are designed to live off your good name. But also realize they have an even better identity—a royal spiritual identity. Each is a child of the King of Kings.

Our task as parents is helping our children discover and begin to understand what their identity is and, practically speaking, what it means. We promise you, it's worth more than warm chocolate-chip cookies, a glass of milk, and a magazine subscription.

Help Your Children Understand God's Character

The process of equipping your children to embrace a clear spiritual identity begins with their basic knowledge of who God is and what He is like. A. W. Tozer states it succinctly: "What comes into our minds when we think about God is the most important thing about us."[1] Helping your children to think correctly about God, who He is, and what He has done for them will ultimately transform their lives. When we understand and think rightly about who God is and His love for us, we can begin to think accurately about ourselves.

In essence, it is impossible to truly embrace your spiritual identity without a growing understanding of who God is: His attributes, His personality, and

His character. It could easily be said that you are helping your children embark on a lifelong journey of discovering that God is God and they are *not*. You will find that as you disciple your children, you will unearth magnificent new vistas of who God is for yourselves as parents.

As I was selling magazine subscriptions and talking with people who had known my dad for a lot longer than I had, I found out that my dad's integrity in how he did business and related to people was like granite, solid. I had experienced that with my dad, but hearing about his character from others caused me to appreciate him even more. And as his son, I felt my backbone straighten to want to be like him. Likewise, beginning to understand God's character is the basis of your children realizing who they are, experiencing true humility, and beginning to truly grasp the depths of their spiritual identity.

Discover the Benefits of God's Attributes

As you teach your children about God, point them to an application of different ways they can trust Him. Here are some statements by Bill Bright, from the study guide to his book *God: Discover His Character*.

Because God is a personal Spirit . . . I will seek fellowship with Him.
Because God is all powerful . . . He can help me with anything.
Because God is ever present . . . He is always with me.
Because God knows everything . . . I will go to Him with all my questions and concerns.
Because God is sovereign . . . I will joyfully submit to His will.
Because God is holy . . . I will devote myself to Him in purity, worship, and service.
Because God is absolute truth . . . I will believe what He says.
Because God is righteous . . . I will live by His standards.
Because God is just . . . He will always treat me fairly.
Because God is love . . . He is unconditionally committed to my well-being.
Because God is merciful . . . He forgives me of my sins when I sincerely confess them.
Because God is faithful . . . I will trust Him to always keep His promises.
Because God never changes . . . my future is secure and eternal.

Bill Bright, the late cofounder of Cru, repeatedly spoke of God's character being central to understanding our spiritual identity. His excellent book about the attributes of God, *God: Discover His Character*, was a classic work reminding us that understanding God's attributes helps us know Him and grow in our trust of Him. "Because God knows everything," he wrote, "I will go to Him with all my questions and concerns. Because God is sovereign . . . I will joyfully submit to His will." (Check out the sidebar for the entire list of attributes and what our responses should be.)

Consider using dinner as a time to read the Bible together and discuss the stories and their application to your lives. From there, you can help your children notice and understand these attributes of God. Find ways of talking about these attributes of God in everyday circumstances in your family's life.

Your Child Is an Image Bearer of God

As I made my way throughout the county raising money for our prom, invariably, after I introduced myself as Hook Rainey's son, people would say, "Of course. You look just like your dad—the spittin' image of Hook." Even as a teen I kind of liked that, because my dad was handsome.

You and your child were made "in the spittin' image" of One far greater than any man. Genesis 1:27 records our sacred origin: "God created man in his own image, in the image of God he created him; male and female he created them." What does it mean to be created in the image of God? How does this distinguish humans from the rest of creation—animals, birds, and sea creatures?

As image bearers, we are embedded with some of the attributes of God. We are like God in that we have personality. We can think, make choices, create life, and nurture life. We can dream dreams and imagine new ideas. Like God, we can love, relate to others, and feel and express emotion. And though your children will not likely embrace this for a while, we were made to work just as God did in the first six days of creation.

Have you ever seen a cow or a bird stare enraptured at a magnificent sunset or kneel as it worships God? No, because animals were not made with this godlike capacity. The fact that we are made in God's likeness makes us different from any created thing, including angels. It gives our lives dignity, purpose, and meaning.

We can't fully comprehend it, but every person is an image bearer. Explain to your child that God has given us the noble task of showing the world what He is like—compassionate and caring in His perfect love; full of mercy, grace, and forgiveness; righteous and just; filled with loving-kindness in how He deals with people. We are to mirror that kindness in everyday life.

Instruct and remind your children even from an early age that their lives should honor God and show Him off to the world.

Your Child Is a Member of the Ultimate Royal Family

All of England and most of the world are fascinated with the United Kingdom's royal family. The monarchy has served Great Britain's subjects for hundreds of years, and we all marvel at the birth of a new prince, knowing that someday he could be the king of England.

One of the most important discoveries you help your child make is that, at the moment he places his faith in Jesus as his Savior and Lord, he becomes a child of God. John 1:12 declares your child's new identity: "But to all who did receive him, who believed in his name, he gave the right to become children of God." John goes on to tell us we are "born of God" (verse 13), or "born again" (3:3).

Explain to your child that this isn't just any family he's been "born again" into, but the ultimate royal family, led by the King of Kings and Lord of Lords. If you were to compile a list kings throughout the history of humankind, it would include thousands of kings from hundreds of kingdoms and countries. Discuss with your child what it means that Jesus is the King of Kings and Lord of Lords. This is his King, his Savior, and his royal family.

Consider discussing what it might be like if he were a member of the royal family of Great Britain—the places he'd be able to go, people he'd meet, and privileges he'd experience. Then talk about what it means if he is born again into the King of King's royal family. And talk about the promise of Jesus and the mansion that He is preparing for us:

Let not your hearts be troubled. Believe in God; believe also in me. In my Father's house are many rooms. If it were not so, would I have told you that I go to prepare a place for you? And if I go and prepare a place for you, I will come again and will take you to myself, that where I am you may be also.

John 14:1–3

What a King. What a royal family. What a mansion. What a future and hope. What a spiritual identity.

> **Y**ou need to tell your kids every day, "God loves you, and He made you just the way you are. Your identity is safe in Him because you're a child of the King."
>
> PHIL VISCHER

Your Child Has a Divine Mission and Message

Author C. S. Lewis wrote in *Mere Christianity*, "Every Christian is to become a little Christ. The whole purpose of becoming a Christian is simply nothing else."[2] God's divine purpose for everyone is to grow more like Jesus in all His attributes of love, grace, mercy, and peace as we live on this planet. And the more we grow more like Him, the more we understand that Christ came not just to reconcile us to God and satisfy our needs and desires; He came to enlist us.

> All this is from God, who through Christ reconciled us to himself and gave us the ministry of reconciliation; that is, in Christ God was reconciling the world to himself, not counting their trespasses against them, and entrusting to us the message of reconciliation. Therefore, we are ambassadors for Christ, God making his appeal through us.
>
> 2 Corinthians 5:18–20

As your children learn to follow Christ, they will discover another noble feature of their spiritual identity: Jesus wants to commission them to be His ambassadors. Just as ambassadors represent their homeland in another country, we represent Christ to a world full of people who need Him. We'll further unpack what being an ambassador for the King means in chapter 18.

Being an ambassador means standing for Him, speaking for Him. It isn't about accomplishing great feats, though that may happen. It's about representing Christ wherever we go. It's about loving people with the love of Christ, sharing the good news, and explaining how they can be forgiven by God and reconciled to Him.

It may be difficult to look at a three-year-old and envision him or her as an ambassador of Christ. But that changes as your children grow older and start realizing there is a lot wrong with this world. They will want to make a difference. Invite those conversations. Listen to their dreams, their desires to change the world, and encourage them to pursue their ideas as much as they can. Help them begin to think about their unique gifts, abilities, and interests, and how God might want to use them for His big purposes.

Begin the process of introducing the character qualities of God, like His sovereignty, to your children so they have a greater context for their lives and understand that nothing happens to them apart from God's control. It's not a mistake that they live in a specific neighborhood or attend a specific school. It helps them view their circumstances in a different way—that God wants to use them as His ambassadors wherever they are.

Every person alive has an assignment as image bearer to uniquely reflect God to others. Your children have the capacity to honor God with their lives and represent Him to the world.

Think of yourselves as your children's tour guides in a lifelong discovery of what the Scriptures say about their divine purpose. Whet their appetites by sharing with them that God has a very special mission for their lives. He has

Our Amazing Identity in Christ

When a child or adult places faith in Jesus Christ as Savior and Lord, he or she becomes a new creation. Scripture tells us:

- We are given a new name (Revelation 2:17).
- We have a new heavenly Father (2 Corinthians 6:18).
- We receive a divine assignment (Ephesians 2:10; 2 Corinthians 5:17, 20).
- We can look forward to a new home—heaven (Luke 10:20; Revelation 21:1–4).

Here's a suggestion for a family devotion. Look up these Scriptures with your children and figure out what each one has to say about our identity in Christ:

John 1:12	Romans 6:6
Ephesians 1:5	1 Corinthians 12:27
Colossians 2:9–10	1 Corinthians 6:19–20
1 Corinthians 6:17	1 Peter 2:9

gifted them with abilities, personality, and certain qualities that will result in a unique plan just for them.

We wanted our children to know that it would be better to be a garbage collector in the will of God than to be on the mission field just to please their parents. It's not about us and our ambitions for our children; it's all about what God has for them. Each has a spiritual identity as God's child that has been created for a purpose that only he or she can fulfill.

Help Your Children Grow Hearts for God

Throughout this book we've mentioned repeatedly the need to focus on the hearts of your children. Much more important than forcing them to behave well is helping them understand that they cannot change their propensity to sin, to be selfish. They need Christ in their hearts. They need to grow in their relationship with God. They need to identify themselves as followers of Christ.

When our younger girls were teens, we were seeing lots of heart issues we didn't like—bad attitudes, snippy comments, and general complaining. One weeknight after dinner, I (Dennis) had an inspiration. I told both girls we would pay them to do a Bible study. Naturally, they rolled their eyes in exasperation and asked, "Do we have to?"

We sat them at the dining room table, handed each one a fat Bible concordance, and told them their assignment was to use the concordance to find all the verses they could with the word *heart*, and to add an observation of what each verse said about their hearts. Whoever found the most verses in thirty minutes would win the "competition." We explained that we would pay the winner twenty-five cents for every verse she found.

Competition that includes money almost always motivates kids! Both girls really wanted to be the winner, so their earlier lack of interest suddenly vaporized. When the time was up, each had a long list of qualities she'd found about hearts. We had them read the ones they liked best or felt were most helpful or meaningful. For thiry minutes they focused on God's Word, saw what He valued. And we happily rewarded them. It was a good investment.

Did their hearts change immediately and forever? No. But it was another step, another deposit in their understanding of their need to pursue God, seek His truth, and learn to trust Him with their lives.

What kind of heart do you want your children to have when you finish this parenting journey?

What kind of heart do you want them to have as they walk into the uncertainty of a world where you will not be present every day and your voice will likely become much less influential?

Do you want your children to have hearts that are kind, loving, clear, pure, generous, open, whole, wise, strong, willing, teachable, glad, full of understanding, focused, faithful, happy, and joyful (just a few of the descriptors our girls discovered)? Then teach them to trust in God in the spirit of Psalm 28:7: "The Lord is my strength and my shield; in Him my heart trusts, and I am helped."

Your children need spiritual role models besides their parents. One easy way to inspire your children to great faith and also to expand their knowledge is to read them great books about faith heroes. Two of our favorites are Corrie ten Boom's *The Hiding Place* and Brother Andrew's *God's Smuggler*, both set in the era of World War II. Or read Barbara's books *Growing Together in Forgiveness* and *Growing Together in Courage*, each of which contains seven faith stories about Christians around the world. Stories such as these will influence your children and add other voices to yours calling them to follow God's ways.

The bedrock of a solid spiritual identity is all about the heart. To whom does your child's heart belong? Who is influencing your child's heart?

Tim Kimmel says we parent well when we know how long our child will live, because "your child will live for eternity." Psalm 84:5 says, "Blessed are those whose strength is in you, in whose heart are the highways to Zion." Open the doors of your children's hearts so that they understand what it means to be a follower of Christ. Encourage this relationship that will last forever.

Nothing Is More Important

In the introduction to this section, we offered this definition: "My identity tells me who I am as a unique person on earth and what my purpose in life is." Your children's spiritual identity does the most to help them understand who they are and why they are here.

Because of our relationship with God, we understand these things:

- "I was made in the image of God."
- "God made me to have a relationship with Him."

When Other Family Influences ——————
Lead Away from Christ

If you are not married to your child's other parent, and the other home is a negative influence on his or her faith, resist the temptation to limit the other parent's contact with the child. That tends to backfire on you and doesn't respect the parent's right to be with the child. You must find other ways of influencing your children. Here are some suggestions.

Make the most of your time with your children; model the Christian walk and impress on them the decrees of God (Deuteronomy 6:4–9). Parents whose children are witnessing differing values will have to be even more intentional in their faith training.

One useful strategy is utilizing "spiritual inoculations." Medical inoculations are controlled injections of a virus that allow the body to develop antibodies that can combat a live virus, if ever encountered. Similarly, spiritual inoculations discuss viewpoints that oppose the Word of God and then teach biblical concepts that help children combat them. For example, if you're watching a TV program that glorifies greed, talk about it with your kids and present a more godly view of money management and stewardship.

It's important that you remain neutral about the other parent; the inoculation cannot be a personal attack. A comment like, "Your father shouldn't be lying to his boss—he is so self-centered," pulls on children's loyalties and burdens them with your judgment. Ironically, it also diminishes your influence as they react defensively against your negativity.

A more appropriate response is, "Some people believe lying is fine when it serves a purpose. But God is truth, and He wants us to be honest, as well. Let's talk about how you can practice that in every aspect of your life."

You may have to endure seasons of prodigal living as your children try out the values of the other home. Children may experiment with the "easier, less demanding" lifestyle of the other home, especially during the teen or young adult years when they are deciding whether the faith they've been handed ("inherited faith") will become their own ("owned faith"). Lovingly admonish them toward the Lord (not away from the other parent), and be close enough to reach when they repent, as many children and young adults will return to the wisdom of your values.

Pray daily for the strength to walk in the light and introduce your children to Jesus at each and every opportunity. Your model is a powerful bridge to their personal commitment to Christ. Do all that you can to take your kids by the hand and lead them in the way of the Master (Ephesians 6:4).

Ron Deal

Adapted from *The Smart Stepfamily* (2014) by Ron L. Deal, Bethany House Publishers, a division of Baker Publishing Group. Used with permission. All rights to this material are reserved.

- "As I develop a heart for God, I grow to become more like Him."
- "I am a follower of Christ."
- "I belong to a community, a larger body of believers."
- "God wants to use me to represent Him as His ambassador."

If your children understand these truths, they will be able to stand strong in their identity, no matter what challenges may come their way.

16 Sexual Identity

It's time for Christians to do what leaders like Paul and Peter did—study and engage society with boldness, graciousness, and complete dependence on God.

Caleb Kaltenbach

Spoken-word artist Jackie Hill Perry has written and spoken on many occasions about her fatherless childhood and being raised by a single mom, about her aunt who faithfully took her to church, and about the confusion that swirled in her heart regarding her identity and feelings of attraction to other young women. Her present-tense story is a relevant one for today. Jackie is a twentysomething woman who is eagerly showing other women where truth is found.

> I understand how it feels to be in love with a woman. To want nothing more than to be with her forever. Feeling as if the universe has played a cruel joke on your heart by allowing it to fall into the hands of a creature that looks just like you. . . .
>
> At the age of seventeen, I finally made the decision to pursue these desires. . . . I enjoyed these relationships and loved these women a lot. And it came to the point that I was willing to forsake all, including my soul, to enjoy their love on earth.

... At the age of nineteen, my superficial reality was shaken up by a deeper love, one from the outside—one that I'd heard of before but never experienced.... My eyes were opened, and I began to believe everything God says in his word. I began to believe that what he says about sin, death, and hell were completely true.

God put this impression on my heart: "Jackie, you have to believe that my word is true even if it contradicts how you feel." Wow! This is right. Either I trust in his word or I trust my own feelings. Either I look to him for the pleasure my soul craves or I search for it in lesser things. Either I walk in obedience to what he says or I reject his truth as if it were a lie.[1]

We decided early in the process of raising our children that if we didn't know what our convictions were about the issues swirling in the culture, then we would not be able to train our children to know how to think critically or help shape their convictions. We concluded that all of our convictions were a choice of whom we chose to believe as our authority. Like Jackie, we had to turn away from what the culture was advocating and base our convictions on what God has said. Some of the issues today have changed, but the challenge is the same: Will you teach your children to follow the truth of God, or modern feelings that question everything true with the ancient rebuttal "Has God said . . . ?"

If you are to raise your arrow to fly straight in a world that wants to take it off the bull's-eye, you will need to determine who your authority is going to be on sexual identity issues and related questions. To lead your children wisely, you must first know what *you* believe about gender identity, sexual identity, the definition of marriage, and God's intentions from the beginning.

It's Pretty Simple Really

Restating the obvious, the Bible begins with the clear creation of two sexes and genders, male and female. *Sex* refers to our reproductive biology, and *gender* refers to the social manifestation of our biological sex. God didn't stutter when He declared in Genesis 1:27, "So God created man in his own image, in the image of God he created him; male and female he created them." This passage of Scripture teaches three things:

- First, **God is the Creator**. Three times in twenty-two words, God makes it clear He is the Creator of humankind. As such, He has authority to design people, His creation, as He wants. Because He is good and perfect, we can and should trust Him.

- Second, **God chose to create them in His image**, in His likeness. Both male and female were made to reflect God, to look like Him, to act like Him, to do the same kind of work God does.
- And third, **God created male and female to be complementary**, not identical, not interchangeable. God chose to make Adam incomplete without Eve (Genesis 2:18). Apart from Eve, Adam was still an image bearer, but the image of God he reflected was limited. So God fashioned a balancing partner, a woman with obvious physical differences, but also different emotional, spiritual, and relational capacities. Together these two image bearers are tasked with ruling over God's creation.

Nowhere in the other sixty-five books of Scripture do we find a third sex identified as an alternative to male and female. Today's more than fifty so-called gender identities, or social manifestations of our sex, force new dilemmas upon already beleaguered parents and confusing influences on our children.

Our assignment as parents is to confirm and affirm the sexual identity God has made clear at birth. Embrace God's created design and teach your sons and daughters the wonder and glory of their identity as male or female.

How Male and Female Are Alike

In the beginning God stated a clear purpose for Adam and Eve. He expressed their combined and equal mission in three sentences:

1. "Let us make man in our image, after our likeness. And let them have dominion over the fish of the sea and over the birds of the heavens and over the livestock and over all the earth" (Genesis 1:26).

    God intends for His children, male and female, to be image bearers and **reflect who He is** to others. He also created both Adam and Eve to **rule, or reign, over His creation.**

2. "Be fruitful and multiply and fill the earth and subdue it, and have dominion . . . over every living thing that moves on the earth" (Genesis 1:28).

His second intention is that this couple, this man and woman, would **produce godly children** who would in turn reflect God to their generation.

3. "For this reason a man shall leave his father and his mother, and be joined to his wife; and they shall become one flesh" (Genesis 2:24 NASB).

His third intention is **marriage between a man and a woman**, both for the reflection of His image to others and for the procreation of children. In this verse, the narrator summarizes all God's stated purposes for marriage—"for this reason." Adam and Eve's union defines the norm for every other marriage that follows. And their roles within marriage define God's intention for gender roles within every other marriage that follows.

Stated another way, it is God the Creator, not man, who has the authority to define marriage and how a husband and wife are to assume their respective responsibilities in marriage.

How Male and Female Are Different

We believe the Bible clearly teaches that God created men and women and made them distinct as male and female. Humankind has blurred those differences. The world wants to homogenize the sexes. And the enemy has created so much distrust between men and women, both inside and outside the Christian community, that we can't have helpful, hopeful conversations about the obvious differences and how to relate with wisdom and respect. The result in parents? Lack of clear beliefs. Result in children? Confusion and collusion.

As you teach your children about their gender and sexual identity, you'll need to learn the nuanced differences God has hardwired in making them male and female. Think this through as parents so that you have a good understanding from which to have these conversations with your children. It's a challenge to teach gender differences without defaulting to cultural roles, stereotypes, and assumptions that have distorted God's design. Learning to identify and affirm the differences between male and female is important to create stability emotionally, intellectually, and spiritually. Parents have been tasked by God with this teaching responsibility, and they need to be careful to base their teaching upon biblical truth.

So how do you teach your son what it means to be a boy and eventually a man? How is he different from girls? What do you teach your daughter about being uniquely female as distinct from boys? What sets her apart from a boy? And how do you coach your children to appreciate the differences and relate with respect to the opposite sex?

Though books could be written on this topic, we want to share some high-level talking points to have with your children. Our goal is to focus on God's original intentions, knowing that none of us can know His purposes fully because of our fallen state and our very limited ability to understand an infinite God. We are not attempting to address all the complexities in male and female relationships that have resulted from sin. We want to help you think about your children's differences as boys and girls and to give you the unique essence of what we believe God has built into male and female. Genesis 1 and 2 are the only glimpses we have into human life that isn't marred by sin. So let's look at those as yet untarnished people. We start with men because God began by creating Adam first.

Men were designed to be warriors and protectors

God designed men to be protectors of women, children, their communities, and their nations. Their naturally greater physical strength (on average, not in every specific case) is not an accident, but a good indication of God's intentions. Men have always been at the front lines of battle in wars and in most moral conflicts. It doesn't mean women can't join in and help, but men's temperaments and physical bodies are better suited for physical battles and hard physical labor.

Teach your sons to use their strength to protect girls, especially their sisters, and not to beat up on and wrestle with girls. Boys are loud and rough and hurt each other physically often (see our daughter Ashley's sidebar about this on page 71). As a mom, I was always afraid our two boys would really hurt one another, enough to send one of them to the emergency room. I was truly relieved they both arrived at adulthood without permanent scars from all their fighting, shoving, and rough play. As your sons grow older, teach them how to protect a young lady's sexual innocence (and never abuse her in any way) and her heart in relationships.

Encourage your boys to use their desire to be strong, even when they are little, to lift heavy things as a way to help others. Help them learn to use their strength to care for animals, to be good shepherds of other living things. Even at a young age, boys love showing their muscles and being needed for safety—like the time my four-year-old grandson said he'd hold the ladder steady for me while I climbed it to help paint their living room. He was so proud to be making me safe. Affirm that God-given desire and capacity.

Women are not to take their husband's role as the primary protector, nor would many women want to. If an angry neighbor is pounding on the front door, your husband should be the one to answer the door and deal with the situation. If sounds of an intruder wake you at night, your husband should be the one to check out the noises even if he is afraid.

Women protect, too. Moms physically protect their children, especially when they are little. Moms are also often the first line of defense against emotional and psychological attacks from bullies. I was a vigilant protector of my children's hearts and minds. I monitored television, movies, phones, friends, and other influences that came at our kids. Dennis did this with me, but as I was the one who was with the children more, I led this charge with them. God made both men and women with protective functions, yet with different purposes and in different spheres—and with men having the primary protective responsibility for their families. It's one way we complement each other as a team.

Help your sons and daughters understand they both have a protective gift that needs to be expressed but that they will express it differently—and that it is good.

The biblical principle here is that the stronger protect the weaker and men are to sacrifice for the well-being of women and children. It's why most men gave the seats in the lifeboats to the women and children as the *Titanic* was sinking. The responsibility to be courageous protectors is something that moms and dads should encourage and build into their boys as they grow.

As men exercise their warrior and protective responsibility, they are also to protect others from sin. Adam is described in the New Testament as "a type of the one [Jesus] who was to come" (Romans 5:14), indicating Adam had a protective spiritual responsibility in the garden, anticipating the work Jesus would come to do on our behalf. Adam's work was to be preventative against evil, for sin had not yet entered the garden. He was to be the first line of defense against Satan, who God knew would in time tempt them both. But Adam was passive and failed to protect Eve.

Teach your sons the importance of resisting sin, of modeling for others, siblings, and friends a high standard of excellence in living. When they are

older and have dating relationships, boys should be the ones primarily responsible for protecting the relationships from straying into sinful behavior. Call
them up to nobility as young men. Their hearts desire it. God made them to
protect, warn, and save others.

Likewise, women can and should help protect against sin. Teaching your
children, guiding their thinking, helping them know right from wrong are
all ways moms fulfill their responsibility as daughters of the King to protect
from sin. Train your daughters to be mindful of this responsibility as they
grow into their teen years and relate to teen boys. Help them understand that
one way they can protect young men is by how they dress and relate to them.

Again, the Bible teaches that we should all encourage one another to be on
guard against sin. While this assignment is not exclusive to men and boys, it
is an area where men and boys are intentionally trained to step up to their responsibilities, to provide direction, and not to be passive but to be courageous
warriors and protectors. We need more men who are acting like real men!

Men were made to initiate and lead with love and self-sacrifice

Following God's creation story again, there is a purpose in His created
order, making man before He made woman. In the time of the Old Testament,
there was a well-known principle that the firstborn was to be the leader. When
God created Adam first and then Eve, God revealed His intention that this
"firstborn" was to be the leader (1 Timothy 2:13).

One reason that seems fairly obvious is that Adam was supposed to lead
Eve in following God. He gave Adam the instructions on what to eat and not
eat in the garden in Genesis 2:16–17 before Eve was even created. Therefore,
it seems God's intention was for Adam to take the initiative to communicate
God's instruction to Eve. In the words of our friend Robert Lewis, creator of
Men's Fraternity, real men "reject passivity and accept responsibility." Again,
we know the sad result when Adam failed to initiate, to protect Eve from the
snare of the serpent.

Proactive leadership driven by a servant spirit should be the mark of your
boys as they become men. Train your sons to reject passivity by demonstrating
common courtesies to girls and women. At the heart of these courtesies is the
moral goodness of a sacrificial and servant spirit that says, "I'm choosing to
give my life in this small way to honor you as a girl or woman." We believe
we need a revival of these common courtesies!

Girls should be taught to encourage and support young men as they take initiative and as they step out to lead. As we've already mentioned, men are prone to passivity. Equip your daughters with the understanding that they have a unique, God-given ability to powerfully affirm and support the men around them as they see them initiating and leading in good ways.

But equally important, our daughters should be taught not to follow or enable any inappropriate or selfish leadership of boys or men that would lead to sin. Girls should be empowered to bravely refuse to follow boys who lead them in ways contrary to God's best.

Taking the initiative is one of the primary responsibilities for men, but women can also take the initiative. I (Barbara) took the initiative to teach our boys to learn to help me with tasks like bringing in groceries or unloading luggage or carrying overflowing laundry baskets down the stairs. I talked to them about looking for ways to serve and help, not just waiting to be told what to do. I was thinking ahead to the day they would be married and have wives who would be delighted to have a husband who led them, sacrificially served them, and knew how to help in these ways.

Men were made to be providers

Men were to provide the means and create a safe place to live physically, emotionally, and spiritually. Because of our biological differences, specifically pregnancy and nursing, it is not always possible for women to also attend to full-time employment or work. The ultimate responsibility has historically fallen on men, and it mirrors the work of managing the earth in the garden. Of course women can and do work very hard to help in providing for their families. Again, women assist in every culture in the world, but the primary responsibility for providing still belongs to men.

Women were created to be life givers

Our friend Dr. Dennis Burke has said, "The first woman was taken from the first man, but every person since has been taken from woman" (see 1 Corinthians 11:12). God's clear design for women is to create life, to be life givers, filling the earth with true godly image bearers.

Beyond conception, birth, and nursing, women have a great capacity to nurture life, not only in their children but also in others and other living things. I love growing things, restoring old furniture to new life, encouraging my daughters to grow in Christ as they work hard raising their kids, and mentoring other younger women in the faith. All of these are life-giving actions.

We recently had dinner with a woman who has four children and more than a dozen grandchildren. When asked what she was passionate about, she replied, "I am focused on praying for and bringing spiritual life to my children and grandchildren." She is modeling life-giving generationally to her family.

Most little girls naturally gravitate to dolls and the nurturing of babies of all kinds more than boys do. Affirm this God-created nurturing seed. And if your daughter would rather play sports, it doesn't mean she's not a nurturer. It's in her but may not blossom until later in her life.

And yes, nurturing others is something men are responsible for as well. Both men and women are charged by God to mentor and disciple younger men and women. There is nurturing involved in the disciple-making process. But by God's design, women are called and equipped to nurture in ways that men can't.

Women were fashioned to be helpers

God is the one who said, "It is not good that the man should be alone; I will make him a helper fit for him" (Genesis 2:18). It was God who made the first woman: Eve was made *from* Adam and *for* Adam with this purpose of being a helper in mind. Helper is a title of great honor and privilege because it is also the name of the Holy Spirit. Just as the Holy Spirit is our constant companion working on our behalf, so women as helpers can give companionship, comfort, and guidance; they can teach truth; if God calls them to marriage, they can intercede on behalf of their husbands; and they can intercede for children and others in need in their communities. Women were made to mimic this supportive life-giving work of the Spirit as Helper.

Sadly, this high title and calling has become synonymous with hired help or being second-class, but that was never God's intention. A helper was fashioned—a word which also implies beauty—for the purpose of completing the man, making him whole, since God had just said Adam was incomplete. In other words, God made man incomplete ("not good that the man should be alone") and inadequate on his own, and he was made whole by what only a woman can bring. Men need female thinking, feeling, perspective, experience, and viewpoints to round out, complete, and balance their knowledge, which is always only partial.

We taught our girls that their voices mattered, that their perspectives, experiences, and feelings were equally valid in our family. No one person or gender was more valuable or important than another. We taught our sons to listen to their sisters and to value them and their wisdom. We encouraged our girls to get involved in ways in which God might use their gifts to benefit others.

Likewise, even though helping is not one of man's primary responsibilities, men can and should also be helpers, but in ways that are unique to them in balance and in harmony with their other responsibilities. A husband who helps his wife with her responsibilities is using his initiative and strength to serve her sacrificially.

These qualities and distinctives, though similar, are like two sides of a coin. God intended that you can't have one without the other. Both are needed.

When Your Children Ask Questions

- First, be a safe person for your children. Don't bristle or freak out when they share with you their doubts about God, their confusion around issues of sexual identity, and their failures. As a parent, become the trusted source of love, wisdom, and forgiveness.
- Teach your sons and daughters to celebrate and enjoy both their equality in the image of God and their God-given differences as male and female.
- Train your child with the understanding that all human beings are broken by sin, which includes matters of gender and sexual identity. All need God's forgiveness.
- Guide your children to be compassionate toward friends or neighbors struggling with gender identity. Let the love of Christ rule.
- Help your children know how to speak the truth in love with gentleness.
- Teach your children the concept of two worldviews: a Biblical worldview with God at the center and the Scriptures as the authority, and a secular worldview that places man at the center and as the authority.
- Help your children understand feelings are usually a poor authority for most decisions, especially questions of gender identity or expressing sexual passions, and that differences in reproductive organs, not changing feelings, indicate whether someone is a boy or a girl.

We recommend *True Identity* by John C. Majors and FamilyLife's *Passport2Identity for Young Men* and *Passport2Identity for Young Women* for discussing matters of sexual identity during the middle teen years of ages fourteen through sixteen.

Both are necessary. Both send a message regarding the value of that coin, and in our genders, both send messages that are needed to accurately exalt God's image on earth.

After the Fall

We have sought to focus on the ideal of God's original intentions for us as male and female, to help you identify the essence of maleness and femaleness in your sons and daughters.

After Adam and Eve sinned, they experienced the unknown emotions of shame and fear, impacting their relationship. They hid from God, signaling that the vertical relationship of men and women with God and the horizontal relationship of men and women were changed forever. The result of sin has been thousands of years of rigid and distorted roles, unequal gender value, and damaging assumptions of purpose and worth.

Into the now broken lives of Adam and Eve, God explained how sin would impact male-female relationships, both sexually and socially. All aspects of our maleness and femaleness were damaged. In the New Testament God calls us back to His design by describing male and female relationships both in marriage (Ephesians 5:22–33; 1 Peter 3:1–7; Titus 2:1–8) and outside marriage. His desire for men and women is that we live holy lives pleasing to Him and for all that we do to be governed by love.

In the endless grace of God, when we follow His truth and purposes, He gives us tastes of the fulfillment He intended in the garden. As Jackie said at the beginning of this chapter, "Either I trust in his word or I trust my own feelings. Either I look to him for the pleasure my soul craves or I search for it in lesser things. Either I walk in obedience to what he says or I reject his truth as if it were a lie." This is the crux of guiding your children to a healthy sexual and gender identity.

A Challenging Assignment

When we started our work with families in 1976, we could never have imagined that families today would be dealing with the sexual and gender issues that are swirling today. As never before, you as parents need to unashamedly and repeatedly enter your children's world and engage them in meaningful conversations around these issues. These are not days to retreat from your children's lives; they need you to be there with them. You don't have to have all the answers; in fact, we've found that it's okay to tell your children that you don't have all the answers, but that you aren't going to leave them alone to find the answers on their own. You are there to help them begin to craft their convictions and encourage them to be compassionate with those who do not believe as they do.

Ask God for wisdom in how to train and guide your children, and keep on building the bridge of your relationship with them.

17 An Intentional Approach to the Birds and the Bees

We should not be ashamed to discuss what God was not ashamed to create.

Dr. Howard Hendricks

When our oldest were eight and almost seven, we decided we'd watch PBS's *Nova* episode "The Miracle of Birth," which we'd previewed earlier. Barbara was either pregnant or had recently given birth, so the topic was a normal part of our daily life. The production was excellent and accurately portrayed the wonder of new life. We felt it was an age-appropriate documentary for our older two children.

We made popcorn one night after dinner, settled on the couch together, and watched in wonder as the documentary showed herds of sperm swimming their way toward an egg to fertilize it. When the credits rolled, we were not prepared for any questions, let alone the question that our daughter Ashley asked: "How did the sperm get into the mommy's tummy?"

I did what most dads do—shot a nervous glance at Barbara and punted. I said, "Uh, well . . . you and I . . . uh . . . well, let's talk about that next week on our ski trip."

Secretly, I was hoping she'd forget.

One week later, Ashley and I were riding the ski lift for our first run of the day. Ashley, who has always loved science, pulled her goggles off her face, looked me straight in the eyes, and said, "Okay, Dad. How'd that sperm get in the mommy's tummy?"

So . . . being the spiritual leader of our family, I pulled my ski goggles down over my eyes. . . . No, I really didn't do that, but I wanted to. I said, "Well, mommies and daddies who are married to one another really do love one another, and they express their love in bed. And . . . uh . . . they take their clothes off, and after kissing for a while, the daddy puts his penis into the mommy's vagina. After a while a bunch of those sperm come out. Just like in the movie, they swim their way up to the egg. Sometimes they make it, and the egg and sperm unite to become a baby that the mommy carries in her tummy for nine months and then births like in the movie."

I'm sure that I exceeded my allotted pauses for such a conversation, but when it was over, she said, "Okay." And that was it. Phew. I survived. No further questions and discussions. We got off the lift and enjoyed skiing the rest of the day.

I thought I'd accomplished my mission for the day. But when we arrived back at our condo to sit by the fire, warm up, and down another round of hot chocolate, our son Benjamin joined us. Almost on cue, for another classic Rainey family moment, Benjamin asked, "So how does the sperm get in there?"

Being the courageous leader of an organization designed to help families in matters such as these, I turned to Ashley and said, "Princess, tell Benjamin what I told you!" I wanted to hear what Ashley had heard me say. (Does that sound like a lame excuse? Okay, it is!)

Ashley nailed it as she repeated, almost word for word and very matter-of-factly, what I'd said to her. Her brother seemed to shrink in his chair at the mere thought of what he was hearing.

Gratefully, he also had no further questions. This was the first he'd ever heard of it. The poor boy was likely in a state of shock!

We share that story because we want you to be ones who give your children this information. Being proactive—on the offensive, out ahead of your children—is indispensible to successful parenting. Especially on this topic. *Be engaged, be thinking ahead, be anticipating, be intentional, be on the alert!* Be the first one to give them the facts. Don't play catch-up.

Yes, it's awkward, but that's okay. God designed the family to be a safe place to engage in some of life's most sacred and sweet moments. The Rocky Mountain ski-lift story remains one of our fondest memories, and it gave us courage for four more conversations with our other children. Once you've had a couple of conversations, they aren't nearly as challenging as the first one.

Would You Rather Play Offense or Defense?

Sex education really consists of two connected subjects. First, there's the "birds and the bees" information about human reproduction. Then there's the morality of sex, and of course that's the more problematic issue. Looking at the vast changes in our culture today leaves us with the utmost respect for the challenges you as parents will face.

Take a moment and reflect back on your sex education: Where and from whom did you first hear about sex? What was the impact of what you heard? Was it a positive experience that felt healthy, good, and honorable? Or was it something secretive, dirty, perhaps even shameful—something you dared not repeat? What kind of experience do you want your children to remember?

Chances are your sex education came from friends or from the media. Most adults learned little from their parents.

The bottom line: Your children are going to learn about sex. You need to determine whether they will hear about it from you, parents who have sought to embrace and communicate God's view of sex, or see it on a screen shoved in front of their faces by a peer. One of our grandsons almost had pornographic photos air-dropped into his digital device, and he didn't even ask to receive them. He turned his air drop off just in time. It's better for your kids to hear the truth from you first, and probably earlier than you ever intended.

Will you go on the offensive, where you can control the messaging about sex, or will you play defense against voices that will not present sex as the wholesome, sacred intimacy that God designed it to be? After raising six children to adulthood, and playing way too much defense, we can promise you that going on the offensive is the best choice.

Going on the Offensive, Part One

Here's your challenge: As parents, you should consider drafting a simple plan for your children that clarifies *what* you will say about sex and *when* you will say it. Here are some suggestions for what to put into this plan.

- Affirm the sexual identity of your son or daughter. This begins soon after birth; as you change diapers, you can tell them they are fearfully and wonderfully made.

- Agree upon a vocabulary to talk about specific body parts. Don't send confusing messages with words that are silly or crass.

- Find a good series of books that explain sex and human reproduction, written to different ages starting at two to three years old. Reading books on this topic with your child on your lap deposits the information in a warm, comforting way and is much easier than face-to-face! (See our recommended resources at the end of this book.)

- Plan to involve both parents in speaking into each child's sexual education and sexual identity development. Be united in this effort.

- Don't be afraid to give information earlier than you would normally think. Better a little information too early from you than delaying their curiosity until they hear elsewhere.

- Consider milestone moments to have significant conversations in advance of major changes in your child's life. Remember the Old Testament story of Daniel? He made up his mind in advance that he would not defile himself with the king's food. Get out in front by asking yourself, "What are the issues my child will face in the coming two to three years?" An early milestone moment is starting preschool or kindergarten, when they are likely to hear stories or see images on screens when you aren't around.

- Milestone moment: Starting in late grade school, teach your sons how to handle sexually aggressive girls. Read Proverbs 5–7. (See also *Aggressive Girls, Clueless Boys* in our recommended resources.)

- Milestone moment: Before puberty, take your preteen through *Passport-2Purity*, a weekend getaway resource that guides parents and children ages nine to twelve through the issues they'll face during adolescence. Preadolescence is a great time to drive a truckload of truth into a child's life before the hardwiring of puberty begins and they start to think all parents are dumb. Over a quarter million preadolescents have been through this experience—girls with their moms and sons with their dads. A companion book, *So You're About to Be a Teenager*, is available to read after the *Passport2Purity* getaway.

- Be on the alert at all times, even around your good friends and their families. For example, we know of a ten-year-old boy who was exposed to sex by an eleven-year-old whose parents had no idea he knew anything.

- Milestone moment: Freedom increases dramatically with wheels. Before teens get their driver's license, have conversations about situations they'll face, like being alone with the opposite sex. Peer pressure to go places and do things will increase as your presence decreases when they begin driving.

- Milestone moment: During high school, *Passport2Identity for Young Men* and *Passport2Identity for Young Women* offer fuel for another great getaway. John Majors's book *True Identity* also needs to be read and discussed by parents and child after the getaway.

- Important: Discuss what to do if your children fail. Ask if they've seen images on screens they didn't want to see. Take the initiative. Investigate. Ask questions. Don't assume all is well. Their well-being is your business even if they are angry that you're asking. Discuss the forgiveness of God and His grace toward us. Talk about your love and assure them that you will always love them.

- In this culture, sex education is never a one-and-done discussion. It should be a lifetime conversation with your children. Read the book of Proverbs (especially chapters 5–7) and see that Solomon appealed to his son repeatedly to be wise and not a fool when it came to sexual sin.

Once you have a general plan in place, establish a timeline for discussing specific topics with your child. The following checklist will encourage healthy discussions about sex with your child.

Note: These are *recommended* ages only. Each child matures at his or her own rate, so parents need to use discretion.

Also, specific issues (like modesty, language, movies, etc.) need to be reviewed a number of times, not just when the child is younger.

Birth through age 5

Properly identify body parts: penis, vagina, vulva, breasts
God created them male and female (Genesis 1:27)

Ages 6–10: Basics

"The talk"—basics of human reproduction

Affirm inner beauty, character

Modesty

Manners

Language/swearing

Eyes—movies and television

Terms—sperm, egg, ovulation, intercourse

Not viewing pornography

Aggressive girls preying on clueless boys

Ages 11–12: Shaping convictions

(*Passport2Purity* will help you address most of these issues)

Male and female sexual identity

Puberty—physical, emotional, and relational changes

Wet dreams, erections, masturbation, menstruation (this possibly should be addressed at an earlier age, depending on family history)

Continue discussing how dress/fashion can send signals

Discuss dating, romance, and puppy love

Talk about character qualifications for their dates

Discuss how you plan to interview their dates (not up for debate)

Whom to date

Girls calling boys and boys calling girls

Age to start dating; make a plan (we found later is better than sooner)

Principles for dating

How the opposite sex thinks

Keep physical distance

Virginity and abstinence

Decide in advance how far he or she will go with the opposite sex

Purity, innocence, blamelessness

Masturbation

Eyes—pornography, movies, romance novels

Ages 13–15: Testing convictions

Unpack and discuss what's happening among their peers

Sexual attraction

Music

Continue to discuss the timing of dating

Talk about accountability for dating (interviews, contracts)

Guidelines for when they're with the opposite sex

Continue discussing modesty

How to say no to sexual advances

Reinforcing sexual boundaries/guardrails

Not going into the opposite sex's home if the parents are not there

Not going into the opposite sex's bedroom, ever

Understanding sexual response

Convictions about touching, kissing, petting, intercourse

Ages 16–18: Testing and reinforcing convictions

Continued ongoing discussion of all of the above

Affirm them for convictions and learning from mistakes

Interview your daughter's dates—it's good for them and you

Give a purity locket, ring, or other token that would be meaningful to your son or daughter

Challenge your children to protect their innocence

Challenge your children to protect the innocence of the opposite sex

Don't be afraid to ask how they are handling all that's coming at them

Track with your child on how they are doing, if dating

Don't be afraid to have conversations with a young man if he's getting "physically friendly" with your daughter

College, military service, or beyond school, before marriage

Encourage and cheer them on for right choices

Keep the conversation honest, but not intrusive; ask how life is going in this area

If appropriate, share temptations you had at this time, or even a failure

Don't be afraid to ask your son how prevalent porn is among college guys and how he's doing

Don't be afraid to ask your daughter what the dating or sexual hookup scene is like; ask her about porn, too

Meet the the person your son or daughter is dating for coffee—not for an interview, just a healthy one-on-one conversation

Be available after marriage to dialogue if invited

All of this is a piece of cake, RIGHT?

Going on the Offensive, Part Two

Sex education that stops with the birds and the bees doesn't address the real issue today. Think of your own apprehension as a parent: Are you more worried about how your children learn the facts about sex, or about when they start *having* sex?

Our goal as parents was to teach and encourage our children to *believe and trust in God's view of sex*. Woven into your many discussions of sexuality and gender identity will be God's purposes of sex. Your children need to understand that our biological differences are clearly made for the coupling of a man and a woman in marriage.

We pray you will be the ones to introduce this divine design to your child. Don't leave it to the schools, friends, or social media. Here are some major points you will want to share with your child about God's view of sex.

1. God created sex. Genesis 1:27 tells us, "So God created man in his own image, in the image of God he created him; male and female he created them." The Creator of the universe stamped and embedded His image within us in a way that is somehow mysteriously tied to our sexuality.

2. Sexual intercourse in marriage glorifies God. God was not embarrassed when Adam and Eve had intercourse in the garden. No, God designed the equipment and He blessed the union. When God made them male and female, He said it was "very good" (Genesis 1:31).

3. Sex was created to be enjoyed by a man and a woman in marriage. Sex in marriage is chemically bonding by God's majestic design, which explains why it's not good outside of marriage.

One night one of our teenagers came into our bedroom and said to us, "You know, it really bugs me that you shut your door to your bedroom at ten or ten-thirty at night. I feel like you're shutting us out of your lives."

We replied that this was by design! It gives us a chance to talk and to know each other better.

Neither of us explained *how* we were knowing each other, but it was the idea that we need the opportunity for intimacy—spiritual, relational, and sexual.

4. Sex is for procreation in marriage. God created sex so that we can reproduce children. Genesis 1:28 tells us that God blessed the man and the woman and commanded them to be fruitful and multiply and fill the earth. He is commanding us not just to populate the earth with children, but to reproduce children who know, love, and walk with God and serve His purposes in their generation.

5. Sex in marriage is for protection against immorality. It is a preventative against temptation and sin.

6. Sex was never designed to be between two people of the same sex. Two people of the same sex were not designed by God to naturally fit together. These days our media bombard us with the idea that God created and blesses other kinds of sex. But the Scriptures are very clear about how God created male and female for marriage and procreation.

7. Sex outside of marriage is a sin. God very clearly forbids fornication (1 Corinthians 6:9; Matthew 15:19). Some believe only a cruel God would give teenagers a strong sex drive but then order them not to act upon it until marriage. But when God forbids something, it is for our own good.

These purposes for sexual expression in marriage are a part of how a married couple expresses their sexual identity and uniqueness. Children need to understand these purposes and God's design in order to counter what the world is teaching about sex. It is from your model of committed marital love that a child can best learn what it means to be a man and a woman.

As you talk about all of this, in both planned conversations and casually in matter-of-fact circumstances, teach your children the benefits of following God's plan. This is the good news of waiting until marriage, and they need to know it's worth it. And here is where you might share more of your personal story, judiciously, of course, to illustrate why you are glad you followed God's plan or why you wish you had. Here are some of the benefits.

- You will feel no guilt, no shame, no emotional scars when you hold to a standard of sexual holiness. You won't hear any accusing voices in your own conscience.
- You won't be tempted to compare your future spouse with a past lover.
- You won't have any risk of sexually transmitted diseases.
- You will not face the possibility of bearing a child out of wedlock.
- You will develop the much-needed disciplines of self-control and self-denial, which are necessary for adults—in marriage, in raising children, in jobs, in the church, in your neighborhood. . . . All adult relationships need both of these qualities to be healthy.

The Leaky Balloon

As a parent, be ready to seize a teachable moment with your children, especially your teenagers. You never know when it'll come.

Early one evening, I (Dennis) drove Rebecca, then fourteen, to meet some girlfriends for a bunking party. Her friends were running late. As we sat in the parking lot, somehow the topic turned to boys. Soon we found ourselves in a wonderful conversation about how she was going to relate to the opposite sex.

We talked about everything again—hugging, kissing, petting. We discussed her limits and how far she was going to go with a young man prior to marriage.

I talked to her straight about protecting her purity and innocence. What occurred then was an illustration about sexual purity that was so profound that Rebecca and I still jest about who came up with the idea.

The way I remember it (sorry, Rebecca!) . . . I looked down at the console between us and picked up a water balloon. It was stashed ammo from a huge water balloon fight between us and our teenagers a few days before. (The parents won.)

Holding the water balloon up for her to see, I said, "Let's say this water balloon is filled with your sexual purity and innocence. This is all that you have. How much of it would you want to give away before you are married?"

It didn't take her long to answer that question. "I wouldn't want to give away any of it!"

Then I put it in teenage terms. "Let's say that a young man comes to you and just wants a little kiss—your first kiss and just a little bit of your innocence. What would you do?"

At that point I held the balloon up and pretended to pierce it with an imaginary needle. I added, "The young man says to you, 'It's just a little drop. Just an ever-so-teensy drop. You'll never miss it.'" Not giving her time to respond, I went on.

"And then another boy comes along and he wants another little droplet. And after that, let's say he liked what he got and wants even more of your innocence, so now you've lost several drops." With that I punctured the balloon several times with my imaginary needle.

Talking about Your Sexual Past

The greatest fear for many parents is a child asking, "Did you have sex before marriage?"

Parents should not let past failures disqualify them from teaching biblical standards to their children. We've all lied, yet we still teach our children to tell the truth. We have all stolen something, but that doesn't stop us from teaching that stealing is wrong.

We believe the ultimate enemy of our souls is behind this conspiracy of silence about sex in our homes.

First, know that most children will not ask questions about your past. Teens might, but children won't. If they do, know in advance what you will say. Discuss this with your spouse and determine how you want to handle this as a couple.

Children don't need to hear a detailed confession. But at appropriate ages, you can use your failures as a teaching tool.

Here are some different ways you can begin to answer the question, depending on your level of comfort:

- "That's a good question. Perhaps we can talk about that someday."
- "I ignored what my parents taught me and made some mistakes that I really regret."
- "I did not have a parent who was challenging my standards and calling me to live out convictions based on Scripture. And I had poor judgment."
- "Yes, I made some mistakes, and a part of why I'm having this conversation with you now is to protect you from the consequences of going against what God has prescribed."
- "I made some errors in judgement when I was young, but since we've been married, your parents have been faithful to one another."
- "Some day when you are an adult, if you still want to know, I'll tell you my story."

"There's more," I said, seeing a growing frown on her face. "Then let's say you fall in love and really like a guy and decide that it's okay to give even more of your purity and innocence away."

I paused, looking deep into her wide eyes. "What's going to happen to innocence and purity? How much will you have to give to the man you marry and spend the rest of your life with?"

Silence filled that semidarkened car. Rebecca looked up from the balloon to me.

"It'll all be gone," she said with a tinge of sorrow.

"And how would you have lost your purity and innocence—all at once or little by little?"

She was coming to her own conclusions now. "Little by little."

"That's exactly right," I affirmed her. "And that's how young people today are losing one of the most precious gifts that they can give to another human being; they start by giving it away a drop at a time. Then they give away even more, and the holes get larger and it's no longer drops, but a small stream."

Rebecca understood. That water-filled balloon gave her a wonderful object lesson of what God wanted her to protect as she matured and negotiated adolescence.

Looking back, it was one of those God-ordained moments for a parent and a child. Training your kids about the morality of sex will mean hours of impromptu and intentional talks about dating, resisting peer pressure, avoiding pornography, avoiding tempting situations, and more.

Much more.

This is one of the major tests of faith for kids as they go through the adolescent and the single young adult years: *Will they trust in what God says in His word, no matter what the world is telling them . . . no matter how they feel?*

Talking with Your Kids about Sex

Talking about reproduction and the most intimate nature of what it means to be a man and a woman is not like discussing tomorrow's math test or last night's ball game. When you dare to broach the subject with your child, you communicate, "You are important enough to me that I will risk talking about this uncomfortable topic."

Because you've had this conversation, your child may feel it's safe to talk about other intimate issues with you. It has to be a relief to admit this is a part of his life to someone he can trust, namely his parents.

If you have been faithful in appropriately teaching your child from an early age about sex, you will be tempted to relax when your child hits preadolescence. But preteens and teenagers need moms and dads who stay involved in their lives all the way through their teen years by breaking the silence and discussing matters of human sexuality and sexual response.

And if your child has already passed puberty, remember that it is never too late to initiate conversations. He may not act like it, and he won't say so, but he is feeling insecure, maybe even frightened.

Do you recall how you felt as a teenager? Teens need to have Mom and Dad come alongside them and say, "There are some things I wish I had told you earlier, but I want to tell you now. I want to be a part of your life as you go through what can be some very confusing years. I want to be there for you. I don't want to leave you with your peers or by yourself to deal with this issue."

Men in particular may back off from talking about sex with their teenagers because they just don't know what to say. Or maybe Dad hasn't done a good job in other areas of parenting and feels defeated. Regardless, dads need to pursue their children.

Three Big Ideas for Sex Education

BIG IDEA #1: Parents should consider challenging their children to protect not just their virginity, but their sexual purity, innocence, and experience until they are married.

The apostle Paul's plea in Romans 16:19 is worth considering as a challenge for your children, especially as they go through their teen years: "I want you to be wise as to what is good and innocent as to what is evil."

Now let's get practical. Assuming you agree with what God says in His Word about purity, how will you help your children maintain this conviction to remain pure and innocent until marriage? Paul called the Romans up to a higher standard than just avoiding adultery. How can you do that without being legalistic and judgmental? Talk about it with your spouse or other parents. Discuss: Is it better to have standards or to have no standards?

> If we say Jesus Christ is Lord, we have no right, no freedom to believe anything other than what He has taught. We must submit. We know God has ordained that sexual relationships have one context—heterosexual, monogamous, lifelong partnership. Everything outside of that is ruled out by Scripture, despite our culture saying, "No, there's not a problem." I encourage young people all the time, "Bow down under the dictate of Scripture, and allow your feelings to catch up with your head."
>
> ALISTAIR BEGG

BIG IDEA #2: Will you equip your child to have a more wholesome experience with the opposite sex than you had in your teen years?

Bob Lepine, a friend and cohost of *FamilyLife Today*, asked a group of about one hundred parents, "How many of you would like your child to have a similar experience of what you had in terms of dating growing up?" One or two hands went up cautiously. We've asked the same question and seen similar results. An equally important question is, "What are you doing as a parent to engage your children on the issues of dating and sex and to give them a better experience than what you had?"

BIG IDEA #3: Let's say your teenage daughter or teenage son comes to you and says, "Mom, Dad, as I begin to date the opposite sex, how far should I go?" Do you know what standard you'd consider challenging your son or daughter with?

Let's talk about *kissing*. We challenged our children to set a goal of not kissing anyone until the wedding ceremony. Now, that likely sounds prehistorically Victorian and totally preposterous to you, and that's fine. But if that standard seems too high, answer this question: What line *will* you challenge your child to draw? If you do not challenge your child with a specific standard, we can promise you that your child will most definitely turn to peers to develop his or her own line and standard. Is that who you want setting the boundaries for your teen?

Years ago, our son Samuel called from the university. I (Dennis) asked if I could ask him a gritty question or two and then if I could use his answer in a book I was writing. Always up to the challenge, Samuel said, "Fine, go for it."

Cautiously I asked, "Have you ever kissed a girl?"

Samuel's reply was quick and firm. "Nope! I am waiting until I get to the wedding altar."

Probing deeper, I asked, "Have you ever been tempted?"

"Sure," he said. "But I try to stay out of situations where that temptation can occur."

"When were you tempted?"

I could almost hear him smile over the phone, "Oh, it was before I decided on my standards, in the seventh grade with a girl I liked."

Now, the reason I share that story is twofold: First, many young men and women today are taking a similar stand for personal purity. And second, Samuel was tempted the most before he established his own standards. We weren't challenging our preteens and teens with that standard before he was in middle school.

I also should mention that Samuel made it—the first woman he kissed was his wife, Stephanie, during their wedding ceremony!

We occasionally asked our teenage daughters questions to help them form their own conclusions: "Are you going to allow a young man to kiss you? Why? Why not? How will you handle it if a boy tries to kiss you? What are your feelings about that?"

We've talked with teens about the two types of kisses. One is a kiss of pure affection. It's the kiss on the cheek or forehead, or a peck on the lips. The other is a kiss that asks for or demands a response. A sexual response. It is a passionate kiss.

Consider asking your teen, "If you are going to kiss, which kind of kiss are you going to do? What if your date initiates an affectionate kiss and it turns into a passionate kiss? What are you going to do then?" Even a simple first-time kiss on the lips can quickly move to a passionate kiss.

A question every preteen and teenager ought to grapple with is this: "How much of your own sexual passion and responsiveness do you want to experience outside of marriage?" In the end, it really is up to the individual, but you can build some firebreaks by helping your son or daughter to determine in advance where he or she is going to draw the line.

Now let's talk about *touching*. Today, teenagers are so comfortable and friendly with the opposite sex that they don't think anything about giving each other back rubs and frontal hugs or sitting on each other's laps. This kind of physical contact is common even in most church youth groups. Most teens would think it odd or outdated to be questioned on this type of behavior.

Your children need to understand how dangerous touching can be and how quickly it sparks passion. They know it feels good; that's why they do it. Holding hands can quickly lead to kissing, passionate kissing, caressing, petting, and more.

We cannot emphasize enough that your home environment must be safe—one of love, encouragement, security, and forgiveness if you are going to challenge your teens to high moral standards. If your home life is characterized by fear and legalism, your children will likely rebel.

Challenge your teenagers to holiness in this area, knowing that they may fall short. We believe it's better to have the highest of standards in sex and dating—held before our teens with enormous amounts of love, encouragement, and grace—than to conform to the confusing morality of the world. The Scriptures give parents of teens a great reminder: "Love covers a multitude of sins" (1 Peter 4:8).

Section Five

Mission

He is no fool to give that which he cannot keep, to gain that which he cannot lose.

Jim Elliott, martyred at age twenty-five

Our lives begin to end the day we are silent about things that matter.

Martin Luther King Jr.

Life is either a great adventure or it's nothing.

Helen Keller

The only thing worse than being blind is having sight, but no vision.

Helen Keller

This final section reflects the meta story of God's work throughout all of human history: God's grand purpose and design for the family was for it to be the birthplace of the gospel, the emissary to the world of God's message of the cross and redemption. The family is where you see the transfer of the truth of God and the experience of God from one generation to another.

As we've journeyed with you through this book, we have sought to encourage you in coaching and training your children in how to love God and others, in knowing how to be a wise builder of enduring character, and in helping children find their identity in Christ. All three of these hallmarks of Christian faith and practice are leveraged in the final element of raising children: releasing your child to fulfill the Master's mission for his or her life.

The concept of mission is that of being sent on an important task or assignment. One of the most important ways you can shape your children's lives is by being purposeful about their lives and evaluating how they are stewarding their talents, gifts, abilities, experiences, and passions.

Your Child: God's Work of Art

Every parent and every child is designed by God for a mission. Paul writes in Ephesians 2:10, "For we are his workmanship, created in Christ Jesus for good works, which God prepared beforehand, that we should walk in them."

This passage was written to believers in Jesus Christ, those who had been saved by grace through faith. Note three profound statements about your children and their mission:

- The word *workmanship* literally means "work of art." Each life is a unique, exquisite masterpiece.
- Every child is not just any work of art, but *God's* work of art—divine artistry, handcrafted by heavenly fingerprints and design ingenuity.
- A child's life is hardwired with a spiritual DNA that will be the source of good works created by God for him or her to execute. These good works will demand a child's courage, faith, and obedience.

Take a step back from your child and consider that he or she is not just some random, purposeless composition of the more than 7×10^{27} atoms in the human body (that's seven billion billion billion atoms!). Your child is a spiritual treasure trove, God's intricate work of art, marked with a divine purpose and set apart for a mission handcrafted by almighty God.

Your child is a unique image bearer of the God who also created the universe with two trillion galaxies. If your child is a believer, committed to Jesus Christ, he or she has a significant assignment of good works in God's kingdom labor.

As parents, you are the initial, temporary stewards of all that God has wrapped up in the lives of each of your children. You are in the most influential position to aid in your children's discovery of the "good works" that God has prepared for them.

Guiding Your Children in the Discovery of Their Mission

Here are some ideas for helping your children to discover their mission:

1. Evaluate your own life. Are you a person on a mission? How would you describe the mission God has given you? Are you excited about fulfilling God's mission, and are you talking about it with your children as you do life together?

2. Ask God to give you discernment to spot your children's gifts, abilities, passions, and burdens—their "missional DNA"—as they begin to emerge. Begin to rough out a picture of who they are and what they truly seem to care about. What lights their fire? Start a digital diary where you can enter ideas and observations about your child's talents and passions. It may take a while, but the "missional DNA" will begin to emerge.

3. Affirm and encourage your child when you see him or her operating in what appears to be a sweet spot of his or her gifts and wiring. This will become increasingly important during the awkward years of adolescence when nearly all teens need someone speaking truth to them. Don't be surprised if your child has difficulty believing it.

4. Use a date night with your spouse to sharpen your inventory of your child's life. Discuss what each of you are observing in your child, and talk about how you can better develop your child's gifts, talents, and passions.

5. Live your own life "on mission." Talk about what your mission is at the dinner table, as you run errands with your kids, or perhaps on a date with your child. Talk about your passions, your dreams, and how you've developed your mission over your lifetime. If possible, consider inviting your child to join you in executing your mission. If you are looking for additional reading material on this subject, dig into Dennis's book *Choosing a Life That Matters* and Rick Warren's *The Purpose Driven Life*.

6. Fan the flames of your child's dreams. Perhaps ask, "If you could do anything in the world and couldn't fail, what would you do and why?" Or read this quote from A. W. Tozer at the dinner table and discuss: "God is looking for those with whom He can do the impossible—what a pity that we plan only the things that we can do by ourselves."[1]

7. If possible, use testing services as children move into their middle teens and beyond. This was invaluable to us in presenting an objective view of one child's gifts and motivations. Ultimately, it helped us know how to encourage and motivate that child.

8. Encourage and affirm small and big steps of faith. Stepping up and out in faith to use a gift can feel very risky to some children. Memorize Hebrews 11:6 with your children and applaud them when they show initiative.

9. Teach how to process failures—and that they are not final. Don't rescue children from failure; it may be one of the best tutors in their lives. Study men and women who failed. For example, Thomas Edison failed thousands of times before he ultimately succeeded in inventing the lightbulb.

10. Be a person of faith, too. We had to deal with our fears when our son came home from college and said he wanted to go live in Estonia, the former Soviet state, for a year and help introduce students to Jesus Christ. He worked with students at Tallinn University in Estonia's capital. You may be surprised to learn that parents are the number one reason college graduates don't go into the ministry—Christian parents block their kids from going. Personally, we wouldn't want to be the parents blocking one of our children from doing what God had called him or her to do!

11. Pray with and for your child, for the fulfillment of God's mission for his or her life.

12. Read Ephesians 2:10 as a family and assign an older child (a teenager) to lead the family in a devotion about it a couple of weeks later. Then talk about how each would apply that passage of Scripture to his or her life. Do the same with Matthew 6:33 and Matthew 28:19–20. Note the context of this latter passage, where Jesus gave His Great Commission as He spoke His last words to His disciples: "All authority in heaven and on earth has been given to me. Go therefore and make disciples of all nations, baptizing them in the name of the Father and of the Son and of the Holy Spirit, teaching them to observe all that I have commanded you. And behold, I am with you always, to the end of the age."

13. Discuss this Ethiopian proverb at dinner: "The feet take a person where one's heart is."

14. Assign one of your children to read Katie Davis Majors's book *Daring to Hope* and then give a report about it to the family. Tighten your seat belts, for this is quite a story of faith by a remarkable young lady.

Your Arrow: Receive . . . Raise . . . Release

What an assignment and mission you are on—to receive your children as God's gifts and begin this epic adventure of raising them to be all that God designed them to be. What an honor to be called Mommy or Daddy and to be given the significant assignment of releasing them. This is no small task, but a tremendous privilege given to us as parents for a season.

John Wesley's Prayer

Lord, I am no longer my own, but Yours.
Put me to what You will. Rank me with whom You will.
Let me be employed by You or laid aside for You,
exalted for You, or brought low for You.
Let me have all things. Let me have nothing.
I freely and heartily yield all things to Your pleasure and disposal.
And now, O glorious and blessed God, Father, Son, and Holy Spirit,
You are mine and I am yours.
So be it.
Amen.

18 Your Home, His Embassy

You are the only Bible some unbelievers will ever read.

John MacArthur

In our nation's capital of Washington, DC, is a beautiful tree-framed street with large, grand buildings. The area is called Embassy Row for its collection of residences where ambassadors from other countries live and do official business with our government on behalf of their own home countries.

Years ago, two men had a vision for a different kind of embassy, a Christian Embassy. With plenty of prayer and work, this idea eventually blossomed into a real functioning embassy in a beautiful home just off Embassy Row. Its goal was to be a spiritual resource to leaders working in Congress, the executive branch, and the diplomatic community.

One of the founders, Dr. Bill Bright, shared with me (Dennis) that this embassy's purpose was to welcome American leaders and emissaries from other nations with the hope of eventually introducing them to the King of Kings. At embassy dinners, government leaders and dignitaries from various nations heard world-renowned educators, doctors, corporate leaders, authors, Christian leaders, and entertainment personalities tell about their relationship with Jesus Christ.

Bright, the cofounder of Cru (formerly Campus Crusade for Christ), had a vision that each and every follower of Christ would become an ambassador for Jesus Christ. The apostle Paul introduced this concept in his letter to the church at Corinth: "Therefore, we are ambassadors for Christ, God making his appeal through us. We implore you on behalf of Christ, be reconciled to God" (2 Corinthians 5:20).

If your life has been purchased by Christ's death, burial, and resurrection . . .

if you belong to Him . . .

if your children belong to Him . . .

then you are all His representatives, His ambassadors.

And if you are ambassadors, *then your home is His embassy.*

Making an Embassy

Thinking of your home as much more than a haven or refueling stop elevates its atmosphere and purpose. It also lifts the value of everyone who lives within. It sets a vision that this earth is not our home—we belong to the King of Kings, and our citizenship is in heaven. It invites the presence of God into our everyday lives.

And it involves everyone—parents and children—in the work of mission, of reaching out with the love of God to all who need to know God.

Here are three facts about embassies to help you see your home as His residence.

1. An embassy is one country's headquarters in another country. Your home can be God's embassy to your neighborhood. He has filled your residence with His people from His kingdom or country.

- Think for a moment: Whom or what do your home and family currently represent?
- Do you own your home, or does your Father?
- What difference would it make in your life and in the lives of your children if you began to think and act as an emissary of heaven and of the King of Kings?

2. The laws and customs of the home country are observed within the walls of the embassy. Framed photos of the current president and historical figures like George Washington are proudly displayed in American embassies

around the world. Even the food served reflects the home cuisine. At the American embassy in Beijing, China, for instance, the American staff always celebrates Thanksgiving on the same day they would if still living in their homeland.

- When guests walk through your home, do they see that it is a home ruled by the King?
- Is your home governed by His calendar? If so, how have you practically transmitted the values of being a citizen of heaven to your children around the major Christian holidays?
- Does your family truly celebrate the holy days that matter most to Him?

3. An ambassador is an honored representative of one country to another. That person is chosen carefully; you don't want your representative embarrassing your country.

- When you and your kids walk out of your embassy's door, are you aware you are in a foreign country, on mission?
- How is your family representing your homeland, your King?
- How are you empowering your children to be emissaries of the King's agenda in a foreign land?

If your children feel their lives matter to the King of Kings, if they are aware that their choices and actions reflect back on Jesus and also on your home and family as His embassy, they will feel purpose and value on earth. We don't mean placing the weight of the world on your children. It's not their sole responsibility to change the world, but knowing they are ambassadors of the King will impart meaning and value to your children's lives.

Belonging to a King is life-giving!

What Matters Is Not the Size of Your Home, but the Size of Your Heart

Walking through the market with a basket on her arm, a slightly bent silver-haired woman named Ludmilla buys some tea, some rolls, and a few other small items. She returns home, where next to her front door is a square brass plaque with the words "Embassy of the Kingdom of Heaven."

Once inside, Ludmilla puts away her purchases and readies her small kitchen table with lunch. Her home is filled with photos of her family—children, grandchildren, great-grandchildren . . . and her husband, who died in 2002.

Soon there is a knock on the door, and a woman comes in. She tells Ludmilla that she is a widow, and her family is struggling financially. Her husband died four years earlier, and this day he would have turned seventy. They talk and sip their tea, and soon they are praying through their tears.

Ludmilla sees her home as a hideaway for anyone in need at any time. Some friends and family call ahead to schedule their visits; others drop by unannounced. She says her favorites are the ones who surprise her—because the Holy Spirit is there, telling her what to say and do and how to love that person.

> This is our time on the history line of God. This is it. What will we do with the one deep exhale of God on this earth? For we are but a vapor and we have to make it count. We're on. Direct us, Lord, and get us on our feet.
>
> BETH MOORE

"My home is an extension of Christ's kingdom," Ludmilla says. "It's a place where people can come and look for help if they're in trouble or have a need. The Bible says the kingdom of heaven is joy and peace in the Holy Spirit. That is the atmosphere I want here at the embassy."

I (Barbara) have never met Ludmilla; all I know is what I see in the video I've watched many times. She was eighty-two at the time of film and lived in the Czech Republic. It would be difficult to find a better example of someone who sees her home as an embassy.

"It's an honor for me to be an instrument of God's love and His wisdom every day," Ludmilla says. "We often don't realize that all believers are called to be representatives of the kingdom of heaven. We are all ambassadors. The Lord Jesus didn't choose to do it any other way. He simply entrusted us."[1]

Welcoming the World

Ludmilla's story illustrates one of the best ways to use your home as an embassy—practicing hospitality. There are many ways you can open up your home to people in need.

Consider Dave and Lida, empty nesters who own a four-bedroom home. They keep their extra bedrooms clean and ready to be filled with whoever might need them. Their town is known for a certain type of medical treatment that families travel across the country for. Dave and Lida heard of a patient who was traveling frequently to the local treatment center, so they offered the patient and his family a free stay in their home for the duration of his treatments. They haven't cured his sickness or paid off his medical bills, but they've given him shelter, food, rides, friendship—*home*—in the middle of very difficult times.

Making your home an embassy means that your children inevitably become involved in the mission. They help welcome guests, they play with the children. Your home can also become a peace-filled place for their friends to enjoy.

But we don't have to be in our embassy home to offer people hospitality. We "embrace" people even when we give a waiter a kind word and a generous tip, when we sit with a friend on a triumphant day or one when she can't stop crying because of loss. We communicate a taste of God's tenderness, warmth, and purposeful, well-planned love for us.

When you are aware of being the King's ambassador, your everyday errands, meetings, and tasks take on new meaning. As we, His containers of grace, interact with others, we can extend that touch of God to someone else. I am often unaware when God uses me to remind others of His presence. My senses are too often dulled by self-preoccupation. But He is not as limited as I imagine. Not as invisible as He seems. We walk by faith, not by sight.

And the same is true of your children. If they know Jesus, they are taking Him to school, to a friend's house, to piano lessons. Because your children need to embrace a sense of mission to eventually discover their own destiny, it's important to teach them that God has a purpose and calling for their lives. Nurturing your home as an embassy will support and encourage that yet unknown call God has placed in the hearts of your children.

In her book *Raising Grateful Kids in an Entitled World*, author and blogger Kristen Welch writes,

> For many years, our family lived a good, often intentional life inside our four walls. We focused on ourselves—what we needed, what we loved, what we wanted. We spent time together, reading the Bible, playing games, focusing on our little family. I think taking care of your family, dreaming a little, splurging

at times is great, but when that's all we do, we are creating a self-awareness void. The best way to fill that empty place is by serving others.[2]

Rather than allowing your home to function like a biome, self-contained and self-serving—consider casting a vision for your home as an embassy, a place where each person learns to live beyond oneself, for others, all for the kingdom of heaven.

Remodeling Your Home into an Embassy of the King

An embassy is sometimes called a diplomatic mission. Just as a diplomat's mission is to represent his or her homeland and its governing authority, your mission is to represent your heavenly homeland and your King.

1. Like real ambassadors, know as much as you can about your true homeland and your King. This will help you accurately represent Him to anyone who asks or who comes to you or your home embassy for help. Does this sound like a repeated theme you've heard in this book? We hope so. That means studying the Bible, which is God's message of love to us and to all people of all nations.

2. Ask your King every day what He has for you to do for Him. Earthly ambassadors get messages from their home countries with requests to meet with certain officials or to tour local cities to get to know the people. They are always on mission. God has the same kind of instructions for us, too. But we have to ask, and listen carefully for Him to answer, and then we must follow. The

> **Y**ou have the privilege of participating with our living Lord in the fulfillment for His Great Commission in our generation. In my opinion, the only way to change the world is to change individuals. Changed people, in sufficient numbers, will produce changed campuses, changed communities, changed cities, states and nations—yes, in a very real sense, a changed world. Jesus Christ is the only One who can change people from within. You can help to change the world by introducing people to Jesus Christ.
>
> BILL BRIGHT

Holy Spirit is infinitely creative in how He wants us to represent Jesus here on earth. Listen carefully to Him.

3. Listen for His directions. The Bible tells us God's Holy Spirit will be our instructor. He will tell us what to say (Luke 21:13–15), lead or show us whom to talk to (Acts 8:27–29), help us remember all Jesus said (John 14:26), and guide us (John 16:13). The ultimate experience of a lifetime is to know you are being used by almighty God to accomplish His agenda on planet earth.

4. Watch for angels! One more verse about your home being an embassy is Hebrews 13:2, which encourages us be hospitable to strangers because sometimes they are angels! Verse 13 reminds us to remember prisoners and to visit them. Being an ambassador sometimes means going to others, not just having them in your own home.

Remember, an embassy doesn't exist so that a nation's representatives can enjoy each other in a nice building. No, their mission is like a nerve center for relating to the foreign nation around them, for recruiting new citizens, and for assisting its own citizens with the difficulties in living away from home.

Is that the kind of family your household wants to be, a residence of ambassadors of all ages who use all that God has poured into you—your education, your finances, your home, your talents, your time—to love other people as He would?

We hope you want your home to be a place where, because God so generously pours into you, you pour generously right into the world around you. We hope you and your children will want to serve others to honor our King—so that others can know Him and become citizens of the country that lasts forever.

Why Does This Matter to Me As a Parent?

If you are an ambassador and your home is an embassy, that changes everything.

- Your life and your children's lives are sacred. Our bodies are the temple of the living God; therefore, our everyday moments matter.
- Jesus lived in obscurity for thirty years, and we know every moment of His life counted. Can we believe the same is true for us, especially moms, who so often live hidden lives?

- In the hidden work of your embassy, there is significance, daily eternal value. Dallas Willard writes that where "transformation is actually carried out is in our real life, where we dwell with God and our neighbors. . . . First we must accept the circumstances we constantly find ourselves in as the place of God's kingdom and blessing. God has yet to bless anyone except where they actually are."[3]

- Caring for our bodies and the bodies of our children is caring for eternal souls, for the two are inextricably entwined.

- Creating order out of endless disorder is daily mimicking our Creator, who hovered over the formless void and with His word changed everything.

- Our bodies were made for worship. Nurturing these sacred containers of God's presence on earth is an assignment whose value we vastly underestimate. C. S. Lewis described the holy wonder of our bodies this way: "The dullest and most uninteresting person you can talk to may one day be a creature which, if you saw it now, you would be strongly tempted to worship. . . . There are no *ordinary* people. You have never talked to a mere mortal."[4]

- Rightly reordering our view of ourselves, our children, and our homes in light of how God views everything will greatly impact how you parent. Failures can be redeemed, fresh beginnings can start every single day, and eyes can be opened to see God anew when we invite Him to live and work in and through us as we live and work and are daily transformed in His embassy.

Think of the indescribable privilege the Creator of the universe has given you: You are raising the next generation of emissaries to the world. Steward the lives of these young ambassadors well.

19 Releasing Your Arrows

Begin with the end in mind.

Stephen R. Covey, *The 7 Habits of Highly Effective People*

It was a scorching, humid August day in Oxford, Mississippi. We were sweating on the outside and our hearts were melting on the inside—we were carrying boxes, hangers draped with clothes, and suitcases up eight floors to Ashley's dorm room at the University of Mississippi.

After eighteen years in the quiver, our first arrow was about to be launched. Ashley was our Princess. We knew this day was going to be a toughie. She was leaving the nest . . . going to college . . . all by herself.

As we helped her move in, I watched Barbara find all kinds of things to hang, straighten, and tidy up. She was stretching out the time, stalling, putting off the inevitable hug and good-bye. A lump is forming in my throat and tears in my eyes as I relive the moment.

Archers will tell you to purchase an armguard before you let go of your first arrow. It's a piece of leather you strap on your forearm to absorb string slap when you release an arrow.

Note to parents on releasing their arrows: String slap is very painful. When the arrow is notched, pulled back, and released, you will discover one important thing: They don't make a string-slap guard for parents' hearts.

As the three of us walked one last time down all eight flights of stairs and into the parking lot where our empty pickup truck was parked, neither of us was prepared for the bittersweet emotion that was about to ambush us. As I prepared to pray for Ashley, I heard the words of the apostle Paul in my ears:

> Therefore, my beloved, as you have always obeyed, so now, not only as in my presence but much more in my absence . . . that you may be blameless and innocent, children of God without blemish in the midst of a crooked and twisted generation, among whom you shine as lights in the world, holding fast to the word of life, so that in the day of Christ I may be proud that I did not run in vain or labor in vain.
>
> Philippians 2:12–16

As we walked across the hot pavement of the dorm parking lot, my eyes met Barbara's and saw that hers were already red with emotion. Finally, we reached the pickup. Now *both* of us were stalling . . . a mom and dad wanting to make sure Ashley knew how much we loved her, to call us and her family, to remember to check the oil in her car, etc.

Barbara and I encircled Ashley in a family hug, and I attempted to say, "Let's pray," but I was already crying so hard that the words didn't come out. By the time we bowed our heads, both Barbara and I were crying so hard neither of us could choke out a prayer. As we sobbed, I asked Ashley to pray. It was a pitiful scene . . . our daughter had to pray for herself!

Then we all laughed and brushed away our tears, said our final goodbyes, and got in the pickup, which felt really empty now. Silent, too. Neither of us could talk.

As we pulled out of the parking lot, we looked back to the front of the dorm. There was our Princess, standing alone on the sidewalk with a big grin on her face, waving good-bye. That scene made us cry even more. Then through my sobs I choked out these words: "That does it! There's not enough left of my heart to do this five more times with the rest of our children. I'm going to hire Rent-a-Daddy to do it for me!" And we both burst out laughing again through our tears.

Now that we've released all six of our arrows, we can tell you that it really doesn't get any easier. Intellectually, releasing your child makes sense. It has to happen. It's right. It's good.

But you still feel string slap when you *really* let go.

From the Hand of a Warrior

Parenting is one long process of crafting each of your arrows to fly, aiming them, and letting go. It starts out with a series of small releases in which you give your children greater independence: teaching them to feed themselves, sending them to school, teaching them to drive.

At each stage, you teach and train the child in what to do and in how to handle this new responsibility. Your hope is that, over time, your child moves from dependence on you to total dependence upon Jesus Christ at the final release—leaving home for college, marriage, a job, or military service. As we said earlier in the book, you seek to connect your children to God so they don't need to remain connected to you.

We find it interesting that when God inspired the words of Scripture, He could have chosen any image or metaphor to represent children and their parents. He didn't say children are "like a staff in the hand of a shepherd" or "like a shovel in the hand of a gardener."

No, He said, "Like *arrows* in the hand of a *warrior* are the children of one's youth" (Psalm 127:4, emphasis added). It's clearly a battlefield metaphor.

Your children were not given to just anyone, but given to you, and you are called to be like a warrior.

> **K**eep in mind that the goal of our discipline is always weaning them from us, their earthly parents who love them incompletely, to a heavenly Father who loves them completely unconditionally.
>
> SUSAN YATES

Parenting isn't a hobby. It's not a sport. It's not playing house, just for fun. It's not about your children's comfort. You will be releasing your children into a very real spiritual battlefield against a very evil and crafty enemy. Your arrow was given to you by God not to keep in your quiver, but to craft, test, aim, and let go for God's glory and for God's kingdom impact on planet earth.

The apostle Paul recognized the enemy and this battlefield, giving us a sobering warning in Ephesians 6:10–12:

Finally, be strong in the Lord and in the strength of His might. Put on the whole armor of God, that you may be able to stand firm against the schemes of the devil. For we do not wrestle against flesh and blood, but against the rulers, against the authorities, against the cosmic powers over this present darkness, against the spiritual forces of evil in the heavenly places.

Paul wouldn't be challenging us to put on armor if there wasn't the need for spiritual protection. We aren't speaking here of culture wars. We are not talking about political parties or the state of our schools or what's going on in the media. This is about living our lives in a world system that has never reflected biblical values, where we are discouraged from believing that God exists or wants to play a part in our lives. This is the world you live in, and it's the world for which you are preparing your children to take flight in and have an impact.

You are raising a vulnerable child in the midst of a smoke-filled, invisible spiritual battlefield. That's always been true for generations of followers of Christ. We aren't talking about protecting your child from knee scrapes and

Release Points

While the ultimate release for a child is when they leave home to live on their own, there are many other smaller release points for children. These earlier occasions provide you with opportunities to train and prepare them for the level of independence each one offers. Here are some earlier release points:

- Feeding themselves
- Walking on their own
- Going to school
- Sleepovers
- Spending a week with grandparents or relatives without their parents
- Allowances—learning to save, give, purchase their own clothes, and generally handle their money
- Having a smartphone
- Driving
- Working a part-time job
- Group dating and individual dating
- Curfews (by their senior year, we allowed our kids to determine their own hours)

The goal is to build character and shape your children's ability to make wise decisions—and helping them work through failures—while they are living under your roof.

flesh wounds, but spiritual, emotional, moral, and sexual lacerations that not only can scar a child's soul, but can impact the generations that follow.

Once again, A. W. Tozer challenges believers to be on the alert as we go into "lion country" and engage in spiritual battle against our adversary, the devil, who is described as in 1 Peter 5:8 as a "lion, seeking someone to devour." Tozer says, "It is a delightful thing when you know that you are close enough to the adversary that you can hear him roar! Too many Christians never get into 'lion country' at all!"[1]

Winston Churchill believed the battlefield is the place where great issues are resolved. After more than four decades of working with families, we agree. We believe that the great issues of our day will never be decided by pursuing comfort, sipping lemonade in a hammock. Rather, it will be through well-equipped children who are learning how to invade lion country. Just as Churchill refused to negotiate until the adversary had capitulated, neither can we afford to give into temptation or compromise.

One last caution to you as a warrior: If you want your arrows to hit the target, then neither you nor your child can become a casualty. Be on the alert. Stand firm in the faith (1 Peter 5:6–11).

What's Your Target?

Every arrow has a mission for which it and it alone was designed to fulfill. You can't ensure your arrow hits the bull's-eye, but you can point it in the right direction.

The *Peanuts* cartoon character Lucy captures what has been a problem for parents for centuries. Comparing life to a deck chair on a cruise ship, she quips to Charlie Brown, "Some people place their chairs facing the rear of the ship so they can see where they've been. Other people face their chairs forward . . . to see where they're going! . . . . Charlie Brown, which way is your deck chair facing?" Charlie Brown replies, "I've never been able to get one unfolded."[2]

As a parent, what is it that you are trying to see produced in your child? What's your target?

I was talking recently with a good friend and warrior for Christ, Kerry Bradley. He's father to three adult children and served as the CEO of a five-billion-dollar company. I asked, "What would be your coaching advice for parents who are raising their children to be released?"

His response was a good one: "Your job for twenty-one years is to raise your children to become God-honoring, effective adults who want to fulfill God's mission for their lives. Your goal is not to be your children's friend, but their coach, their guide, and their teacher in these years of training called parenting."

Our target was similar. We both agreed our bull's-eye was this: "I have no greater joy than to hear that my children are walking in the truth" (3 John v. 4).

Whether you are a single parent, in a blended family, or in a nuclear family, that should be the goal, the target. We like this statement that is frequently attributed to German pastor Dietrich Bonhoeffer, who was martyred at the age of thirty-nine: "It is the righteous man who lives for the next generation."

We wanted to release our arrows into an adulthood where they were impacting their world for Christ—and training their own children to do the same. And though our children are as imperfect as their parents, it's been a joy to watch them leading small-group Bible studies, counseling couples in their marriages, ministering to orphans, serving on different church and ministry boards, working in the schools, ministering to their co-workers, and much more. We've been very proud to watch our kids buy into God's mission for their lives.

> I **want** kids to be able to make decisions, to be good decision-makers. That's not to say they're not going to make mistakes. Who lives a mistake-free life? And do we make mistakes that we regret? Of course we do. But God frequently uses those mistakes, the things we regret, in a far more powerful way than those times when we're just cruising along and doing great.
>
> KAREN FITZPATRICK

What If You Don't Want to Let Go?

Leaving Ashley at college was one of the hardest things we've ever done. But if we don't release our children, we are robbing them from becoming independently dependent on God. Prolonging their adolescence potentially creates an emotional cripple in a dysfunctional parent-child relationship.

Four tips for letting go:

> # We need to prepare our kids to be launched as an arrow, not a boomerang.
>
> BRYAN LORITTS

1. Be careful that you don't hold on too long. One dad removed this obstacle by declaring, "You will always be my son, but you are no longer my boy." Making this declaration creates accountability. You may unintentionally revert to treating him like a boy, and if you do, your son needs to be empowered to call you out. Ditto for daughters. Don't lengthen the apron strings. Cut 'em.

2. Agree with your spouse that you won't build a child-centric marriage. Too many parents arrive at the release point, let go, turn around to take their spouse's hand, and find it's not there. Your marriage must be built to outlast your children.

3. Don't stay big. Our friend Jane Ann Smith gave us some sage advice when it comes to releasing your adult children. Throughout all of our children's lives, Mom and Dad have been big. We've ensured their survival, invested in their well-being, been a constant in their lives. But when it's time for the release, Jane Ann advises that "our adult children need us to become smaller in their lives, not bigger." Jesus' cousin John the Baptist understood this concept when he said, "He must increase, but I must decrease" (John 3:30). Are you ready to get small?

4. CAUTION: Prepare for the pink slip. Realize that you are in the only profession where, if you do your job, you're guaranteed to be fired! Moms especially feel this. *Barbara and Susan's Guide to the Empty Nest*, a book Barbara coauthored with Susan Yates, contains sage advice about this stage. Husbands need to process "the firing" with their wives. They need to plan together for their next stage of life.

Send Them, Don't Just Let Go

As each of our two sons approached high school graduation, we marked the moment by organizing a breakfast to which we invited several men who had influenced their lives. Each man shared some great counsel about going to college and manhood issues. We recorded what they said and had it transcribed. For one of our daughters, we created a notebook with letters written by women who had impacted her life.

Bless them as they go. Don't just passively let them go. Instead, give them a transgenerational commissioning. Challenge them with a vision for influencing at least two generations beyond their own. Consider formalizing the release by writing a blessing and having it framed; then read it to your child as you aim and let go.

Ramen Noodles Are a Great Teacher

When children are released, they should feel your approval, affirmation, and love—and they should feel freedom from your day-to-day rule or demands. You no longer tell them what to do!

Released children should feel a growing sense of responsibility for their own life, but not abandonment from their parents. A couple of our daughters expressed that they felt too much space from us, that we didn't stay connected enough.

And they should feel an emerging sense of identity, of who God made them to be, and a realization that they have to figure out this thing called mission.

What they don't need to feel is your arms pulling them back. And they don't need to feel like you will rescue them from their mistakes or from adult responsibilities.

As our children went to college, we purposefully gave them a very modest living allowance. We will never forget the time one of them called from college to complain she was eating ramen noodles all weekend—she had joined a health club and didn't have any money left over. We expressed compassion and sadness, and then encouraged our college student to get a part-time job!

Another child came home during sophomore year and complained there wasn't enough money to do the things his friends did. We empathized for a few moments, but then we said, "You know that we love you. You are becoming an adult, with adult tastes and desires, which is all very good. However, as your parents, we are not committed to subsidizing your adult lifestyle. We suggest you do what we did in college and find a way to earn money to fund those desires."

I asked one of our sons if he'd ever been afraid of me as his dad. I was surprised when he quickly said, "Yes! When you gave me my first credit card when I was a sophomore at the university. You

> It's a lot easier to let them go, even though you're sad, when you've spent these eighteen years preparing them to take off on their own.
>
> TIM KIMMEL

told me that if I didn't pay it off each month and had to pay even one penny of interest, you would drive three and a half hours to school and kick my tail!"

Our children also knew that after graduation from college, they were welcome to come home for the summer. Within three or four months they would need to find employment and move out on their own. This was good for them—and us!

Finally, tell your children that if God blesses them with a spouse and they have the incredible privilege of being blessed with arrows in their quiver, then you want to challenge them to be warriors and to equip their own arrows for spiritual battle and impact.

"Dad, This Is My Mission Field"

On the day we took our second child, Benjamin, to college, I was helping him unload his clothing and move his gear into his room. We rested on the tailgate of a pickup truck and watched other students coming in. Their arms were loaded with cases of beer and sacks of liquor. It was just three o'clock, and some of them were already completely wasted.

As I sat there, I was suddenly overtaken by fear. I wondered if all of our efforts as parents, all of the hours of discipline, building character, and helping Benjamin face issues in his life had adequately prepared my son. Would he pass the test?

I turned to Benjamin and looked him in the eye. "Son, I've got to tell you that watching all these young men get wasted on booze really causes me to question the wisdom of sending you into the midst of all this."

There was only a brief silence, and he returned my gaze. "Dad, this is my mission field," he replied. "It's going to be tough, but if it was easy, these guys wouldn't need Jesus Christ. This is what you and Mom have trained me for. God has led me, and He will protect me."

> You do your children a big disservice when you hover over them, when you protect them, when you isolate them until they go off to college. You haven't prepared them for that. That's why so many Christian kids just fall off the boat there. They have not been prepared to think and live on their own.
>
> DARCY KIMMEL

There I sat, rebuked by my eighteen-year-old son. He was a young man of faith.

"Dad, I see your fear, and I know you have a concern," he said. "I want you to know that God has sent me to this fraternity. I feel like He has led me to impact this fraternity for Jesus Christ. And I am going to be okay. You pray for me, but I am going to be okay."

And both Benjamin and his brother, Samuel, did just fine.

On their own, our children must be prepared to make the choice to be different—not to be pious or religious, but to be a young person who operates on firmly held personal convictions.

Like arrows in the hand of a warrior . . . Will you receive your children as a gift, raise them to follow Christ, and release them for impact?

Your arrow was made by God for this moment in His Big Story. Let the arrow fly.

With These Hands

There are three stages in any great work of God: . . . impossible . . . difficult
. . . done.

Hudson Taylor

Mark DeYmaz was born out of wedlock in 1961, an only child, to a single mother, Dorothy. Mark was a latchkey kid because Dorothy worked two jobs to support her son. But that's not all she did to love and support her son. One night, Dorothy prayed him into the kingdom of God.

In the winter of 1977, when Mark was living apart from God and without Christ in his life, he was awakened by the sound of loud cries permeating the one-bedroom apartment he shared with his mother. Realizing she was not in her bed, he became frightened and quietly tiptoed out of the room to investigate. With each step he took, the cries grew louder and he grew increasingly scared. Passing the small bathroom and then the kitchen, Mark soon reached the living room; there, peering into the darkness, he saw in the far corner of the room his mother on her knees crying out to God. Her words, distorted by her agony, were indecipherable to him, but in that moment, he had no doubt: His mother was praying for him.

Years later, in May 1994, as the student ministries pastor at our church and with his mother in mind, Mark penned the following poem to share at a ceremony for graduating high school seniors. Barbara and I were there that night with our firstborn son, Ben. At the end of the evening, Mark invited us and all the other parents present to stand behind our sons and daughters and to lay hands upon them. As we did this, tears streaming down our faces, Mark read the poem in prayer.

To this day, we have never forgotten the significance of that moment as we launched Ben into adulthood. In the days to come, we pray you, too, will recognize the significance of the launch, of all such parental efforts, and ultimately, of the power of prayer.

With These Hands

With these hands . . .

> I gently cradled this child.
> Held him close to my heart.
> Nursed his wounds and calmed her fears,
> And rocked this child fast asleep.

With these hands . . .

> I made his lunches, and
> Drove the car that carried her to school.
> Snapped endless pictures, wrapped countless gifts,
>   Then did my best to assemble those gifts!
> Combed his hair and wiped her tear,
> Let her know that I was near . . .
> To nurse his wounds, and heal her heart when it would break . . .

With these hands, I made mistakes

And with these hands, I prayed, and prayed . . . and prayed.

These hands are feeble.
These hands are worn.
These hands can no longer calm the storms.
These hands have done all they can do.
These hands now release this child, my child, to You.

For Your hands are able.
Your hands are strong.
Your hands alone can calm the storms.
Your hands will continue to do what they so gifted do.
To shape his life and make her new.

Into Your hands, receive this child,
For my child I now give back to You.

In the strong name of Jesus,
And with all my heart I pray . . .

Amen

> Dr. Mark DeYmaz, founding pastor and directional leader,
> Mosaic Church of Central Arkansas; cofounder and president,
> Mosaix Global Network; author, *Building a Healthy Multi-Ethnic
> Church* and *Multiethnic Conversations*

Recommended Resources

For Your Marriage

The Art of Marriage: Getting to the Heart of God's Design, video series and small-group kit, hosted by Dennis and Barbara Rainey, FamilyLife Publishing

Moments Together for Couples: 365 Daily Devotions for Drawing Near to God and One Another by Dennis and Barbara Rainey, Bethany House Publishers

Moments with You: Daily Connections for Couples by Dennis and Barbara Rainey, Bethany House Publishers

Weekend to Remember marriage getaway, FamilyLife

Character

Age of Opportunity: A Biblical Guide to Parenting Teens by Paul David Tripp, P & R Publishing

Aggressive Girls, Clueless Boys: 7 Conversations You Must Have with Your Son [and 7 Questions You Should Ask Your Daughter] by Dennis Rainey, FamilyLife Publishing

The Christian Parenting Handbook: 50 Heart-Based Strategies for All the Stages of Your Child's Life by D. Scott Turansky and Joanne Miller, RN, BSN, Thomas Nelson

The Heart of Anger: Practical Help for the Prevention and Cure of Anger in Children by Lou Priolo, Grace and Truth Books

Interviewing Your Daughter's Date: 30 Minutes Man-to-Man by Dennis Rainey, FamilyLife Publishing

Parenting in the Pew: Guiding Your Children into the Joy of Worship by Robbie Castleman, IVP Books

Passport2Purity Getaway Kit: A Life-Changing Weekend with Your Preteen by Dennis and Barbara Rainey, FamilyLife Publishing

Raising a Modern-Day Knight: A Father's Role in Guiding His Son to Authentic Manhood by Robert Lewis, Focus on the Family

Shepherding a Child's Heart by Tedd Tripp, Shepherd Press

Stepping Up: A Call to Courageous Living Video Series by Dennis Rainey, FamilyLife Publishing

Stepping Up: A Call to Courageous Manhood by Dennis Rainey, FamilyLife Publishing

Strengthening Your Kids' Faith

Grace Based Parenting: Set Your Family Free by Tim Kimmel, Thomas Nelson

Growing a Spiritually Strong Family by Dennis and Barbara Rainey, Multnomah

Passport2Purity Getaway Kit: A Life-Changing Weekend with Your Preteen by Dennis and Barbara Rainey, FamilyLife Publishing

Why Christian Kids Rebel: Trading Heartache for Hope by Tim Kimmel, Thomas Nelson

Disciplining Children

Grace Based Discipline: How to Be at Your Best When Your Kids Are at Their Worst by Karis Kimmel Murray, Family Matters

Letting Go: Rugged Love for Wayward Souls by Dave Harvey and Paul Gilbert, Zondervan

Identity

Aggressive Girls, Clueless Boys: 7 Conversations You Must Have with Your Son [and 7 Questions You Should Ask Your Daughter] by Dennis Rainey, FamilyLife Publishing

Passport2Identity for Young Men: Getaway Kit, Dennis Rainey et al., FamilyLife Publishing

Passport2Identity for Young Women: Getaway Kit, Barbara Rainey et al., FamilyLife Publishing

Relentless Parenting: The Critical Pursuit of Your Teen's Heart by Brian and Angela Haynes, Randall House

So You're About to Be a Teenager: Godly Advice for Preteens on Friends, Love, Sex, Faith and Other Life Issues by Dennis and Barbara Rainey with Samuel Rainey and Rebecca Rainey, Thomas Nelson

True Identity: Finding Significance and Freedom through Who You Are in Christ by John C. Majors, Bethany House Publishers

Sex Education

How and When to Tell Your Kids about Sex: A Lifelong Approach to Shaping Your Child's Sexual Character by Stan and Brenna Jones, NavPress

Passport2Purity Getaway Kit: A Life-Changing Weekend with Your Preteen by Dennis and Barbara Rainey, FamilyLife Publishing

The Talks: A Parent's Guide to Critical Conversations about Sex, Dating, and Other Unmentionables by Barrett and Jenifer Johnson, INFO for Families

Legacy

Building Strong Families by Dennis Rainey, ed., Crossway Books

Choosing a Life That Matters: 7 Decisions You'll Never Regreat by Dennis Rainey, Bethany House Publishers

Total Family Makeover: 8 Practical Steps to Making Disciples at Home by Melissa Spoelstra, Abingdon Press

Blended Family

Daily Encouragement for the Smart Stepfamily by Ron L. Deal and Dianne Neal Matthews, Bethany House Publishers

Dating and the Single Parent by Ron L. Deal, Bethany House Publishers

The Smart Stepfamily Marriage: Keys to Success in the Blended Family by Ron L. Deal and David H. Olson, Bethany House Publishers

The Smart Stepfamily: Seven Steps to a Healthy Family by Ron L. Deal, Bethany House Publishers

Empty Nest/Adult Children

Barbara and Susan's Guide to the Empty Nest: Discovering New Purpose, Passion, and Your Next Great Adventure by Barbara Rainey and Susan Yates, Bethany House Publishers

Notes

Section One: A Parakeet Teaches God's Love

1. Barna Research Group, *Six Tech Habits Changing the American Home*, April 18, 2017, https://www.barna.com/research/6-tech-habits-changing-american-home/.
2. Ewan McGregor, BrainyQuote.com, Xplore Inc, 2018, accessed April 16, 2018, https://www.brainyquote.com/quotes/ewan_mcgregor_581715.

Chapter 1: Like Arrows

1. Neil Postman, *The Disappearance of Childhood* (New York: Delacorte Press, 1982), xi.

Chapter 5: Bridge Building Lanes Two and Three: Pursuing and Forgiving

1. Adapted from *Men of Action*, Spring 1992, 5.

Chapter 6: Teaching Love for Others

1. C. S. Lewis, *The Weight of Glory* (New York: HarperOne, 2001), 46.

Section Three: Building Character

1. Samuel Taylor Coleridge, *Specimens of the Table Talk of the Late Samuel Taylor Coleridge*, vol. 1 (London: John Murray, 1835), 191.
2. "Minnesota Crime Commission Report," *Journal of the American Institute of Criminal Law and Criminology* 18, no. 1 (May 1927).
3. Henry Cloud and John Townsend, *Raising Great Kids: A Comprehensive Guide to Parenting with Grace and Truth* (Grand Rapids, MI: Zondervan, 1999), 29.

Chapter 8: A Plan for Building Character

1. Benjamin Franklin, *Poor Richard's Almanack* (Waterloo, IA: U.S.C. Publishing, 1914), 26.

Chapter 9: How God Builds Character in Us

1. Laura Story, "Blessings," CD, track 5, *Blessings*, independent, 2011.

Chapter 10: Building Character in Your Children

1. Voddie Baucham Jr., *Family Driven Faith: Doing What It Takes to Raise Sons and Daughters Who Walk with God* (Wheaton, IL: Crossway, 2007), 95.
2. Albert Einstein, ThinkExist.com, accessed April 16, 2018, http://thinkexist.com/quotation/setting_an_example_is_not_the_main_means_of/145964.html.
3. C. S. Lewis, *Mere Christianity* (New York: HarperOne, 2001), 38.

Chapter 11: Using Discipline to Build Character

1. Associated Press, "'Meanest Mom on Planet' Sells Teen Son's Car after Finding Booze under Seat," Fox News, January 9, 2008, http://www.foxnews.com/story/2008/01/09/meanest-mom-on-planet-sells-teen-son-car-after-finding-booze-under-seat.html; Monica Hesse, "'Meanest Mom' Sells Son's Car, Family Gets Quite a Ride," *Washington Post*, January 11, 2008, http://www.washingtonpost.com/wp-dyn/content/article/2008/01/10/AR2008011003852.html.
2. C. S. Lewis, *The Problem of Pain* (New York: HarperOne, 2001), 91.
3. Martin Luther, AZ Quotes, accessed April 17, 2018, http://www.azquotes.com/quote/562902.

Chapter 12: What about Spanking?

1. Julie Crandall, "Poll: Most Approve of Spanking Kids," ABC News, November 8, 2017, http://abcnews.go.com/US/story?id=90406&page=1.
2. Jessica Samakow, "What Science Says about Using Physical Force to Punish a Child," HuffPost, September 18, 2014, https://www.huffingtonpost.com/2014/09/18/adrian-peterson-corporal-punishment-science_n_5831962.html.

Chapter 13: Smartphones for Smart Families

1. Lesbian, Gay, Bisexual, Transgender, Transsexual, Queer, Questioning, Intersex, Asexual, Ally, Pansexual.
2. Sherry Turkle, *The Second Self: Computers and the Human Spirit*, twentieth anniversary edition (Cambridge, MA: MIT Press, 2005), 311.
3. Roald Dahl, *Charlie and the Chocolate Factory* (New York: Puffin Books, 1968, 2013), 139.
4. Blaise Pascal, *Pensées* 171.
5. G. K. Chesterton, *Orthodoxy* (London: John Lane Company, 1909), chap. 6, https://books.google.com/books?id=p7UEAQAAIAAJ.
6. Have no fear. Axis has resources on Finstagrams, sneaky apps, porn, sexting, and whatever the new thing is at Axis.org. Check out our parent guides and *The Culture Translator* weekly email.

Section Four: What Is Identity?

1. BBC, *Henry Faulds 1843–1930*, accessed March 26, 2018, http://www.bbc.co.uk/history/historic_figures/faulds_henry.shtml; Gavan Tredoux, "Henry Faulds: The Invention of a Fingerprinter," Galton.org, December 2003, http://galton.org/fingerprints/faulds.htm.

Chapter 14: Emotional Identity

1. Erica Komisar, *Being There: Why Prioritizing Motherhood in the First Three Years Matters* (New York: TarcherPerigee, 2017).
2. Erica Komisar, "The Politicization of Motherhood," interview by James Taranto, *Wall Street Journal*, October 17, 2017, https://www.wsj.com/articles/the-politicization-of-motherhood-1509144044.
3. Komisar, "The Politicization of Motherhood."

Chapter 15: Spiritual Identity

1. A. W. Tozer, *Knowledge of the Holy* (New York: Harper and Row, 1961) in *A. W. Tozer: Three Classics in One Volume* (Chicago: Moody Publishers, 2018), 13.
2. Lewis, *Mere Christianity*, 177.

Chapter 16: Sexual Identity

1. Jackie Hill-Perry, "Love Letter to a Lesbian," Desiring God, July 20, 2013, https://www.desiringgod.org/articles/love-letter-to-a-lesbian.

Section Five: Mission

1. A. W. Tozer, AZ Quotes, accessed April 17, 2018, http://www.azquotes.com/quote/589330.

Chapter 18: Your Home, His Embassy

1. The Czech *"Embassy of the Kingdom of Heaven,"* Deidox Films, video, 4:58, accessed April 25, 2018, https://deidox.org/film/woman-lives-at-embassy-of-kingdom-of-heaven/.
2. Kristen Welch, *Raising Grateful Kids in an Entitled World: How One Family Learned That Saying No Can Lead to Life's Biggest Yes* (Carol Stream, IL: Tyndale Momentum, 2015), 81–82.
3. Dallas Willard, *The Divine Conspiracy: Rediscovering Our Hidden Life in God* (New York: HarperCollins, 1998), 347–348.
4. Lewis, *Weight of Glory*, 45–46.

Chapter 19: Releasing Your Arrows

1. A. W. Tozer, *Tozer Speaks: 128 Compelling and Authoritative Teachings of A. W. Tozer*, vol. 1 (Camp Hill, PA: WingSpread Publishers, 1994), book four, preface.
2. Charles Schulz, *Peanuts*, March 15, 1981, accessed April 26, 2018, http://www.gocomics.com/peanuts/1981/03/15.

Dennis and Barbara Rainey have been married since 1972 and are the parents of six married children and proud Papa and Mimi to a growing number of grandchildren—soon to be twenty-four as of this writing.

The Raineys are cofounders of FamilyLife, where Dennis served as president and CEO and also hosts the daily radio program *FamilyLife Today*. Barbara created Ever Thine Home, a collection of beautiful and biblical products women can use to make their homes a witness for their faith. She loves to encourage younger women through her blog at EverThineHome. com. They have spoken at more than 150 Weekend to Remember marriage getaways and conferences around the world and have authored more than 50 books and Bible studies, including the bestselling *Moments with You* and *Moments Together for Couples*.

Barbara loves to create and make all things beautiful. She enjoys working in her garden and finally convinced Dennis to enjoy it with her. Dennis loves to hunt, fly-fish, and cook—he makes the world's best black bean soup, blackened salmon, and chateaubriand with béarnaise sauce, and he will share the recipes for a modest fortune. Dennis has also joined Barbara in becoming a champion for reclaiming Easter and its message of redemption. The Raineys live in central Arkansas.

Learn more about the Raineys at www.FamilyLifeToday.com and www .EverThineHome.com.

familylife's art of
parenting™

There is an approach to parenting that can reduce the stress and increase the harmony in your home. Based on decades of teaching from Dennis and Barbara Rainey, and featuring insights from other parenting advisors, *FamilyLife's Art of Parenting*™ small-group curriculum highlights the core issues that every parent and child need to address together.

The eight sessions are:

THE GOAL OF *Parenting*

FORMING *Character*

APPLYING *Discipline*

BUILDING *Relationships*

UNDERSTANDING *Identity*

NURTURING *Identity*

PREPARING FOR *Mission*

THE POWER OF *Family*

From the creators of the highly successful *The Art of Marriage*® series, this small-group series includes:

🍂 Two DVDs, each featuring 4 sessions

🍂 One workbook

🍂 One small-group leader guide

🍂 Two "Arrow Charts" for completing the parenting projects

🍂 One copy of the book, *The Art of Parenting* by Dennis and Barbara Rainey

🍂 One copy of the *Like Arrows* movie on DVD

To order your kit visit **FamilyLife.com/parentingkit**
or call 1-800-FL-TODAY.

More Resources from Dennis and Barbara Rainey!

Visit familylife.com for additional information.

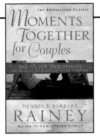